Apostles
of
Mediæval Europe

Destruction of the Idol Swantevit. — P. 249.

Apostles

of

Mediæval Europe

BY THE

REV. GEORGE F. MACLEAR

Essay Index Reprint Series

BOOKS FOR LIBRARIES PRESS

FREEPORT, NEW YORK

First Published 1869
Reprinted 1972

Library of Congress Cataloging in Publication Data

Maclear, George Frederick, 1833-1902.
  Apostles of mediaeval Europe.

  (Essay index reprint series)
  Reprint of the 1869 ed.
  1. Missionaries. 2. Missions--Europe. I. Title.
BV3700.M27 1972   266'.0092'2   72-624
ISBN 0-8369-2803-2

PRINTED IN THE UNITED STATES OF AMERICA
BY
NEW WORLD BOOK MANUFACTURING CO., INC.
HALLANDALE, FLORIDA 33009

PREFACE.

THESE Lives are naturally based, to a considerable extent, on my *History of Christian Missions in the Middle Ages*, which I have at times been advised to publish in a somewhat more popular form, but the numerous notes and references there given have been omitted, while the Lives themselves have been re-cast, and in some cases entirely re-written.

The Mediæval Period is apt to be altogether overlooked in modern accounts of Christian Missions, and yet it was fertile in noble and heroic men, who laid the foundations of many of the Churches of Modern Europe, and into whose labours we have entered.

If we remember to make due allowance for the Age in which they lived, we shall, I think, conclude that the roll of missionary heroes, since the days of the Apostles, can point to few more glorious names than of some of those whose Memoirs are recorded in the following pages.

G. F. M.

BUDE, CORNWALL, *Aug.* 13, 1869.

LIST OF ILLUSTRATIONS.

CONTENTS.

CHAPTER XI.

CHAPTER XII.

CHAPTER XIII.

CHAPTER XIV.

CHAPTER XV.

CHAPTER XVI.

CHAPTER XVII.

CHAPTER XVIII.

CHAPTER XIX.

CHAPTER XX.

APOSTLES

MEDIÆVAL EUROPE.

INTRODUCTION.

AT the commencement of an account of some of the apostles of Mediæval Europe, it may be well to notice briefly some of the chief characteristics of the mediæval period itself, and especially of the mission field then presented to the Church, and the work she was called upon to accomplish.

During the first four hundred years of her existence, the Christian Church had not, except in the extreme East, extended her conquests far beyond the limits of the Roman empire.

Her territorial field may be said to have mainly included the countries immediately bordering upon the Mediterranean Sea, Numidia and Egypt, Palestine and Asia Minor, Greece, Italy, and Southern Gaul, the very centre of the old world and its heathen culture.

Within this area the kingdom of heaven had been establishing itself gradually and silently. The word, indeed, had been running very swiftly, but it was the word of him, whose early life had been spent in an obscure village of Palestine, and who had died the death of the malefactor and the slave. The mustard seed and the hidden leaven, had, even as he had predicted, been true figures of its progress, overlooked by the world, yet penetrating the world with its secret and subduing force.

There is a mystery, as has been often observed, about the planting of the early Church in various places. Who knows for certain how that congregation originated which was already at Damascus when the disciple of Gamaliel went thither breathing forth threatening and slaughter against those of the way? Who can throw any clear light on the planting of the first Church of Rome, to which St. Paul addresses so many salutations? Who, again, so laboured in establishing the early Church of France, that in the second and third centuries a Pothinus and an Irenæus could enter into their labours? Who, lastly, can give any certain account of the origin of the early British Church?

Thus for a long period the work of the Church was almost imperceptible in the great Roman world. Its going forth was not proclaimed on the housetop or in the market-place. The new faith made its way from below rather than from above. Not many wise, not many mighty, not many noble, were amongst those first called to join its ranks. In the literal sense of the word, it worked its way at first " underground, under camp and palace, under senate and forum, as unknown, and yet well known; as dying, and, behold, it lived !" [1]

But at length the leaven began to pervade the whole mass of society. In spite of contempt and outrage, the glad tidings found eager listeners. Philosophers might scoff at the first believers. Politicians might suspect them. The populace might pursue them with ferocious yells. A Nero might persecute them to avert general detestation from himself; a Hadrian and a Trajan, as deeming them guilty of insubordination or treason; a Marcus Aurelius and a Decius, from horror at the public calamities of the empire ; a Diocletian, as recognising in the new and mysterious society a formidable rival to be put down and crushed. But there were at all times those to whom the new faith spake as never man spake. There were always the children by whom its wisdom was justified.

The story of Justin Martyr, who, after trying every other system in vain, was advised by the aged stranger on the sea-shore to inquire into the "new philosophy," was, no doubt, the story of many. Self-convicted of his impotency to regenerate himself, man cried out with Seneca, "O that one would stretch out his hand!" and sighed for relief from the endless strife of discordant systems. The religions of heathenism had taken deep root neither in the intellect, the conscience, nor the affections of mankind.

[1] Stanley's "Lectures on Ecclesiastical History," Introd. p. xxxviii.

Art and literature, philosophy and politics, had done their utmost, and yet man had not attained that which he felt he needed. His soul still thirsted; it had reached no fountain of living water.

To these deep-felt wants the Gospel responded, and thus exerted a direct, a divine influence. It calmed the clashing creeds of heathendom by proclaiming the unity of the Godhead. It attracted the hearts of men by its revelation of his true character as a Father. It proclaimed the glad tidings of his infinite love as displayed in the incarnation of his Eternal Son. It assuaged the sense of guilt by pointing to the sacrifice of the Cross. It strengthened the power of hope by bringing to light life and immortality, and the glory of the world to come.

And while it thus proved its adaptation to the wants of men, it manifested its divine power sometimes in miracles and signs, the echoes of the Apostolic ages, often in the constancy of its martyrs under persecution, oftener still in the upright walk, the holiness, the charity of its teachers. What they effected directly was effected as powerfully, though indirectly, by Christian captives, Christian colonists, Christian soldiers. Apologists, before long, like Irenæus and Justin, Cyprian and Athenagoras, Origen and Tertullian, justified the claims of the new faith to be the true philosophy. The Fathers of the East moulded its creeds. The Empire of the West bequeathed to it its organization and its laws. With Constantine it was publicly recognised as the religion of the State; and at length the symbol of the most degrading punishment the Roman could inflict on the malefactor and the slave became the symbol of an empire's creed, and was blazoned on the conqueror's banner.

But when the Iron Kingdom had run its course, a very different work was proposed to the energies of the Christian teachers. As the Roman empire sank beneath her feet, its last embers trampled out by Alaric, the Church found herself confronted with one of the most stupendous tasks that could have been presented to her to accomplish.

Scarcely recovering herself from the shock of the barbarian invasions, she was called to train and civilize races fresh from their native wilds, filled with all the ardour and impetuosity of youth, and ignorant of the first principles of order and settled life.

For centuries had they been gathering from afar, and now they were precipitated over the face of Europe. Celt and Teuton, Sclave and Hun, followed each other in quick succession, with strange language and strange customs, to fill the abyss of servitude and corruption in which the Roman empire had disappeared, and to infuse a new life-blood into its effete civilization.

And what was the condition of the provinces of the great empire where they now appeared, and which they made a beaten highway for their passage?

Little change for the better had their social and domestic life experienced as the ring of empire had widened more and more. Crushed under a weight of merciless taxation, drained of their population by repeated levies for the imperial armies, Italy and

Gaul, and even more distant provinces, had almost ceased to till the soil. Many tracts were given up to the wasteful tenure of discharged soldiers, or were cultivated by the manacled hands of slaves. Native chieftains, aspiring to the pomp and state of the Roman patrician, exalted themselves to their fancied dignity on the ruins of the yeomanry class. " The old tenantry, or clansmen, were ejected from their ancient holdings, to constitute from the aggregation of them one of those vast estates, or *latifundia*, which were cultivated entirely by slaves for the behoof of the proprietors alone. From them they drew the means of boundless self-indulgence, but left to the husbandman nothing beyond the most scanty allowance of the bare necessaries of human existence ; and when they were hurried by fatigue, by want, and by sickness to premature graves, they recruited their number from the Roman slave-markets." [1]

And when this work of depopulation had been going on for centuries, what was likely to be the condition of the more remote country districts in Gaul or Italy, when they were exposed to the ravages of tribes as careless of the arts of agriculture as the imperial legions they had expelled ?

As it was in the days of the Judges in Israel, so was it now. The villages ceased [2] throughout the land. Towns deserted by their inhabitants completely disappeared, or could be traced only by the

---

[1] Sir James Stephen's " Lectures on the History of France," vol. i. p. 27.
[2] Judg. v. 7.

attentive traveller, with the utmost difficulty, under the thick overgrowth of dense woods. Temples and baths, villas and streets, became a mass of crumbling ruins, over which the tangled underwood gradually extended its sway, till at length it joined the immense and impenetrable forests, which always were a prominent feature in the scenery of Gaul and Germany, and formed, by the thick growth of maple and birch, aspen and witch-elm, a boundless wilderness of forest trees.

"On the north of the Rhine alone," writes Montalembert, "six great deserts existed at the end of the sixth century—the desert of Reome, between Tonnerre and Montbard; the desert of Morvan; the desert of Jura; the desert of the Vosges; the desert of Switzerland, between Bienne and Lucerne; and the desert of Gruyere, between the Savine and the Aar. Advancing towards the north, the wooded regions become more and more profound and extensive. Even in the provinces least depopulated and best cultivated, through the most favourable soils and climates, long wooded lines extended from north to south, and from the rising to the setting sun, connecting the great masses of forest with each other, surrounding and enveloping Gaul as in a vast network of shade and silence."

"We must imagine Gaul," he continues, "and all the neighbouring countries, the whole extent of France, Switzerland, Belgium, and both banks of the Rhine—that is to say, the richest and most populous countries of modern Europe—covered with forests such as are scarcely to be seen in America, and of which there does not remain the slightest trace in the ancient world. We must figure to ourselves these masses of sombre and impenetrable wood covering hills and valleys, the high table-land as well as the marshy bottoms, broken here and there by watercourses which laboriously forced a way for themselves across the roots of fallen trees; perpetually divided by bogs and marshes which swallowed up the animals or men who were so ill-advised as to risk themselves there; and inhabited by innumerable wild beasts, whose ferocity had scarcely been accustomed to fly before man, and of which many different species have since almost completely disappeared from our country." [1]

And now, as from the gloom of these solitudes the new tribes, wild and wasteful, without prudence or forethought or steady industry, issued forth upon the towns and cities of Southern Europe, according as internal war or factions drove them to seek new homes, and gradually settled down in their midst, a grave question arose. Who would have the courage to seek out these wild races? Who would brave all dangers in preaching to them the word of life? Who would plunge into the darkness of these forests, proclaim the divine message to the inhabitants that dwelt around, improve their infant agriculture, and instil amongst them the first principles of civilization?

This was the question, and we shall see how it was answered. At this critical period, when the founda-

---

[1] Montalembert's "Monks of the West," vol. ii. pp. 319, 320, English Translation.

tions of the great deep seemed to be broken up, and chaos to have come back to earth, we shall take our stand to watch how the Christian Church set out on her great work; how she sent forth men who did not count their lives dear unto them, if they might win over to the fold of Christ the multitudes that bade them come over and help them.

Mindful of the difficulties to be encountered in making the effort at all, and of the features of the times when it was made, we shall not expect perfection of men who partook of the common infirmities of our nature; we shall rather rejoice to trace from time to time the fulfilment of the Divine word, *Behold I am with you alway, even unto the end of the world,*[1] and to observe how the Lord of the harvest was pleased in the darkest times *to send forth labourers into his harvest.*[2]

---

[1] St. Matt. xxviii. 20.   [2] St. Matt. ix. 38.

CHAPTER I.

AND, first, it will be well to notice some of the more striking features, moral and religious, of the nations which now awaited the missionary zeal of the Christian Church. As an outline is all that can possibly be attempted, we may, sinking minor divergences of race, and regarding them solely in their social and religious aspects, arrange these nations under the several groups of Celts, Teutons, and Sclaves.

1. With the first group indeed we shall be but very partially concerned. The Celtic races had, except in Ireland and Northern Britain, to a great extent become amalgamated with the institutions, feelings, and social life of their Roman conquerors, and had learned to ascribe to their deities the attributes of the gods of Rome. We are therefore hardly concerned with their religious creed, except so far as they formed an advanced outpost among the Western nations, and, when evangelized by Christian missionaries, became, in their turn, signally ardent and successful preachers of their newly-adopted faith.

The Commentaries of Cæsar give us the earliest sketch of the social and moral features of the Celtic character. During his campaigns, which lasted upwards of fourteen years, and cost him two millions of men, this great commander had ample opportunities of becoming acquainted with them, and he has described with minute accuracy their gigantic stature, fair complexions, enormous muscular strength, and love of personal decoration.[1]

Fond of war, hot of temper, but simple and void of malice, they knew little of that personal liberty, which was the proud characteristic of the Teuton. While the meanest Teuton was independent and free, the lower orders among the Celts were little better than in a state of slavery, for all real freedom and power centred in their chieftains.

The same great warrior has given us the fullest account of the Druids, the all-powerful religious order of the Celtic tribes. Under their various divisions, they were at once the ministers of a theocracy and the judges and legislators of the people. Enjoying an immunity from service in the army and the obligation to pay taxes, they instructed the youth of the nation in the mysteries of learning, the majority of which they veiled in inviolable secrecy, and did not suffer to be committed to writing. The chief doctrine, however, that they did impart, seems to have been the immortality of the soul, or rather its transmigration to another body, to which was added instruction in the nature and motions of the sun, moon, and stars, and the power and greatness of the immortal gods.

Though proscribed by successive Roman generals,

[1] Cæsar, "De Bel. Gall." vi. 13.

and nominally exterminated in Britain by Suetonius
Paulinus, Druidism lingered on for centuries in Ireland
and the Scottish Highlands. In the "Book of Armagh"
the monarch of Ireland is represented, at the arrival
of St. Patrick, as having in his service his soothsayer
and magicians, his augurs and diviners. A member of
the same order withstood with the utmost pertinacity
the first preaching of St. Columba in Scotland,[1] and
in the "Book of Leinster" we find an early Irish king
asking the Druids to ascertain for him by their arts
the events that were to happen to him during the
ensuing year.

Almost of equal rank with the Druids was the
Ollamh, the "bard" or "gleeman," and only a step
lower stood the Seanchaidhe, the "historian" or
"story-teller." The person of the former was regarded
as inviolate. With the princes and the Druids, he took
part in the great national assemblies; he ranked next
to the monarch himself, had a fixed title in the chieftain's territory, besides ample perquisites for himself
and his attendants, and by carrying or sending his
wand to any person or place he conferred a temporary
sanctuary from injury or arrest.

As to the Celtic religious belief, however modified
it may have been by subsequent contact with Roman
or Teutonic systems, it is clear that in its original

---

1 See Adamnan's "Life of St. Columba," by Reeves, p. 74 *n.* In
the Irish MS. of St. Paul's Epistles at Wurtzburg the gloss on Jannes
and Jambres, in 2 Tim. iii. 8, is *duo Druidæ Ægyptiaci.* In an
ancient hymn, ascribed to St. Columba, we find the expression,
"Christ the Son of God *is my Druid.*"—Miscell. Irish Arch. Soc.
i. 8.

form it was essentially the worship of the powers of nature. Highest in the Celtic pantheon was the sun, the "life of everything," the "source of all being," who shared the devotion of his worshippers with the moon and stars, with genii of the hills and the valley, of the grove and the spring. The sacred principle of fire also received special adoration. The season of the vernal equinox was ushered in by the sacred festival of the Bel-tine, or "the lucky fire," and was celebrated with those peculiar rites, which once from every hill-top in Ireland welcomed the return of the solar beams and the banishment of winter's gloom, but now linger only in the popular sports of May Day.

The records of missionary labour in Ireland and Scotland do not make any special mention of those numerous gods, which Cæsar describes as worshipped in Gaul, and to which he has transferred the attributes of the deities of Rome. But the apostle of Ireland is represented in the earliest annals as recalling his converts from the worship not only of spectres and genii, but of idols also, the greatest of which, the image of Crom-cruach,[1] stood on the plain of Magh Slecht, "the Plain of Adoration," in the county of Cavan, and was the chief object of native worship till its destruction by him.

As a rule, however, the original form of the Druidic

---

[1] "Supposed to have been also termed *Crom-dubh*, 'the black stooping-stone,' and to have given rise to the name of *Cromdubh* or *Cromduff* Sunday, by which the last Sunday in summer, or the Sunday next before All Saints' Day, is commonly known in Ireland."—Todd's "Life of St. Patrick," p. 128.

ritual was marked by much simplicity. The shadow
of the sacred grove, or the wide-spreading oak with its
mystic misletoe, was the Druid's temple ; the hill-top,
with its cromlech or altar-stone, his nearest approach
to architecture ; while the triple procession round the
sacred circle from east to west, the search for the
misletoe on the sixth day of the moon, the sacrifice of
the milk-white bull, and the usual methods of augury
and divination, constituted the chief portion of his
sacred rites. But at particular times the earnest
craving to appease offended powers, or the dread of
sudden danger, or the outbreak of some terrible pestilence, suggested the offering of those sacrifices of
human beings which Cæsar has described, and which
long continued to be the custom of the Celtic tribes.

2. With this outline of Celtic superstitions, we must
pass on to the Teuton. Under this generic name we
include not only the inhabitants of the extensive
region ; which, bounded by the Baltic on the north, the
Rhine on the west, the Vistula and Oder on the east,
may be called, with tolerable accuracy, the European
home of the Teutonic tribes, but also those hardy
Northmen, whose gaudy but terrible barks bore them,
during the eighth and ninth centuries, from their
homes in Denmark and Sweden to be the scourge of
the European shores.

Differ as these undoubtedly did in minor points, in
all the essentials of their moral and religious character
they were similar, and for our purposes it will suffice
to speak of them together.

The earliest Teutonic doctrine, then, appears to

have recognised one Supreme Being, whom it represents as Master of the universe, whom all things obey.

"Who is first and eldest of the gods?" it is asked in the Edda, and the answer is, "He is called Allfadir in our tongue. He lives from all ages, and rules over his realm, and sways all things, great and small; he made heaven and earth, and *the lift*—that is, the sky —and all that belongs to them; and, what is more, He made man, and gave him a soul that shall live and never perish, though the body rot to mould or burn to ashes. His is an infinite power, a boundless knowledge, an incorruptible justice. He cannot be confined within the enclosure of walls, or represented by any likeness to the human figure."[1]

Such appears to have been the primitive faith. Allfadir would be a name naturally dear to a people which as yet had hardly passed the limits of the patriarchal state, amongst whom every father of a family was at once a priest and king in his own house.

But the idea of a pure spirit was too refined to retain any lasting hold on the mind and conscience. It lost its original distinctness, and retired more and more into the background, surviving only as the feeble echo of an older and purer creed. Just as the Aryan in crossing the Hindu Alps was spellbound by the new and beauteous world into which he was transplanted, so the Teuton, in the course of his migrations towards colder climes, bowed down

[1] See Dasent's "Norsemen in Iceland," p. 187, and compare Tacitus, "Germania," chap. ix.

before the wild and overbearing powers of nature, and
then out of nature-worship arose an elaborate form
of hero-worship, the adoration of the conquerors of
nature, that is, of man himself, with his virtues and
his vices.

From the Invisible One emanates, so thought the
Teuton, an infinite number of inferior deities, whose
temple is every part of the invisible world. Hence
nature was to be venerated in all her forms and mani-
festations. The heavenly bodies, the sun and moon
and stars ; the earth, with its trees and springs, its
fountains and hills ; the sea, with its ebb and flow,
its storm and calm ;—all were regarded with deepest
reverence. And since all nature was but an organ
and instrument of deity, it was of the utmost importance to pay attention even to the most indifferent
phenomena. Nothing was too trifling. The quivering
leaf, the crackling flame, the falling thunderbolt, the
flight or singing of birds, the neighing of horses, man's
dreams and visions, even the movements of his pulse,
all needed attention, all might give some sign from
the other world.

Hence the peculiar regard that was paid, amongst
all the Teutonic nations, Gothic, Saxon, and Scandinavian, to oracles and divinations, to auspices,
presages, and lots. Hence the functions of the pro-
phetess and the sibyl, of the enchanter, the interpreter
of dreams, the diviner by offering-cups,[1] or the entrails
of victims, or human sacrifices. Hence the raisers of
storms, the Runic sticks, and all the usual instru-

[1] Comp. Gen. xliv. 5.

ments of heathenism for exploring the secrets either
of the past or the future. Upsal was the Teutonic
Delphi, as famous for its oracles as for its sacrifices.
Here might be found diviners, both male and female,
who could supply runes to secure victory in the
battle, to preserve from poison, to heal bodily infirmities, or to chase away melancholy.[1] Thus all
nature had a voice which could speak, and to which
all men were bound to hearken. The skies, the
woods, the waters, were the Teuton's books, his
oracles, his divinities.

But nature-worship did not satisfy. The Teuton
ceased in time to quail before her mighty powers.
He learnt to defy the wind and storm, the frost and
cold. So nature-worship became entangled with a
complicated system of human gods.

The first and eldest of the gods, we saw, was
Allfadir, Odin, or Wotan. But in process of time
the great Father was resolved into his attributes.
His power was divided amongst a number of inferior
divinities, sprung from himself, to each of whom he
had imparted a portion of his greatness. Hence the
twelve Æsir and the twelve Asyniar. Moreover, as
in the Hindu mythology, Brahm is almost forgotten
before Vishnu, or the more terrible Siva and Kali, so
Odin shared the worship of his votaries with Thor
the "Thunderer," the "chief of the gods in strength

---

[1] The "Indiculus Superstitionum" and the Lives of the Mediæval
Missionaries afford an insight into the various kinds of Teutonic
sorcery. Comp. the letter of Boniface to Cuthbert, Ep. lxiii. ed. Migne,
and the appendix to Kemble's "Saxons in England," vol. i.

and might;" with Týr, the Teutonic Mars, the
"bravest of all the gods, the giver of victory, and god
of battle;" with Freyr, the god of fertility, of seed-
time and harvest, of marriage and fruitfulness; with
Baldr, fairest of all the sons of Odin, the Phœbus
Apollo of the Teuton, "the restorer of peace, the
maker-up of quarrels;" while Frigga, Odin's wife,
presided over the sweet spring-time and the rising
seed, with her attendants, Fulla, "plenty," Hlin,
"warmth," and Gna, "the sweet and gentle breeze."

The Æsir and the Asyniar were the blithe, beneficent powers. But the Teuton could not look out
upon the natural world, without tracing in its contra-
dictory phenomena the operation of other powers,
dark and sinister, which had brought about a convul-
sion in high places, and with whose machinations
the human race had become entangled. Hence the
belief in monstrous fiends and giants, cruel, powerful,
and inexorable. Chief of these was Loki, the
"calumniator and backbiter of the gods," "the grand
contriver of deceit and fraud." In his form he was
fairer than any of human mould, but his mind was
evil, his nature feeble, and "he cheated in all things,
and in the arts of perfidy and craft he had no equal."
Once the friend and associate of the Æsir, united
with them in sacred brotherhood, he fell like Lucifer
from his high estate, and terrible was his threefold
offspring,—the first, Fenris-wolf; the second, Mid-
gard's worm; the third, a daughter, Hel, the goddess
of death. These are the enemies of the Æsir, the
authors of disquiet and strife, and with their entrance

into the Teutonic and Scandinavian mythology the older and milder religion assumed a more warlike and savage character. Instead of ruling the world in peace, the "Father of gods and men" became Valfadir, the god of battles, the "terrible and severe god," who prepared for the warrior the feast in Valhalla.[1]

Such, roughly and briefly, were the outlines of the Teuton's creed, to which everywhere and at all times he clung, and for which he died, for it was "the transfiguration of the natural man, with all his virtues and vices, with all his feelings, and passions, and natural affections."[2] Hence the free and easy way in which the Teuton regarded his gods. If he honoured them right, and offered the due sacrifices, he claimed his reward. If he considered himself unfairly treated, he openly reproved them, forsook their worship, and destroyed their temples.

For though it may be true that in early times the Teuton knew nothing of temples made with hands, that the Deity, whom no enclosure could contain, or mortal form represent, received the adoration of his worshippers in the obscurity of the wood, or on the lonely mountain-top, yet without doubt the introduction of an elaborate form of polytheism brought with it in time a more elaborate form of external worship.

The transition from the sacred oak-grove to the

[1] See Dasent's "Norsemen in Iceland," p. 191 ; "Prose Edda, p. 446.
[2] Dasent's "Burnt Njal," I. xvii.

hill altar and the cairn was easy. Equally easy the
transition thence to the temple of wood, with its nave
and shrine, its "holy place," and its "holy of holies."
In the Norse temples, formed doubtless on a plan
common in earlier times, the images of the gods
stood on a platform in the shrine. In front of them
was the altar, on which burnt the holy fire. On it,
too, was laid the great ring, which, stained with the
sacred blood, was placed in the hand of all such as
were about to take any solemn oath. Hard by also
was the brazen vessel, in which the blood of the
slaughtered victims was caught, and the brush or
twig wherewith the worshippers were sprinkled, while
they stood behind a partition-wall opposite the platform of the gods, and from this outer court beheld
the ceremonies.

The temple of Upsal, the Teutonic Delphi, was in
circumference not less than nine hundred ells, and
glittered on all sides with gold. In it Odin was
represented with a sword in his hand, while on his
left stood Thor, with the insignia of a crown, a
sceptre, and a hammer, and on his right Freyja, an
hermaphrodite, with many emblems characteristic of
productiveness. Near Eresburg, on the Drimel, stood,
till the times of Charlemagne, the celebrated Teutonic idol, called the Irmin-Saule.[1] On a high stone
column rose the figure of a gigantic warrior, girt with
a sword, holding in his right hand a banner, on which
was painted a bright red rose, in his left hand a

[1] Meibomius, "De Irminsula;" Adam Brem. i. 6; Akerman's "Pagan
Saxondom," p. xxi.

balance. The crest of the warrior's helmet was a
cock; on his breast was figured a bear; on the
shield was the representation of a lion in a field full
of flowers. The image itself was eleven feet in height,
and of a light red colour. Its base was of rude stone,
surrounded with belts of orichalcum, of which the
upper and lower were gilded. It was the largest idol
of all Saxony, and pictures of it were suspended in
other temples, and its priests enjoyed a high reputation. It was believed to be able to aid the warrior
in the din of battle, who oftentimes rode round it,
and murmured to it his prayers. Sometimes it was
borne into the field, and when the conflict was over,
all the prisoners, and all who had disgraced themselves by cowardice, were immolated at its feet.[1]

The offerings presented in these temples consisted
of all living things—sheep, oxen, swine, and especially
horses. The latter sacrifice was particularly characteristic of the Germanic races. The victims having
been slaughtered before the images of the gods, the
heads were by preference offered to them, and with
the hides were fixed or hung on trees in the sacred
groves. The blood was caught in the blood-bowl,
and sprinkled with the blood-twig on the altar, the
images, and the people, while the fat was used for
anointing the images themselves, which were afterwards rubbed dry. The flesh was boiled down in
caldrons over fires placed along the whole length of
the nave. Round these the worshippers took their
seats, and ate the flesh and partook of the broth,

[1] See Dasent's "Burnt Njal," I. xxxix.

while the chief to whom the temple belonged blessed the cups of mead or beer in honour of Odin, Freyr, Thor, Frigga, and, last, of departed friends. Then the rest in order took the cup, and each made his prayer or offered his vow; and so the feast went on, terminating too often in riot and drunkenness.

Such were the usual sacrifices. On great occasions, however, human victims were offered, especially slaves, criminals, and captives. This custom was common to all the Germanic races. But at Upsal the ninth month in each year—and every ninth year appear to have been specially set apart for these sacrifices. On such occasions, the presence of the king, together with all citizens of importance, was deemed absolutely essential. Human victims appear to have been offered either as sacrifices of atonement, or to appease the wrath of malign deities, or as propitiatory sacrifices to the dead in the nether world.[1] In seasons of more than ordinary calamity, the king himself was expected to lay down his life. Thus, on the occasion of a great dearth, the first king of Vermaland, in Sweden, was burnt in honour of Odin. Again, in a great sea-fight with the Jomsburg pirates, the jarl Hakon offered up his son to obtain the victory; and Aun, another king of Sweden, immolated at the shrine of Odin nine of his sons, in order that his own life might be prolonged.

3. But it is now time to glance at the third group of nations, the Sclavonic.

---

[1] See Bartholini's "Antiq. Danicæ," pp. 388-396; Adam Brem. "Gesta PP. Hammaburg," iv. 26.

On a map of Europe in the beginning of the sixth
century we find the Sclaves represented as forming
three principal branches, or aggregates of tribes.
Towards the east, resting on the Euxine, and extending from the Dniester to the Dnieper and the
Don, are the Antes, the progenitors of the great Russian people. Towards the west, resting on the Baltic,
are the Venedi, or Wends. Between the two inter-
vene the Slavenes, a nomad race blending sometimes
with the eastern, sometimes with the western branch.

The first coming of the Sclaves was peaceful. They
occupied quietly such lands as their Teutonic brethren
left them, and thence pushed forward to the south
and west, building trading cities like Kieff and Novgorod and Arcona, sinking mines in Germany, smelt-
ing and casting metals, preparing salt, and planting
fruit-trees, leading a quiet and contented life.

Early writers uniformly speak of them in favourable
terms. Procopius describes them as free from malice
and fraud, generous and hospitable. Adam of Bremen
extols their kindness and courtesy towards strangers.[1]
But they became at an early period the victims of
unparalleled oppressions, and the consequences could
be traced with terrible clearness in the change which
their national character underwent. Under the iron
heel of the Germans on the north, of the Turks on
the south, and afterwards of the Mongols on the east,
their veracity and good faith were exchanged for du-
plicity and cunning. At first they displayed all the

[1] "Hist. Eccles." ii. 12 ; and compare the letter of Boniface to Ethelbald, Ep. lxii. ed. Migne.

characteristics of the pastoral tribe. Living in huts
of rough timber in the depths of forests, or along the
banks of rivers, they tended their numerous flocks of
sheep and cattle, defending themselves in time of war
with nothing but a shield for a weapon of defence, and
for offence a bow and a quiver of poisoned arrows,
or the lasso. But after centuries of oppression they
became demoralized and debased. Submissive in
adversity, they were tyrants in their hour of power,
and obtained a notoriety for cruelties practised only
amongst the most savage nations.

Procopius sketches the chief features of their religious system. "The Sclavonians," he says, "worship
one god, the 'Maker of the Thunder,' whom they hold
to be the only lord of the universe, and to whom
they offer cattle and different kinds of victims. They
do not believe in fate, or that it has any power over
mortals. Whenever they are in danger of death,
either from illness or from the enemy, they make
vows to God to offer sacrifices if they should be saved.
When the peril is over, they fulfil their vows, and
believe that it was this which saved them. They also
worship rivers, nymphs, and some other deities, to
whom they offer sacrifices, making divinations at the
same time."[1]

Later writers give us further particulars, from which
it would appear that the Sclavonic religion was marked
on the one hand by the worship of the gladdening, fruc-
tifying powers of nature, and on the other by the de-
precation of dark and sinister powers, who manifested

[1] Procopius, "De Bello Gothico."

their malignant arts by creating discord, sickness, and death. The first was symbolized by Lada, the goddess of love and pleasure; Kupala, the god of the fruits of the earth; Koleda, the god of festivals, who delighted in offerings of fruits, and rejoiced in songs and dances round lighted fires. Of the second, the chief was Zernabog, "the black deity," whose name recalls the Matchi Manito of the Mexicans, and who, like the latter, was approached with fear and horror, and propitiated with human sacrifices.

The Lord of Thunder was worshipped at Kieff and Novgorod under the name of Peroun, and in Moravia his idol was of wood, with the head of silver. At Rugen were the images of Porenut, "the god of the seasons," with four faces and a fifth on his breast; and of Rhugevit, "the god of war," with seven faces, and seven swords suspended at his side and an eighth in his hand.

At Romove, in Prussia, as late even as the year A.D. 1230, three gods were especially worshipped; Percunos, "the god of thunder," Potrimpos, "the god of corn and fruits," Picullos, " the god of the infernal regions." The face of the first was expressive of extreme anger, his head being wreathed with a crown of flames; the second was represented by a beardless youth, and wore a chaplet of green leaves and ears of corn; the face of the third was pale, the beard snow-white, the eyes looking downwards on the ground.

But the most famous idol, at least of the Baltic Sclavonians, was Sviantovit, or Swantevit. His temple was at Arcona, the capital of the island of Rugen, and was not destroyed till the year A.D. 1168. A Danish historian [1] informs us that the temple, which was of wood and beautifully constructed, rose from a level spot in the midst of the town. It had two enclosures. The outer consisted of a wall with a roof painted red; the interior was hung with tapestry and ornamented with paintings.

The idol, which stood in the sanctuary, was of gigantic size, with four heads and as many necks, two chests, and two backs, one turned to the right, the other to the left. In his right hand the god held a horn made of various metals, which was once a year filled with mead by the attendant priest. His left arm was bent towards his side in the form of a bow. He was arrayed in a long flowing robe reaching down to the feet, while around him lay his bridle, and a sword of enormous size with a beautiful hilt and scabbard.

The worship of the idol was defrayed by an annual tax, payable by every inhabitant of the island, by a third of the spoils taken in war, and by the numerous votive offerings sent to the temple by neighbouring chiefs. A regiment of three hundred chosen cavalry was specially dedicated to his service, who went forth to fight in his name, and brought back the booty, which the priest made up into various ornaments for the shrine.

The god himself was believed to accompany his votaries to the battle-field on a white horse, which specially belonged to him. It was a sin to pull a hair

---

[1] Saxon Grammaticus, " Hist. Danicæ," lib. xiv.: compare also Herbordi " Vita Ottonis," ii. 31 ; Pertz, " Mon. Germ." xii. 794.

from his mane or tail, and the priest alone might feed or mount him. This horse was especially consulted on going forth to war, for it was believed to be able to reveal the secrets of the future. When the tribe wished to declare war, three rows of spears were laid down before the temple, solemn prayers were then offered up, and the horse was led forth by the priest. If, in passing over these spears, he lifted his right foot first, then the war would be prosperous; if the left, or both together, it was a fatal omen, and the expedition was given up.

The most solemn festival was after harvest. On this occasion the people of Rugen assembled, offered sacrifices of cattle, and held a solemn feast. The priest, conspicuous for his long hair and beard, first carefully swept the sanctuary, holding his breath lest the divine presence should be defiled, and if he wished to respire, retiring into the open air. On the morning of the festival he brought forth to the assembled people the sacred mead-cup, which he took from the idol's hand. If the mead had decreased therein, he announced the fact to the worshippers, and bade them beware of scarcity; if it had increased, it was an omen of abundance. The old liquor was then poured forth as a libation at the foot of the idol, and the priest, refilling it, engaged in solemn supplication for the people, that they might be prosperous and have victory in war. He then emptied the horn at a single draught, and once more refilling it, placed it in the right hand of the idol, where it remained till the next year.

Round cakes of flour and honey were then offered, and the priest concluded the ceremony by blessing the people in the name of the god, exhorting them to frequent sacrifice, and promising them, as their reward, victory both by sea and land. The rest of the day was spent in feasting on the remains of the offerings, and the people were taught that on this occasion intemperance was a virtue, sobriety a sin.[1]

Such is the account given by a contemporary writer of this celebrated Sclavonic idol; and it gives us a very vivid idea of Sclavonic worship as it was observed as late even as the middle of the twelfth century. The belief in fairies and sprites, in water-nymphs and wood-nymphs, in sorcery and magic, was as active amongst the Sclavonians as amongst their Teutonic brethren, while the respect paid by them to their priests, who united civil and religious functions, was as submissive as that of the Celt to his Druid teacher.

[1] " Historiæ Danicæ," lib. xiv.

CHAPTER II.

WITH this sketch of the religious systems of the three great groups of nations now presented to the missionary zeal of the Christian Church, we pass on to describe the lives and labours of some of those who devoted themselves to the work of communicating to them the word of life.

We might have expected that it would be necessary to begin with those who went forth from the long-established churches of the Continent. But it is not so. It is true that instances are not wanting of men who left these churches to evangelize the heathen tribes around them: that Ulphilas laboured with no little success amongst the Goths of Mæsia; that the great Chrysostom founded in Constantinople an institution in which Goths might be trained and educated to preach the Gospel to their fellow-countrymen; [1] that Valentinus won for himself the title of " the apostle of Noricum;" [2] that his work was carried on with

---

[1] Theodoret, " H. E." v. 30.
[2] See Surius, " Acta SS." Aug. 4.

signal success by Severinus;[1] that, after the conversion of Clovis and the foundation of the Frankish Church, Avitus of Vienne, Cæsarius of Arles, and Faustus of Riez, proved what might be done by energy and self-devotion among the masses of heathendom.

But the Frankish Church was not destined to evangelize the rude nations of Europe. The internal dissensions, the constant wars, among the successors of Clovis, were not favourable either to the development of Christianity in their own dominions or its propagation abroad. The rapid accession of wealth more and more tempted the Frankish bishops to live as mere laymen, and the light of their Church grew dim. Not only were the heathen lying around neglected, but within her own territory the Frankish Church saw her own members relapsing in some instances into the old idolatries.

A new influence, therefore, was required if this light was to be rekindled, and the nations of Europe evangelized. And this new influence the providence of God supplied. But to trace its origin we must leave the Continent of Europe for an island high up in the Northern Sea, which the Roman Agricola had once dreamt of invading and holding with a single legion,[2] but where the imperial proconsuls and prætors had never landed, and which was now almost forgotten amidst the breaking up of the Roman empire. In short, we must begin with the great apostle of Ireland, St. Patrick.

[1] See "The Hermits," by Professor Kingsley, pp. 224-246.
[2] Taciti "Vita Agricolæ," ch. xxiv.

The original name of St. Patrick was *Succat,* which is said to signify "strong in war." Patricius appears to have been his Roman name. He was born of Christian parents at some period between A.D. 395 and A.D. 415. His father Calphurnius was a deacon, his grandfather Potitus a priest. Though an ecclesiastic, Calphurnius would seem to have held the rank of decurion,[1] and may therefore have been of Roman or provincial British extraction. His birthplace was a spot which he himself calls Bonavem Taberniæ, and which in all probability may be identified with the modern Kirkpatrick, between Dumbarton and Glasgow.

The parents of Succat, as has been already said, were Christians, and it would seem that the Gospel had been preached to some extent in the neighbourhood of his father's home. Whatever amount, however, of instruction he may have received was rudely interrupted, when he was about sixteen years of age.

The coasts of Scotland were at this time exposed to the frequent incursions of Irish chieftains, who landed in their swift barks, ravaged the country, and having carried off as many of the inhabitants as they could, consigned them to slavery. In one of these expeditions the house of Calphurnius was attacked, and Succat, with two of his sisters and many of his countrymen, was carried away, and conveyed to the north of Ireland.

Here he was purchased as a slave by Michul or

[1] "S. Patricii Ep. ad Coroticum;" Todd's "Life of St. Patrick," p. 354.

Milchu, a chief of North Dalaradia, who dwelt in the
valley of the Braid, near Mount Slemish, in the
county of Antrim. The work assigned him was that
of attending his master's flocks and herds, and in his
" Confession," which he wrote towards the close of his
life, he describes how he wandered over the bleak
mountains, often drenched with the rains, and numbed
with the frosts. His period of servitude lasted six
years ; and during this time he would seem to have
made himself acquainted with the language of the
native tribes, and to have learnt their habits and
modes of life. At length he succeeded in effecting
his escape to the sea-side, where he took ship and
after a tempestuous passage, regained his father's
house. His stay, however, was destined to be very
short. In a predatory excursion he was a second
time taken captive, and again, after a brief interval,
succeeded in making his escape.[1]

Had he listened to his parents, he would now have
remained with them, but he was bent on a very different occupation. " The Divine Voice," he says,
"frequently admonished me to consider whence I
derived the wisdom which was in me, who once knew
neither the number of my days nor was acquainted with
God; and whence I obtained afterwards so great and
salutary a gift as to know and to love God." During the
weary hours, moreover, of his captivity, he had often
reflected how blessed a thing it would be if he, to
whom it had been given to know the true God and

[1] This second captivity, however, appears somewhat doubtful. See
Todd's " Life of St. Patrick," pp. 375, 376.

his Son Jesus Christ, could carry the glad tidings to his master's people and the land of his exile.

One night, he tells us, he had a dream, in which he thought he saw a man coming from Ireland with a number of letters. One of these he gave him to read, and in the beginning occurred the words, " The voice of the Irish." While he was reading it, he thought he heard a voice calling to him across the Western Sea, " We entreat thee, holy youth, to come and walk among us."

Obedient, therefore, to what he deemed to be a plain leading from heaven, and resisting the arguments and entreaties of relatives and friends, who mocked at his enthusiastic resolve, he set out for the monasteries southern France, there to prepare himself for the work of preaching the Gospel in the land of his captivity. Amidst the conflicting legends which now follow him at every step, it seems probable that he repaired to the monastic schools of Tours, Auxerre, and Lerins, where he studied, and was employed for some little time in pastoral duties, having been ordained successively deacon and priest.

There, too, he would seem to have been elevated to the episcopate, and thence with a band of fellow-labourers he set sail for Ireland, about the middle of the fifth century. Landing on one of the islands off the coast of Dublin, he and his companions tried unsuccessfully to obtain provisions, which they greatly needed. Thence sailing northwards, they put in at a strait called Brene, and after landing at the south-western extremity of Strangford

S.L. VII. D

Lough,[1] advanced some considerable way into the interior.

They had not gone far before they encountered a native chief named Dichu, at the head of a band of men. Mistaking St. Patrick for the leader of one of the many pirate crews, which at that time often appeared upon the coast, he was on the point of putting him to death. But struck by the missionary's appearance, and seeing that both he and his companions were unarmed, he hospitably received them into his house. In frequent interviews he now heard the doctrines of the faith, and after a time was baptized, with all his family. According to some authorities, he also bestowed upon his instructor the ground whereon his barn was built; and here arose the celebrated church called *Sabhall Patraic,* "The Barn of Patrick," which still retains the name of Sabhal, or Saul, and is situated about two miles north-east of Downpatrick.

Leaving Saul, the missionaries proceeded to northern Dalaradia, and the residence of St. Patrick's old master, Milchu. But nothing would induce the old chief to receive one who had been once his slave, or to forsake the paganism of his forefathers. His journey thus ineffectual, St. Patrick returned to the district where Dichu resided, and made the neighbourhood for some time his head-quarters.

Thence proceeding southward, he determined to visit the central parts of the island, and especially the famous hill of Tara, where King Laoghaire was about to hold a great religious festival in the presence

[1] Todd's "Life of St. Patrick," pp. 406, 407.

St. Patrick and King Laoghaire.—P. 35.

of all his tributary chieftains, Druids, and bards. In this stronghold of Druidism he resolved to celebrate the approaching festival of Easter, and preach the word to the assembled chiefs. It was Easter Eve, we are told, when he reached the neighbourhood of Tara, and having erected a tent, he made preparations for spending the night with his companions, and kindled a fire for the purpose of preparing food. As the smoke curled upwards in the evening air, it was observed by the Druids in the king's tents, and caused the greatest consternation. To kindle any fire during the solemn assembly of the chiefs, before the king had lighted the sacred flame in the palace of Tara, was a sin of the greatest enormity, and the Druids did not scruple to warn the king that if the fire of the stranger was not extinguished that night, unto him, whose fire it was, would belong the sovereignty of Ireland for ever

Messengers were accordingly sent to discover the authors of the sacrilege, and to order them to appear before Laoghaire. The missionaries went, and their fearlessness when in the presence of the monarch and his nobles won for them a respectful hearing. On the following day St. Patrick again addressed the chiefs, doubtless in their own language, and proclaimed to them the doctrines of the faith. Laoghaire himself, indeed, did not profess to be a convert, but he gave permission to the man of God to preach the word on condition that he did not disturb the peace of the kingdom. During the ensuing week, therefore, when the great public games were celebrated at Tailten, the missionary and his companions addressed themselves to the youngest brother of the king, and were so favourably received that he professed himself a believer, submitted to baptism, and is said to have given the site of a church, called afterwards "The Great Church of Patrick."

The impression thus made upon the chiefs was soon shared by their subjects, and though the pagan party made frequent attempts to put the missionaries to death, from which they narrowly escaped, they were heartily received in Westmeath, Connaught, Mayo, and Ulster, and before long found themselves strong enough to destroy the great idol Crom-cruach, on the plain of Magh Slecht,[1] in the county of Cavan, and, in the district of the clan Amalgaidh, admitted to baptism the seven sons of the king and many of their people.

To the worshippers of the powers of nature, and especially the sun and other heavenly bodies, St. Patrick proclaimed that the great luminary which ruled the day had no self-originated existence, but was created by One, whom he taught them to call God the Father. "Beside him," said he, "there is no other god, nor ever was, nor will be. He was in the beginning before all things, and from him all things are derived, visible and invisible." He told them next of "his only-begotten Son Jesus Christ, who had become man, had conquered death and ascended into heaven, where he sat far above all principalities and powers, and whence he would hereafter come to judge both the quick and the dead, and reward every

---

[1] See O'Curry's Lectures, p. 103 ; O'Donovan's " Tribes and Customs of Hy-Fiachrach," p. 310 *n.* and the Addenda.

man according to his deeds." " Those," he declared,
" who believed in him, would rise again in the glory
of the true Sun, that is, in the glory of Jesus Christ,
being by redemption sons of God and joint-heirs of
the Christ, of whom, and by whom, and to whom, are
all things; for the true Sun, Jesus Christ, will never
wane nor set, nor will any perish who do his will,
but they shall live for ever, even as he liveth for
ever with God the Father Almighty, and the Holy
Spirit, world without end."[1]

Such, as it would seem from his " Confession," was
the Gospel he proclaimed, and his words, confirmed
and illustrated by his own intrepid zeal, ardent love,
and sincere and devoted life, made a deep impression
on the minds of the Celtic chiefs. With the religious
enthusiasm deeply seated in the primitive Celtic
character, which many years before won for St. Paul
so warm a reception in Galatia,[2] their hearts were
touched, and they welcomed the missionary and
believed the word which he preached.

As time went on, the labours of St. Patrick were
lightened by the arrival of the bishops Secundinus,
Auxilius, and Isserninus, whom he had sent either to
France or Britain to receive consecration. Their coming
enabled him to extend the sphere of his operations,
and he undertook missionary tours in Meath, Leinster, Ossory, and Munster. These continued for
several years, during which he was occupied in preaching the word, baptizing new converts, and erecting

[1] See " S. Patricii Confessio," O'Connor, " Script. Hibern." vol. i.
pp. cvi. cxvii.
[2] Gal. iv. 13-15.

churches. Knowing well how much his own acquaintance with the native language had contributed to his
success, he laboured diligently to establish a native
ministry wherever he went. Cautiously selecting from
the higher classes those whose piety and intelligence
seemed to fit them for the work of the ministry, he
established seminaries and monastic schools, where
they were trained and educated ; and to these schools
the young of both sexes flocked with extraordinary
eagerness.

While he was labouring in the south-eastern part
of Munster, a petty prince of Cardiganshire, named
Coroticus, though apparently professing Christianity,
set out from Wales, and descending on the Irish
coast with a band of armed followers, murdered
several of the people, and carried off a large number
with the intention of disposing of them as slaves.
This outrage, perpetrated in one of the districts where
St. Patrick was baptizing, roused his keenest indignation, and he wrote a letter, which he sent by one of
his companions, calling upon Coroticus to restore the
captives, many of whom had been baptized. But his
request being treated with contempt and scorn, he
composed another circular epistle, in which he in-
veighed in the strongest terms against the cruelty
of the marauding tribe and its chief. He contrasted
his conduct with that of the Christians of the Continent, who were in the habit of sending large sums
of money to ransom captives, and concluded by
threatening him and his followers with excommunication, unless he desisted in future from his piratical

habits. What was the result of the epistle is not known, but it is to be feared that the attempt to recover the captives was not successful. Slavery and the trade in slaves was almost more difficult to root out than paganism, and the inhuman traffic was in full activity as late as the tenth century between England and Ireland, and the port of Bristol was one of its principal centres.

Meanwhile, after a somewhat lengthened sojourn in the district of Lowth and parts of Ulster, St. Patrick reached the district of Macha, containing the royal city of Emania, the residence of the kings of Ulster, the remains of which, under the name of the Navan, still exist about two miles west of Armagh. Here he was cordially received by Daire, a wealthy chief, who made over to him a pleasant piece of ground on an eminence, *Druim-saileh*, or "Hill of the Willows." The spot pleased St. Patrick, and here he determined to erect a church. The foundations were accordingly laid, and around it rose by degrees the city of Armagh, the ecclesiastical metropolis of Ireland; and here its founder spent the remainder of his life, only leaving it now and then to visit his favourite retreat at Saul, round which clustered so many associations of his earliest labours, and of his first convert Dichu.

Here, too, having called to his aid the bishops Secundinus, Isserninus, and Auxilius, who next to himself were best qualified by long experience for the work, he proceeded to hold synods and to make regulations for the general government of the churches

he had founded. Again and again he was solicited
to revisit his friends and relatives in Scotland, but
nothing could induce him to leave his post. In his
" Confession," written when far advanced in years, he
touchingly describes how often he had been requested
to come amongst his kinsmen once more, but how a
deep sense of the spiritual love between himself and
his flock ever retained him in Ireland.

It was while he was staying at Saul that the apostle
of Ireland was seized with his last illness. He had
lived to a good old age, and the sunset of his life was
calm and peaceful. Perceiving that his end drew nigh,
and desirous, as we are told, that Armagh should be the
resting-place of his remains, he set out thither, but
was unable to continue the journey. Increasing weakness, and, as it seemed to him, the voice of an angel,
bade him return to the church of his first convert;
and there he closed his eyes in death, probably in
the year A.D. 493,[1] leaving behind him the visible
memorials of a noble work nobly done. He and
his fellow-labourers had made for themselves by the
labours of their own hands civilized dwellings amidst
the tangled forest and the dreary morass. At a time
when clan-feuds and bloodshed were rife, and princes
rose and fell, and all was stormy and changeful, they
had covered the island with monastic schools, where
the Scriptures were studied, ancient books collected
and read, and native missionaries trained for their
own country, and, as we shall see, for the remotest
parts of the European continent.

[1] See Todd's " Life of St. Patrick," p. 497.

CHAPTER III.

ST. COLUMBA.

BUT though dead, the apostle of Ireland still continued to speak in the unremitting energy of his successors. Benignus, the next metropolitan of Armagh, and those who came after him, zealously increased the number of schools and monastic foundations throughout the country; and from one of these went forth the next eminent missionary of whom we shall speak, the founder of the far-famed monastery of Hy or Iona.

Columba, or, according to his Irish name, *Colum*, was born at Gartan, among the wildest of the Donegal mountains, about the year A.D. 521. His father, Feidlimidh, was one of the clan which occupied and gave name to the country round Gartan, and belonged to the royal family of Ireland, being descended from one of the eight sons of King "Niall of the Nine Hostages." His mother, Eithne, was descended from a Leinster family, which also claimed connexion with royalty. Enthusiastic biographers have related how before his birth his mother saw in a vision a beautiful robe placed in her hands by an angel, adorned with pictures of flowers of every hue, which, after a while, he took from her and suffered to float in mid air. As it floated, it grew more and more, till at length it covered all the mountains and the country round, and there came a voice, saying, "Be not sorrowful, O woman, for thou shalt have a son who shall be as one of the prophets of God, and is foreordained by God to be the guide of innumerable souls to their heavenly home."[1]

At his baptism the boy received the name of *Colum*, to which was afterwards added *cille*, or " of the church," from his constant attendance at the church which he frequented in early years. From the home of the priest who baptized him, and imparted to him the first rudiments of a literary education, he was removed to the school of St. Finnian of Moville in Down, thence to the care of a Christian bard in Leinster, and finally to a famous monastic seminary at Clonard.

His education completed, he laid the foundations of several monasteries; one on a hill covered with oaks near Lough Foyle, where in process of time rose the city of Derry, and another at Dairmagh, or Durrow, in the diocese of Meath, of which Bede has made special mention.[2] In the foundation of these and other cells Columba was diligently employed till the year A.D. 561, when he left Ireland on his famous mission to the Highlands of Scotland.

The occasion of this mission arose out of circum-

<hr/>

[1] See Dr. Reeve's edition of " Adamnan's Life of Columba," Pref. p. lxx. *n.*
[2] Bede, "H. E." iii. 4.

stances singularly characteristic of the times in which he lived.

Columba had a passion for borrowing or copying volumes and manuscripts in the various monasteries. On one occasion he paid a visit to St. Finnian at Drom Finn, in Ulster, and borrowed his copy of the Psalter. Anxious to retain a copy of the volume, and yet afraid that Finnian would not grant permission if he made the request, he resolved upon a stratagem to effect his purpose. Every day he repaired to the church, and when the people had all left, remained behind and transcribed as much as he could of the volume. The circumstance did not escape the notice of St. Finnian, but he resolved to say nothing about the matter till Columba had concluded his labours, when he sent and demanded the book, reminding him that as the original was his, so also was the copy which he had made without his permission. Columba was extremely indignant, and refused outright to comply. Words followed, and it was agreed to refer the dispute to Diarmaid, the king of Ireland.

Accordingly the disputants repaired to Tara, and were admitted to an audience. The case was heard, and at the close Diarmaid gave the curious judgment which to this day is a proverb in Ireland. *Le gach boin a boinin, le gach leabhar a leabhran,* said he ; that is, "To every cow belongeth her little cow or calf," and so to every book belongeth its son book or copy : "therefore the book you wrote, O Colum, belongs by right to Finnian." "That is an unjust decision, O

Diarmaid," was Columba's reply, "and I will avenge it on you."

It happened that at the very time the son of Diarmaid's steward and the son of the King of Connaught, who was a hostage, were playing a game of hurling on the green before the king's palace. A dispute arose between them, in the midst of which the royal hostage struck his playfellow with his hurley and killed him. Thereupon the young prince fled for sanctuary to Columba, who was still in the king's palace. But the king ordered him to be dragged away, and he was put to death for desecrating the precincts of the palace against the ancient law and usage. At this insult Columba was still more indignant, and escaping with difficulty from the court, made his way to the mountains of his native Donegal. Here he was in the midst of relatives and friends, who took up his quarrel, and marched with the men of Tyrone and the King of Connaught to Cooldrevny, between Sligo and Dromcliff, where a battle was fought in which Diarmaid was discomfited.[1]

Meanwhile, though Columba had become reconciled to Diarmaid, his conscience could not forgive

[1] The manuscript of the Psalter, which had been the cause of this strange conflict, was now returned to Columba, and was hereafter known as *The Cathach* or *Book of Battle*, and became the national relic of the clan of the O'Donnells. In an engagement which took place in 1497 between the O'Donnells and the MacDermotts, it was taken into battle enshrined in a sort of portable altar, but was captured by the Mac-Dermotts. They restored it, however, in 1499, and it is now to be seen in the museum of the Royal Irish Academy.—Reeve's Adamnan, p. 249; "Annals of the Four Masters," vol. i. p. 193.

him for having been the cause of so much bloodshed, and he himself became the subject of ecclesiastical censure. A synod was summoned at Teltown, in Meath, and it was agreed that Columba, as a man of blood, and the author of so great a slaughter, ought to quit his country, and win over to Christ from amongst the heathen as many souls as had perished in battle. In this sentence all present concurred, except the famous abbot Brendan, of the monastery of Birr, who protested against it, and St. Finnian of Moville, the old instructor of Columba, who expressed his admiration for his former pupil.

Accordingly, after announcing his intention to his royal relatives, Columba, now in his forty-second year, collected twelve companions, and in the year A.D. 563 embarked in an osier boat covered with skins, and made for the western shore of Scotland. By Pentecost Eve he had reached an island, one of the smaller Hebrides, about three miles long and a mile and a half broad, and separated by a narrow strait from the south-west extremity of the Ross of Mull, and named Hy or Iona. In one of its rocky bays, still called *Port-an-Churaich*, or "The Bay of the Osier Bark," he cast anchor, and climbing the highest point in the island, and perceiving no trace of Ireland on the horizon, deemed that he had reached the scene of his labours.

About sixty years before a portion of the family of Eirc, chief of the Irish Dalriada, had passed over, with a considerable body of followers, to the nearest coast of Argyllshire, where they settled

and founded the kingdom of British Scotia, or Dalriada, gradually establishing themselves in the districts of Cowall, Kintyre, Knapdale, Argyll proper,
Lorn, and, probably, part of Morven, with the islands
of Islay, Iona, and Arran. As yet, however, the
colony had not acquired much strength, and Bruide,
the chief of the northern Picts, was a prince of considerable power, and could bring a formidable force
into the field. Constant warfare gave the colonists
but little leisure for agricultural pursuits, and their
chief occupation consisted in pasturing their flocks
and herds. Numbering it has been thought scarcely
more than half the present population of Glasgow,
they were scattered here and there over the country, the
central district of which consisted of one vast forest,
called "The Caledonian Wood," and abounded in
enormous wild boars and formidable packs of wolves.
The rest of the country was bare and mountainous,
and was covered to a great extent with impassable
fens, through which even the natives could with
difficulty force their way.

Columba's first care, therefore, was to obtain a
grant of the island of Hy, which was freely conceded
by Conall, the chief of the British Dalriada, who
was allied to him by blood. He next proceeded to
erect a monastery, on the model, doubtless, of those
which he had already erected in Ireland, whither, as
he tells us, his mind ever returned with the fondest
regret, and his memory recalled the wind sighing
amongst the oak-groves of Durrow, and the notes of
the cuckoo and the blackbird. The buildings were

of the simplest character, and consisted of a number
of small wattled huts, surrounding a green court,
including a chapel, a dwelling-house for the missionaries, another for the reception of strangers, a refectory
and kitchen, and, outside the trench or rampart, a byre
for the cows, and a barn and storehouse for the grain.

Over this little establishment Columba presided.
He was the abbot, "the father," of the society. In
ecclesiastical rank he was a priest; he officiated at
the altar in the little chapel, and pronounced the
benediction, but did not usurp the functions of a
bishop. The rest of the community were his "family,"
his "children." At first, as we have said, they were
twelve in number and his companions from Ireland;
but before long they received numerous accessions
from the British, and even the Saxon tribes. Living
together under a common rule, they were to cultivate
the virtues of obedience, humility, and chastity; to
regard one another as fellow-soldiers of Jesus Christ,
and their life as a continual warfare under His
banner.

Their rule required them to repair every morning
and evening to the oratory and join in the sacred
services. Every Wednesday and Friday, save only
between Easter and Whitsunday, was a fast-day,
and no food was taken before three in the afternoon,
except on the occasion of the arrival of a stranger,
when the rule was relaxed that they might indulge
their national hospitality. The intervals of devotion
were employed in reading, writing, and labour in the
field. Unremitting diligence was inculcated alike by

the exhortations and example of their abbot, who allowed no hour to pass during which he was not engaged in prayer, reading, writing, or some other employment.

Reading included chiefly the study of the Holy Scripture, especially the Psalter, which was diligently committed to memory, and, besides this, of books in the Greek and Latin languages, and the lives of some of the saints. Writing was the subject of special attention. Columba was distinguished for his devotion to the work of transcription, and the books of Kells and Durrow are wonderful specimens of the perfection which his followers acquired in the art of copying and illuminating service-books and manuscripts. Active outdoor labour was also required of every member of the community. They were expected to till the ground, to sow the corn, to store the grain, to milk the cows, and to guide their boats of osier on the stormy sea.

In each and all of these employments the abbot set an eminent example to the society over which he presided on the seagirt island. He had many natural gifts which fitted him in an eminent degree for his arduous work. Tall of stature, of a vigorous and athletic frame, of a ruddy and joyous countenance, which, his biographer tells us, rejoiced the hearts of those who saw him, he possessed an extraordinary power of winning the love of all with whom he came in contact. He was celebrated also for the power of his voice, which could be heard at an amazing distance. He could render aid when required in any emergency. He could bale the boat, grind the corn in the quern or hand-mill, administer medicine to the sick, and superintend the labours of the farm.

When we add to this that he was of a princely family, we cease to wonder at the influence which he rapidly gained over Conall and the other Dalriadic chiefs. Every day, his biographer tells us, the brethren of Iona could hear loud cries from the other side of the strait which separated them from the island of Mull. These shouts were the signal for the monastery boat to put across and ferry the strangers over to the island, there to seek either material help in alms or medicines, or more frequently to obtain spiritual comfort and admission into the monastery. The narrow enclosure of the island speedily became too small for the crowds that sought admission, and it was necessary to send off numerous colonies to the neighbouring islands and the mainland of Caledonia to found monasteries and build churches, all of which owned allegiance to the abbot of Iona.

But it was not only to the colonists of Dalriada that the missionary believed he had been sent. North and east of the country occupied by the Irish Scots dwelt the Picts, so called from their habit of painting their naked bodies with various colours, whom the Roman arms had never conquered, whom Tacitus describes as the remotest inhabitants of the earth, who successfully opposed the arms of Agricola, drove the Roman legions from Britain, and laid waste the country till the arrival of the Saxons. Crossing Breadalbane, Atholl, and the Grampians, Columba traversed

E

in his skiff Loch Ness, and made his way to the principal fortress of the Pictish chief, Bruidh, the son of Malcolm. This spot, now known as *Craig Phadrick*, about two miles south-west of Inverness, was then the capital of the great chief, and, like the pagan master of the apostle of Ireland, he was exceedingly unwilling to meet the missionary and his companions, and ordered the gates to be closed against him. But Columba went up to the entrance, and had no sooner made the sign of the Cross over it than, according to his biographer, the gates flew open, and admitted him into the presence of the king.

Much alarmed, the Pictish chief received his visitor with peaceful words, and, in spite of all the endeavours of the Druids to put down the new-comer, agreed to befriend him, and confirmed to him the possession of the island of Iona, the sovereignty of which he appears to have disputed with the chief of the Irish Scots. But the favour of Bruidh did not secure for him the friendship of the native priests, who strove in every way to thwart him in his work. They regarded with little favour his endeavours to recall the people from the worship of streams and rivers, of woods and trees, and on one occasion dared him to drink of a sacred stream, the water of which they declared would kill any one who ventured to put it to his lips.[1] Thereupon Columba drank of it in their presence, and thus proved the emptiness of their threats.

Supported, however, as he was by the protection of their chief, they did not venture to offer him any

---

[1] See Adamnan, lib. ii. 2.

personal violence, and Columba occupied himself in constant journeys to and fro, preaching the word, sometimes with, sometimes without, the aid of an interpreter, wherever he could find an ear to listen. But not content with penetrating the forests, the moors, the rocks, and defiles of Scotland, he and his companions courted new dangers and yet greater hardships. Committing themselves to their boats of osier covered with skins, they braved the perils of the Northern Sea, and carried the Cross into the distant Hebrides and Orkney Isles. One monastery the abbot founded at Hymba, and placed in charge of it his maternal uncle Ernan; another he established at Ethica; a third at Elena or Elachnave, "the holy isle;" a fourth in Skye; and memorials of his visits survive to this day in the bay of *Loch Columkille* and the islands called *Eilean Columkille.*

Meanwhile he had never forgotten his native land, or the monasteries he had founded under the oaks of Derry and Durrow, and before long he had an opportunity of rendering important aid in the settlement of the country. On the death of Conall, the Dalriadan king, in A.D. 574, and the succession of his cousin Aidan, Columba was selected to perform the ceremony of coronation, which took place in the monastery of Iona, and marks the beginning of the Scottish monarchy. In the following year he accompanied the newly-crowned king to the Council of Druimceatt, now Drumkeith, in the county of Londonderry.

Two important points awaited discussion and settlement. Hitherto the Dalriadan chiefs had paid tribute to the King of Ireland, on account of that part of the country whence their forefathers had gone forth to the coast of Argyll. The question now arose, should the tribute be any longer paid? The matter was referred to the abbot of Iona, who declined to give an opinion himself, and advised the assembled chiefs to consult St. Colman, an ecclesiastic famous for his legal knowledge. In accordance with his advice the Irish king renounced all right of tribute from the King of the Dalriadans in Scotland, and promises of mutual alliance and hospitality were exchanged between the two monarchs.

The second cause of discussion arose from the overgrown power and degeneracy of the Ollamhs, or bardic Order, which, as we have already seen, ranked next to the king himself. The people never tired of listening to their praises of the national valour, or of the heroic deeds of some national hero, and the bards, strong in their own numbers and the popular affection, did not scruple to lampoon all that gave them any cause of annoyance, or failed to secure their goodwill by costly presents. The consequence was that many of the influential chiefs, stung by their satirical verses, clamoured for the suppression of the Order, and the King of Ireland himself was inclined to direct that they should be banished from the country. Columba, himself a poet, mediated between the bards and the exasperated chiefs. Though the king was eager for their suppression, he stood up for the Order, and ventured to point out that the good wheat ought not to be pulled up with the tares, and to urge the impolicy of suppressing a class so strongly supported by national feeling. After some dispute, his advice prevailed, and it was resolved that the Order should be preserved, but their number limited, and their profession made subject to certain rules.

When the council had broken up, Columba repaired to the monasteries he had founded before his departure for Scotland, inquired into their welfare, and arranged matters of discipline and ritual. Then he returned to Hy, and, with the exception of several short visits to his native land, devoted the rest of his life to the task of superintending the monasteries and churches he had founded in Scotland.

The boats he had used in his earlier expeditions were either the osier canoes covered with skins, such as Cæsar has described, which were usually small and portable, so that he could take one with him to traverse the inland lakes when he visited the Picts, or they were hollowed out of the trunks of trees, such as those still found buried in the bogs of Ireland. But as time went on, and the community at Iona increased, larger vessels were built, which could be navigated like galleys with sail or oar, and a small fleet of barks lay off the island ready for instant use.

In these the missionary and his companions made frequent expeditions amidst the numerous gulfs and straits of the storm-lashed coast. Encouraged by their abbot's example, and instructed by him in seamanship and knowledge of the winds and tides, his disciples learnt to despise the terrors of the deep, navigating their frail vessels even as far as the steeps of St. Kilda, and more northerly still, to the Shetland and Faroe isles, and even Iceland itself, where they left relics of their visits in Celtic books, bells, and crosses.

But our space will not allow of our recounting further incidents in the life of the apostle of Caledonia. We must pass on to the close.

For some time he had had a presentiment of his approaching end, and he had made all preparation for his departure. At length, towards the close of May, A.D. 597, he desired to visit the monks who worked in the fields on the western, the only fertile, side of the island, that he might give them his blessing. His great age prevented his going thither on foot, and he was drawn to the field in a car by oxen. On reaching the field he told them that he had greatly desired to leave the world a month before, on Easter Day, but it had been so ordered that he should wait a little longer, and thus their joyous festival had not been turned 'into mourning. Now, however, he felt his days were very few; and when they wept at the thought of his departure, he bade them be of good cheer, and gave them his last blessing.

On the Saturday in the next week following he went, leaning on one of the brethren, to the granary where the corn was stored, and thanked God that he had provided for the wants of the brotherhood, and that for that year at least there would be no lack of food, though he himself would not share it with them.

Then, perceiving the sorrow of his companion, he continued :—"This day in the Sacred Scriptures is called *Sabbatum,* or *rest;* and truly will it be a day of *rest* to me, for this day shall I bid farewell to the toils of my life and enter into the rest of heaven. For now my Lord Jesus Christ deigns to invite me, and to him shall I at midnight depart."

Then the two turn back towards the monastery; but when they had got half-way, an old white horse, which had been used to carry milk every day from the dairy to the monastery, came towards them, and put his head on his master's shoulder. Columba's companion would have driven him away, but the aged saint forbade him, and, having caressed him for the last time, he went to the summit of a little hillock, and there, lifting up both his hands to heaven, bestowed upon the island and the monastery his solemn blessing.

Descending they entered the little wattled hut, and the saint began to transcribe the 34th Psalm;[1] but on coming to the words in the 11th verse, *They who seek the Lord shall want no manner of thing that is good,* he remarked that he had come to the end of a page, and to a place where he might well stop. "The next words," said he, "*Come, ye children, hearken unto me,* belong rather to my successor than to myself." Then rising he went to vespers, and when they were ended, returned to his cell, and sent his last exhortation by his companion to his disciples, urging them to mutual love and goodwill, and expressing

[1] Psalm xxxiii. 10, 11, in the Vulgate.

his hope of meeting them hereafter. The evening wore on, and on the turn of midnight, as the bell rang for matins, he rose and went to the chapel, and knelt down before the altar in prayer. The lights had not yet been brought in, but his faithful attendant Diarmid found him by groping in the darkness, and supported his head upon his knees till the rest of the brethren entered. Seeing what was rapidly drawing near, they set up a bitter cry, but Columba looked upon them with cheerfulness, and tried to raise his right hand as if to bless them. His voice failing, he could only make the accustomed sign, and, with his hand lifted up in blessing, breathed his last on the morning of Sunday, June the 9th, A.D. 597, in the seventy-seventh year of his age.

CHAPTER IV.

ST. COLUMBANUS.

AND now that we have watched the rise of the Celtic
churches in Ireland and on the western shores of
Scotland, we shall see how they poured back with
interest the gifts of civilization and Christianity on
the Continent of Europe. We have already observed
the fervid zeal with which the disciples of the apostles
of Ireland and Caledonia, despising all perils and
hardships, penetrated the most inaccessible retreats
of Pictish heathenism and the rocky islands of the
northern seas, planting wherever they went the banner
of the Cross. Blending the ardour of Christian enthusiasm with an inextinguishable love of travelling
and adventure, they now began to search out the most
rugged fields of labour amongst the most barbarous
tribes of Switzerland and Germany.

The outward appearance of these Celtic missionaries
must have been very striking. Travelling generally
in companies—the Irish tonsure high on their shaven
heads, their long locks flowing behind, their outfit
a pastoral staff, a leathern water-bottle, a wallet,
a leathern case for their service-books, another con-

taining relics—they flocked across the sea, landed on the western shores of France, and, after paying their devotions at some shrine, generally that óf St. Martin at Tours, pressed on to some forest, and there—all obedient to one man, all, as they styled themselves, "soldiers of Christ"—they settled down, and by dint of great labour cleared some portion of the waste. Before long the wooden huts arose, with the little chapel and round tower or steeple by its side, with the abbot's chamber, the refectory, the kitchen, the barn for the grain, and other buildings; and here they lived, and prayed, and studied, tilling the waste, preaching the word, healing the sick, comforting the afflicted, and teaching the heathen tribes a "more excellent way" than the cruel worship of Odin and of Thor.

One of the earliest and most eminent of these Celtic missionaries must now engage our attention.

Two years before St. Columba sailed for his island home in Iona, Columbanus was born in Leinster, of noble parents, and was placed at a very early age under the venerable Senile, abbot of Cluain-inis, in Lough Erne. Under this able teacher his studies embraced—besides the Holy Scriptures—grammar, rhetoric, and geometry; and his rapid progress was attested by a commentary on the Psalms, which he composed at an early age, besides other religious works. Resolved on embracing the monastic state, he left Cluain-inis for the great monastery of Banchor, on the coast of Ulster, and submitted himself to the discipline of the eminent abbot, St. Comgall. But he could not make up his mind to stay at Banchor. Seized with the yearning after foreign travel which seemed to have taken so many of his countrymen by storm, and eagerly desirous to preach the Gospel to the pagan tribes on the Continent of Europe, he acquainted the abbot with his resolve to leave his own country and his father's house, and labour abroad. In vain St. Comgall remonstrated. Columbanus remained firm, and, at the age of thirty, having selected twelve companions from amongst the brethren,[1] he bade farewell to Ireland, and, after barely touching on the shores of Britain, landed in France in the year A.D. 580.

He found the kingdom of the Franks Christian indeed, but only in name, distracted with furious wars, and neglected by its own bishops. After traversing the country for some time and preaching the word, he arrived in Burgundy, where he was eagerly welcomed by Guntram, the least blameworthy of the grandsons of Clovis. Here he might have found a secure retreat and a sphere of useful labour; but his ascetic spirit longed for a sterner mission field. On the confines of the kingdoms of Austrasia and Burgundy rose the wild and desolate range of the Vosges, and tribes of pagan Suevians roamed over districts once colonized by the Roman legionaries. Here he determined to take up his abode; and with his twelve companions first settled down amidst the ruins of the ancient Roman castle of Anegray. Here and at Luxeuil, where the speedily increasing number of his

[1] See "Vita S. Galli;" Pertz, "Mon. Germ." vol. ii. p. 47.

disciples forced him to lay the foundations of another
monastery, were charms for the severest ascetic.

" Over a range of sixty leagues, and a breadth of ten
or fifteen, nothing was to be seen but parallel chains
of inaccessible defiles, divided by endless forests,
whose bristling pine-woods descended from the peaks
of the highest mountains to overshadow the course
of the rapid and pure streams of the Doubs, the
Dessoubre, and Loue." [1] War and devastation had
well-nigh effaced every trace of Roman colonists.
What their industry had cultivated the sword of the
barbarous invaders, and especially of Attila, had
restored to solitude, and made once more the haunt
of the bear, the bison, and the wolf.

No spot could have been found more suited to the
spirit of Columbanus. Nowhere could he and his
companions better learn to practise self-denial and
inure themselves to the severest hardships. Before
long, at Anegray and Luxeuil, monasteries arose
amidst the waste, on the model of those Columba
had raised under the oaks of Derry. The boundaries
of the monastic colony were duly marked out, and
the forest cleared. Within these rose the humble cells
of thatch and wattles, and conspicuously the church
with the round tower, which could serve as a place of
refuge in times of need. In fields reclaimed from
desolation the seed was sown, and when the summer
had mellowed the waving grain, the brethren reaped
the golden harvest. The mysterious life of the
strangers profoundly moved the hearts of Franks and

---

[1] Montalembert's "Monks of the West," vol. ii. pp. 403, 404.

heathen alike. Hundreds flocked to listen to their
religious instructions ; hundreds more, encouraged by
their labours in clearing and tilling the land, took to
copying their example. At Anegray, at Luxeuil, at
Fontenay, they beheld forests cleared, trees felled,
and the lands ploughed by the same assiduous hands,
all obedient to one head, who sometimes assisted in,
and always encouraged, their labours.

A Rule severer than that of Benedict bound every
member of the increasing fraternity. Incessant toil,
either in the field or in copying and illuminating
manuscripts ; the punctilious observance of repeated
devotional exercises, three by day and three by
night ; the severest discipline, extending to every
motion of the body, and regulating even the tone of
the voice ;—these and other methods were employed
by the enthusiastic abbot in moulding to implicit
obedience those who were admitted to his cloisters.

"Obedience" is the heading of the first chapter of
his Rule, and the question, "What are the limits of
obedience ? " is answered, "Even unto death ; for
unto death Christ submitted himself to the Father
for us." The life of the monastic brother is thus
described :—" Let the monk live under the discipline
of one father, and in the society of many—that
from the one he may learn humility, from the other
patience—from the one silence, from the other gentleness ; let him never gratify his own wishes ; let him
eat whatever he is bidden ; let him possess only what
he receives ; let him perform his allotted task with
diligence ; only when wearied out let him retire to bed ;

let him be compelled to rise before he has slept sufficiently; when he is injured, let him hold his peace;
let him fear the head of the monastery as a master,
and love him as a father; let him believe that whatever he orders is for his good, and obey him without
question, seeing that he is called to obedience, and to
fulfil all that is right; let his fare be homely and
sparing, sufficient to support life without weighing
down the spirit—a little bread, vegetables, pulse, or
flour mixed with water; let this be his diet, as
becometh one who professeth to seek in heaven an
eternal crown."

But the abbot was far from teaching his disciples
that the essence of piety consisted in externals.
Again and again he reminds them that true religion
consists not in the outward humility of the body but
of the heart. He himself ever set them a worthy example. At once practical and contemplative, he would
work as hard as the best of them in clearing the
waste, and then he would penetrate into the deepest
recesses of the forest, there to read and meditate on
the Scriptures, which he always carried with him.
On Sundays and high festivals he abstracted himself
even yet more from outward things. Seeking a cave,
or some other secluded spot, he would devote himself
entirely to prayer and meditation, and so prepare
for celebrating the holy services of the day without
distraction. "Whosoever overcomes himself," he was
wont to say, "treads the world under foot. No one
who spares himself can really hate the world. If
Christ be truly in us, we cannot live to ourselves; if

we have conquered ourselves, we have conquered all
things. If the Creator of all things died for us, that
he might redeem us from sin, ought not we to die
to sin? Let us die unto ourselves. Let us live in
Christ, that Christ may live in us."

These quotations, and others to the same effect
might be easily multiplied, express the innermost
feelings of his heart, and the principles which he
sought to instil into the Order he had founded, in
superintending which he found constant occupation
for upwards of twelve years.

But he was not without his sorrows and anxieties.
Death carried off seventeen of the brethren, and the
abbot buried them in a portion of the forest he had
so lately cleared. Moreover, the severity of his
life and his zeal for monastic discipline excited the
bitter prejudices of the Frankish clergy, whose own
lethargy and worldliness stood rebuked by his self-
denial. The pertinacity also with which he clung
to the customs he had learnt in Ireland, and especially
the time for the observance of Easter, did not mend
matters, and involved him in a correspondence with
Pope Gregory the Great, in which, while expressing
all due respect for his exalted position, he nevertheless stoutly asserted his independence, and declined to
alter the traditions he had received.

Before long his adherence to his Irish customs
induced several bishops of the Frankish Church to
convene a synod and deliberate how they should act
towards the intrepid missionary. Hearing of their
intention, he addressed them in a letter, wherein, after

expressing his thankfulness that they had met on his account, and his wish that they would meet rather oftener, as the canons required, he referred them as regards the Easter question to his correspondence with Gregory, and assured them with pathetic dignity that he was not the author of these differences.

"I came as a stranger amongst you," he says, "in behalf of our common Lord and Master, Jesus Christ. In his name, I beseech you, let me live in peace and quiet, as I have lived for twelve years in these woods beside the bones of my seventeen departed brethren. Let France receive into her bosom all who, if they deserve it, will meet in one heaven. For we have one kingdom promised us, we have one hope of our calling in Christ, with whom we shall reign together if we suffer with him here on earth. Choose ye which rule ye will respecting Easter, remembering the words of the Apostle, *Prove all things, hold fast that which is good.*[1] But let us not quarrel with one another, lest our enemies, the Jews, heretics, and heathen, rejoice in our contention." Then he concludes, "Pray for us, my father, even as we, humble as we are, pray for you. Regard us not as strangers, for we are members together of one Body, whether we be Gauls, or Britons, or Iberians, or to whatever nation we belong. Therefore let us all rejoice in the knowledge of the faith, and in the revelation of the Son of God, and let us strive earnestly to attain together *unto a perfect man, unto the measure of the stature of the fulness of Christ;*[2] in communion with him let us learn to love

---

[1] 1 Thess. v. 21.   [2] Eph. iv. 13.

one another, and pray for one another, that with him
we may together reign for evermore."

Thus with mingled firmness and pathos did the
abbot plead with the Frankish prelates. But he
was soon called to engage in a nobler strife, and to
protest against the vices of the Burgundian court, at
this time ruled by the notorious Brunehaut, who,
expelled from the palace of Theodebert II., king of
Austrasia, had taken up her abode with her younger
son, Thierri. Thierri had given himself up to the un-
bridled indulgence of his lusts, and Brunehaut con-
niving at his licentiousness, opposed in every possible
way the substitution of a lawful wife for his numerous
concubines, and sought to gain a complete ascendency
in his kingdom, and to rule him through his vices.

But the fame of the abbot of Luxeuil attracted
Thierri, who was not without religious instincts, and
he often visited the monastery. Columbanus did
not neglect the opportunity thus afforded him. He
solemnly reproved the king for his disorderly life, and
bade him leave the society of his mistresses for an
alliance with a queen, who might bring him a legitimate heir. The young king promised amendment,
but Brunehaut saw in a legitimate queen a deathblow
to all her influence, and her rage against the abbot
was unbounded ; but she dared not treat him as Didier,
bishop of Vienne, had been treated, who had paid with
his life for boldly rebuking the king's incontinence.
Shortly afterwards, whether at her request or of his own
accord, the abbot visited the palace, and the queen-
mother implored his blessing on Thierri's four illegiti-

mate sons. "These bastards born in sin," was the uncompromising reply, "shall never wield the royal sceptre." Brunehaut, furious, bade the children retire, and from that day forward commenced a series of petty persecutions, cutting off supplies from the Irish monasteries, and stirring up jealousy between them and the neighbouring convents.

Thereupon the abbot determined to repair once more to the court, and to remonstrate with the king himself. It was sunset when he appeared before the palace, and on his arrival being announced, the king ordered a sumptuous supper to be prepared and sent out to him. "It is written," said the abbot, "that the Most High abhors the offerings of the wicked, who wickedly persecute the servants of God, and exclude them not only from their own, but from the habitation of others." Thereupon, according to his biographer, the dishes in a marvellous fashion brake in pieces, and the wine and other viands were spilt upon the ground. Alarmed at the intelligence of what had occurred, Thierri again promised amendment, and Columbanus returned to Luxeuil. Shortly afterwards, however, hearing that the king had relapsed into his old habits, he indited a letter full of the severest rebukes, and threatening him with excommunication if he did not repent.

Brunehaut felt that her turn was now come. She inflamed the mind of the king against his stern monitor; she roused the nobles and courtiers, and appealing to the bishops, endeavoured to rouse their jealousy against the strange monk. At last, stung to

the quick, Thierri repaired to Luxeuil, and demanded
a free entrance to the monastery for himself and his
suite. Nothing daunted, the abbot forbade his advancing a step further. The king ventured as far as
the refectory, but shrunk from proceeding beyond, so
menacing were the other's words. "Thou thinkest,"
said he, with a sneer, "that I shall confer on thee a
martyr's crown ; I am not so utterly foolish as to
gratify thy pride. But since it pleaseth thee to live
apart from all other men, thou shalt go hence by the
way that thou camest."[1]

Columbanus refused to leave the monastery except
by compulsion, whereupon he was forcibly taken and
conducted to Besançon. But he managed to elude his
guards, and made his way back to Luxeuil. Again
he was taken, and with two or three of his companions
was hurried to Auxerre, thence to Nevers, where he was
placed on board a vessel and conveyed down the Loire
to Orleans, and so to Nantes, where he was put on
board a ship bound for Ireland. But a storm arose,
and the vessel was driven back and left high and dry
on the coast of Neustria, nor till the abbot and his
companions had been put safely on shore did the
waters return and float the ship out to sea.

Thus once more in France, Columbanus repaired to
the court of Clotaire II., king of Neustria, who besought
him to remain and hallow his realm with his presence.
The abbot could be persuaded to stay only a few days
at the court, and then, after advising the monarch
about some political matters, requested a safe-conduct

[1] Jonæ "Vita S. Columbani," capp. xix. xx.

to the court of the Austrasian Theodebert. His
request was granted, and he reached his destination
in safety. The King of Austrasia received him with
delight, but could not prevail upon him to remain
more than a brief space in his dominions.

As he was now not far from Luxeuil, not a few of
the brethren flocked around him once more, and rejoiced to see their revered abbot. But pining for the
solitude which had been so long denied him, he resolved to proclaim the faith among the pagan tribes
bordering on the Austrasian confines, and embarking
on the Rhine with a few followers, ascended the river
as far as the lake of Zurich, and halted finally at
Tuggen. Here the tribes of heathen Suevians roamed
up and down the country, and are described as cruel
and impious, offering sacrifice to idols, and addicted
to augury and divination. One of the abbot's companions, an Irish monk named Callech, or Gallus,[1] set
fire to their wooden temples, and flung their idols
into the lake; while on another occasion Columbanus
himself broke one of the vats whence the beer was to
be drawn for a sacred festival in honour of Woden.
These proceedings roused the wrath of the Suevians,
and they drove the missionaries from their country.
Shaking off the dust from their feet, and invoking
terrible maledictions on the natives, Columbanus and
his companions left for Zug, and thence shaped their

---

[1] The practice of Latinizing the Irish names of these early missionaries
was very common. Thus, *Fergal* was called Virgilius ; *Siadhail*, Sedulius ;
Cathal, Cataldus ; *Donnchadh*, Donatus; *Comgall*, Faustus. See
" Ulster Archæol. Journal," vol. vii. p. 242.

course to Arbon, a small town situated about midway along the south bank of the lake of Constance.

Here they found traces of Christianity planted under the Roman or Frankish government, and a priest named Willimar received them with much cordiality. Seven days were spent in pleasant intercourse, and in reply to the inquiries of his visitors Willimar pointed out Bregenz, at the south-eastern extremity of the lake, as well adapted for a centre of missionary activity. A boat was manned by the friendly priest, and Columbanus and his companions made for the spot, and found it well suited for their purpose. Bregenz occupied the site of an ancient Roman camp, and contained the ruins of a church originally dedicated to St. Aurelius. Within the ruins, however, the missionaries found three images of brass gilded, fixed to the wall, which the people were wont to worship as the presiding deities of the place, and to invoke as their protectors.

These strange gods Columbanus resolved to remove, and availing himself of a festival, when great numbers resorted to Bregenz from the country round, he directed Gallus, who was acquainted with the native language, to address the people on the foolishness of their idolatry, and to persuade them to embrace a true faith. His companion complied with his request, and in the presence of a vast multitude proceeded to reason with them on the absurdities of the heathen errors, and to proclaim to them the one living and true God and his Son Jesus Christ. Then taking the idols, he broke them in pieces, and flung them into

the lake, while Columbanus sprinkled the church with
holy water, and cleansed it of the taint of idolatry.
The people were divided: some seeing the inability of
their gods to help themselves, approved the boldness
of the abbot, and were baptized; others went away
filled with anger and bent on revenge.

In spite, however, of the exasperation of the greater
proportion of the inhabitants, Columbanus and his
little colony remained there upwards of three years,
erected a monastery, and cleared a portion of the
forest. At first their hardships were very great, and
Gallus provided for the wants of the community by
making nets and fishing on the lake, which to this day
abounds with many varieties of fish.

One night, we are told, while he was thus engaged,
he overheard the Spirit of the Mountain call to
the Spirit of the Waters, " Arise and hasten to my
assistance ! Behold, strangers have come and driven
me from my temple. Hasten to my aid, and help
me to expel them from the land !" To whom replied the Spirit of the Waters, " Lo! even now one
of them is busy on my surface, but I cannot injure
him. Oftentimes have I desired to break his nets,
but as often have I been baffled by the invocation
of an all-prevailing Name, which never fails to
cross his lips. Thus defended, he always despises
my snares." Gallus shuddered at this unearthly
dialogue, but quickly crossing himself, addressed
the spirits, "I adjure you, in the name of the Lord
Jesus Christ, that ye depart from this place, and never
venture to injure any one any more." He then hastily

made for the shore, and recounted to the abbot what he had heard, who rejoiced at this manifest proof that even the spirits were subject unto the brethren.

Human hostility, however, they found not so easy to overcome. The heathen party roused against them one of the native chieftains, and Columbanus resolved to leave the neighbourhood. At first he thought of going to labour among the Sclavic and Wendish tribes who bordered on the Germanic nations, but forbidden by a dream to undertake this mission, he took with him a single disciple named Attalus, and crossing the Alps, repaired to the court of Agilulf, king of the Lombards, who with his queen, Theodelinda, welcomed him with the utmost cordiality. Agilulf bestowed upon him the territory of Bobbio, situated in a defile of the Apennines, between Genoa and Milan. Here were the ruins of a church dedicated to St. Peter, which Columbanus restored, and with the aid of companions, who quickly joined him, added to it the famous monastery of Bobbio.[1] Here also he welcomed several of the brethren from Luxeuil, who, with the abbot Eustacius at their head, came on an embassy from Clotaire II., now sole king of the Franks, and master of Austrasia, Burgundy, and Neustria, begging him to return to the scene of his early labours. This, however, Columbanus declined to do, and spent the remaining years of his life in his new monastery, and

---

[1] This monastery existed as late even as the year 1803. Its valuable library preserved not only Cicero's treatise " De Republica," but an Irish antiphonarium of the eighth century and an early Irish missal. The name of its founder still survives in St. Columbano, near Lodi.

died at the ripe age of seventy-two, November 21,
A.D. 615.

Meanwhile his companion Callech, better known as
Gallus or St. Gall, prevented by a severe attack of
fever from accompanying his master across the Alps,
remained behind at Bregenz. On his recovery he
sought out his old friend Willimar at Arbon, and in
his society, and that of two of the Luxeuil brethren,
Magnoald and Theodore, found ample employment
for his boat and nets on the waters of the lake.

But soon yearning, like his master, for profounder
solitudes, he determined to seek a retreat in the midst
of the surrounding forests. On communicating his
design to Hildebald, a deacon under Willimar, who
was intimately acquainted with the woods, the latter
tried to dissuade him, by describing the perils of the
forest and the multitude of wild beasts. "If God
be with us," replied Gallus, "who can be against us?
all things work together for good to them that love
God."

Thus overruled, the deacon persuaded him at least
to take some bread and a fishing-net, and after
prayer the two set out on their journey. They had
travelled till nearly three in the afternoon, when the
deacon proposed that they should stop and refresh
themselves before proceeding further. Gallus, however, true to the rule of his master, bade the deacon
do as he pleased, but declared that, for himself, he
was resolved to taste nothing till God should point
out the site of their retreat.

Evening was closing on a long summer's day as they

reached a stream falling down from a rock, where they succeeded in taking a few fish, which the deacon proceeded to broil over a fire, while the other in the meantime retired to seek a quiet spot where he might engage in prayer. He had not gone far when his foot caught in some bushes, and he fell down. The deacon hastened to raise him up, but Gallus declined his aid, saying, "Let me alone: this is my resting-place for life ; here will I dwell." Then rising up, he made a cross of hazel boughs and planted it in the ground, and suspending from it his casket of relics, continued for some time engaged in prayer that God would enable him to erect a monastery on this spot. Their devotions ended, the two partook of supper ; and while the deacon pretended to be asleep, Gallus engaged in conflict with a bear, which, his biographer tells us,[1] in obedience to the words of so holy a man, condescended to lay aside its usual ferocity, and to leave them unharmed.

In the morning the deacon repaired to the stream of the Steinach, and while fishing beheld two demons in the form of women, who pelted him with stones, and imprecated curses on the head of his master. He returned to Gallus, to whose word the demons were found to be as obedient as the bear had been on the preceding night, and forsook the stream. With a present of fish they now made their way back to Willimar, and recounted all that had befallen them.

Shortly afterwards a message from Gunzo, the pagan chieftain who had been instrumental in expelling

[1] " Vita S. Galli," Pertz, "Mon. Germ." vol. ii. p. 9.

Columbanus from the country, summoned Gallus to cure his daughter, who was possessed with a demon. The spirit recognised the voice of him who had spoken words of power on the lake, the maiden recovered, and on her arrival at the court of the King of Austrasia, to whom she was espoused, recounted all that had befallen her, and secretly took the veil, a step which had been suggested by the missionary, and was not resented by the king. The valuable presents which were bestowed upon him in acknowledgment of the benefit he had conferred Gallus distributed among the poor of Arbon. Among them was a silver cup, which one of his disciples begged him to keep for the service of the altar. "Silver and gold have I none," replied the other; "vessels of brass sufficed my master for the celebration of the sacred feast, and they shall be sufficient for me. Let it be given to the poor."

He then retired permanently to his retreat in the forest, where he was joined by a deacon named John, and twelve other monks, with whose assistance he cleared the waste, and erected the famous monastery which now bears his name. The see of Constance falling vacant, he repaired thither with the deacons John and Magnoald on the invitation of the duke, Gunzo, and there met the bishops of Autun, Spires, and Verdun, and a large body of clergy and laity assembled to elect a successor. After some deliberation Gunzo addressed them, and exhorted them to choose a proper bishop according to the canons, and one who would rule his see with diligence.

The eyes of all were fixed upon Gallus, and all agreed that no other was so fitted for the high office. But the missionary declined the proffered honour, remarking that the canons, except in the most urgent cases, did not permit strangers to be ordained bishops of districts of which they were not natives. "But," he added, "I have a deacon of your own people, who is well fitted to fill the office, and I propose him for your acceptance." Thereupon the deacon John, who during their deliberations had retired to the church of St. Stephen, was brought forth with acclamations by the people, presented to the bishops, and forthwith consecrated. Mass was then celebrated, and after reading the Gospel, Gallus was requested to preach to the assembled multitude. Accordingly he commenced his sermon,[1] which the newly elected bishop interpreted.

The discourse was little more than an abridged history of religion, and of the chief events from the Creation to the preaching of the Apostles. The Origin of the world, the Fall of our first parents, the Flood, the Call of Abraham, the miracles of Moses, the kingly period of Israel's history, the calling and functions of the Prophets, the miracle of the Incarnation, the Sufferings, Death, and Resurrection of man's Redeemer, the mission of the Apostles,—each of these points was treated in turn, and made the text of some moral observations.

---

[1] It is given in full in Canisius, "Antiq. Lect." vol. i. p. 784, and the "Acta SS." Oct. 16 ; in an abridged form in Pertz, "Vita S. Galli," vol. ii. p. 14.

Seven days were spent at Constance, and then Gallus returned to his cell in the forest, where he spent the rest of his life, superintending for twelve years the labours of his monastic brethren. Receiving information of the death of his great master, Columbanus, he sent one of his disciples to make inquiries as to the day and hour of his demise, and received in reply a letter from the brethren at Bobbio, and the pastoral staff of the great abbot, which the latter had bequeathed to him. Once, and only once more, did he consent to leave his retreat. At the urgent request of Willimar he paid a visit to him at Arbon, and on the occasion of a solemnity preached to a large congregation. Setting out on his return, he was attacked with fever, and before he could regain his favourite retreat was overtaken by death, on the 16th of October, A.D. 627.

The life of St. Gall, like that of his master, Columbanus, had been eminent for self-denial and usefulness. He had revived the faith in the ancient see of Constance, he had reclaimed from barbarism the district bordering on the Black Forest. He had taught the people the arts of agriculture, as well as the duties of religion, and the humble cell of the apostle of Switzerland became after his death the resort of thousands of pilgrims, and was replaced by a more magnificent edifice, erected under the auspices of Pepin l'Heristal, which during the ninth and tenth centuries was the asylum of learning and one of the most celebrated schools of Europe.

CHAPTER V.

WHILE the work of gradual evangelization was thus proceeding in Southern Germany, the more northern parts of Europe were not overlooked.

Bordering on the kingdom of the Franks, in the early part of the seventh century, was the powerful tribe of the Frisians, the nearest blood-relations of the Anglo-Saxon race. Their authority extended not only over the strip of territory which still recalls the name of the Frieslanders, but a considerable portion also of the Netherlands, and they even encroached upon the Franks in Belgic Gaul.

The natural consequence was, that between the Franks and these outlying tribes, fierce and barbarous, and clinging to their native superstition with fanatical tenacity, a series of border wars was perpetually maintained. The task, therefore, of planting Christianity amongst them was one of the utmost difficulty and peril.

Men, however, were not found wanting to make the attempt. Thus Amandus, who was consecrated a missionary bishop about the year A.D. 628, selected the neighbourhood of Ghent as the centre of his

operations, and strove with some success to win the
pagans to the faith. About the same time Andomar,
or St. Omer, from the monastery of Luxeuil, preached
the word from the neighbourhood of Boulogne as far
as the Scheldt. Ireland also sent over the missionary
bishop Livinus,[1] who left his country with three
companions and suffered martyrdom amongst the
barbarous natives of Brabant and Flanders.

About twelve years later than Amandus, appeared,
in an adjoining district, another Frankish bishop, the
famous St. Eligius, or, as he is better known, St. Eloy.
Born in the year A.D. 588, at Chatelat, a village
about a mile from Limoges, Eligius was remarkable
at an early age for excellence of character and genuine
piety. His father placed him with a goldsmith at
Limoges, and he soon displayed such skill as to attract
the notice of Bobbo, the treasurer of Clotaire II. By
him he was entrusted with a commission for the king,
and the fidelity with which he executed it won for
him the favour of the court, and he was appointed
to superintend the royal mint.

Though surrounded by temptations, in the midst
of a profligate court, he did not forget the Christian
lessons he had learnt in childhood, but became eminent
for the integrity of his life, for his kindness to the
poor, and the interest he took in the relief and redemption of captives. In this latter sphere of charity his
labours were unwearied. Whenever he heard that a
slave was about to be put up for sale, he hurried to the
place and procured his redemption. Bands of twenty,

---

[1] See the "Annales Gaudenses," Pertz, "Mon. Germ." vol. ii. p. 186.

thirty, and even fifty, were thus liberated, and sometimes whole shiploads of slaves, Romans, Gauls,
Britons, Moors, and especially Saxons from Germany,
experienced the benefits of his kindness. To rescue
them from the hardships of the servile lot, he stinted
himself to the last farthing, and all who were willing
to embrace the monastic life he assisted liberally,
hoping to train them as missionaries amongst their
own countrymen. So munificent was he in his chari-
ties, that he was ever surrounded by a crowd of needy
applicants for his bounty, and it became a common
reply to any one inquiring for his house, "Wherever
you see the largest crowd of paupers, there you may
be sure to find Eligius."[1] He was equally earnest in
erecting churches and monasteries.

One of these latter his biographer describes at
length, and we gain a vivid conception of the civilizing
effects of such institutions at this period. Screened
by a lofty mountain and a dense forest, and surrounded by a moat, the gardens of the monastery
were filled with flowers and fruit-trees of every kind,
while a colony of monks employed the intervals of
devotion in various kinds of handicraft, under the
superintending eye of the skilful master of the royal
mint.

Nothing shocked him more in his journeys from
place to place than the sight of the bodies of malefactors hanging on gibbets and slowly rotting in the
air. Wherever he saw such, he always had them
removed and decently interred. On one occasion his

[1] See the Life of Eligius in Surius, "Acta SS." Nov. 30.

attendants had taken down the body of a man who
had been hanged that very morning, and were preparing
his grave, when Eligius fancied he saw a quivering
motion which gave sign of life not being quite extinct.
He immediately used all his efforts to restore vitality,
and was successful. " What a sin it would have been
to have buried this man alive!" was his simple remark
to his followers, anxious to ascribe the man's restoration to miraculous agency: "let him be clothed, and
rest awhile." It was with difficulty, however, that he
rescued him from his accusers, and, in spite of their
furious declamations against any mitigation of his
punishment, succeeded in obtaining his pardon from
the king.

In such works of charity, and the duties of the lower
clerical office, he found ample employment till his
elevation, in the year A.D. 641, to the bishopric of
Noyon opened to him a still more direct and special
sphere of usefulness. His diocese comprised the districts of Noyon, Vermondes, and Tournay, and was
inhabited in great part by barbarous heathen tribes,
who had never yet received the message of the Gospel.
Here, in spite of imminent peril to himself, and amidst
every hardship, he strove to win over, by his consistent
life and ceaseless self=devotion, the savage hearts of his
people. He founded churches and monasteries, and
traversed his diocese in every part, proclaiming the
word to the people, and warning them against their
idolatries.

Fragments of some of his sermons have been preserved by his biographer, which are interesting as

giving us an insight into the way in which, in the seventh century, a bishop like Eligius would provide for the spiritual wants of his people. In these, while, on the one hand, we find exhortations to a diligent cultivation of such Christian graces as love, faith, self-denial, purity, and concord, to a careful attention to Christian ordinances, as prayer, attendance at church, hearing the word, and the reception of the Lord's Supper, we find, on the other, exhortations to avoidance of all such heathen superstitions as were then rife in the country.

In one sermon, after a persistent protest against the idea that men can win the favour of the Almighty by the mere performance of external ceremonies, the bishop proceeds, "It sufficeth not, my brethren, that ye be called Christians, if ye do not the works of a Christian. That man alone is benefited by the name of a Christian, who, with his whole heart, keeps the precepts and laws of Christ, who abstains from theft, from bearing false witness, from lying, from perjury, from adultery, from hatred of his fellow-man, from strife and discord. For these commands Christ himself vouchsafed to give us in his Gospel, saying, *Thou shalt do no murder, thou shalt not commit adultery, thou shalt not steal, thou shalt not bear false witness, honour thy father and thy mother, and love thy neighbour as thyself; whatsoever ye would that men should do unto you, even so do ye unto them, for this is the law and the prophets.* Nay, he adds stronger commands than these, for he says, *Love your enemies: bless them that curse you: do good to them that hate you: pray for them that despitefully use you, and persecute you.*[1] Behold, this is a hard and difficult command, and seems impossible to men, but it has a great reward; for hear what he declares it is, *That ye may be the children of your Father which is in heaven.* Oh, what grace is here! Of ourselves we are not worthy to be his servants, and yet by loving our enemies we become the sons of God. He then who wishes to be a Christian indeed must keep these commandments. He who keepeth them not deceiveth himself. He is a good Christian who putteth his trust not in amulets or devices of demons, but in Christ alone.

"But above all things, if ye would be Christians indeed, beware of resorting to any heathen customs, or consulting in any trial or difficulty soothsayers, fortune-tellers, or diviners. He who doeth thus speedily loseth the grace of his baptism. Let there be amongst you no resorting to auguries or observance of the flight or singing of birds when ye set out on a journey. Rather, when ye undertake a journey or any business, sign yourselves in the name of Christ, repeat the Creed and the Lord's Prayer with faith and devotion, and no enemy will draw nigh to hurt you. No Christian will choose superstitiously a lucky day for going out or coming in, for all days are made by God. No Christian will attend to the moon before commencing any undertaking, or on the first of January will join in foolish and unseemly junketings and frivolity, or nocturnal revellings.

"Neither heaven, nor earth, nor stars, nor any

[1] St. Matt. v. 44.

other creature, is deserving of worship. God alone
is to be adored, for he created and ordained all
things. Heaven indeed is high, and the earth wide,
and the stars passing fair, but far grander and fairer
must he be who made all these things. For if the
things that we see are so incomprehensible and past
understanding, even the various fruits of the earth,
and the beauty of the flowers, and the divers kinds
of animals in earth, air, and water, the instinct of the
provident bee, the wind blowing where it listeth, the
crash of the thunder, the changes of the seasons, the
alternations of day and night; if these things that we
see with our eyes cannot be comprehended by the
mind of man, how shall we comprehend the things we
do not see? Or what kind of Being must he be by
whom all these things are created and sustained?
Fear him, my brethren, before all things, adore and
love him, cleave fast to his longsuffering, and never
despair of his tender mercy."

In other sermons the bishop enlarges on the promises made by the Christian at his baptism, on the
duty of remembering them in the course of daily life,
on the true aspect and responsibility of life as a state
of warfare against sin, and a preparation for the Great
Day, when an account must be given for the deeds
done in the body.

On this latter topic his exhortations are powerful
in their reality and earnestness. "Let us reflect," he
says, "what terror ours will be, when from heaven
the Lord shall come to judge the world, before whom
the elements shall melt in a fervent heat, and heaven

and earth shall tremble, and the powers of the heavens
shall be shaken. Then while the trumpets of the
angels sound, all men, good and evil, shall in a
moment of time rise with the bodies they wore on
earth, and be led before the tribunal of Christ :
then shall all the tribes of the earth mourn, while
he points out to them the marks of the nails wherewith he was pierced for our iniquities, and shall
speak unto them and say, ' I formed thee, O man, of
the dust of the earth ; with my own hands I fashioned
thee and placed thee, all undeserving, in the delights
of Paradise ; but thou didst despise me and my words,
and didst prefer to follow the deceiver, for which
thou wast justly condemned. But yet I did pity thee,
I took upon me thy flesh, I lived on earth amongst
sinners, I endured reproach and stripes for thy sake ;
that I might rescue thee from punishment, I endured
blows and to be spitted on ; that I might restore to
thee the bliss of Paradise, I drank vinegar mingled
with gall. For thy sake was I crowned with thorns,
and crucified, and pierced with the spear. For thy
sake did I die, and was laid in the grave, and descended into Hades, that I might bring thee back to
Paradise. Behold and see what I endured for thy
sake ! Behold the mark of the nails wherewith I was
fixed to the Cross ! I took upon me thy sorrows,
that I might heal thee. I took upon me thy punishment, that I might crown thee with glory. I endured
to die, that thou mightest live for ever. Though I
was invisible, yet for thy sake I became incarnate.
Though I knew no suffering, yet for thy sake I

deigned to suffer. Though I was rich, yet for thy sake I became poor. But thou didst despise my lowliness and my precepts, thou didst obey a deceiver rather than me. My justice, therefore, cannot pronounce any other sentence than such as thine own works deserve. Thou didst choose thine own ways, receive then thine own wages. Thou didst despise light, let darkness then be thy reward. Thou didst love death, depart then to perdition. Thou didst obey the Evil One, go then with him into eternal punishment.' "

In the lips of the preacher these were no empty words. He lived in the constant realization of that awful day whose coming he thus vividly describes. With unwearied activity he persevered in his self-denying labours till his seventieth year. Increasing weakness, at last, warned him that his end was near, and he spoke of it openly on one occasion, as he was walking in Noyon to a church with some of his younger clergy. Noticing a defect in the building which threatened its speedy fall, he sent for a workman to have it repaired. His companions suggested that the repairs should be deferred till such time as they could be completely carried out. " Let it be repaired now, my children," he said ; " for if it is not done now, I shall never live to see it finished." To their expressions of sorrow at such a speedy loss of their friend and guide he replied, that he had long felt the day of his departure was coming, and he would not be sorry to leave the world.

Shortly afterwards worse symptoms appeared, but

he still continued his labours of love, so far as he was able. He employed the last days of his life in solemnly charging his monastic brethren to remember their vows, and not to forsake the flock of Christ, but to labour diligently to carry on his work. When he felt that his hour was really come, clasping his hands in prayer, he said, " Now lettest thou thy servant depart, according to thy word. Remember, O Lord, I am but dust, and enter not into judgment with thy servant. Remember me, O thou that alone art free from sin, Christ the Saviour of the world. Lead me forth from the body of this death, and give me an entrance into thy heavenly kingdom. Thou who hast ever been my protector, into Thy hands I commend my spirit. I know that I do not deserve to behold thy face, but thou knowest how my hope was always in thy mercy, and my trust in thy faithfulness. Receive me, then, according to thy loving-kindness, and let me not be disappointed of my hope." With which words he departed this life A.D. 659.

CHAPTER VI.

WHILE, however, these and other missionary bands were carrying the light of the Gospel into the countries bordering on the northern and eastern parts of France, events had taken place in England destined to exercise a profound influence on the consolidation and development of the churches of the Continent, and the evangelization of the Germanic races.

Some five years before the founder of Luxeuil left Ireland for France, that is, about A.D. 575, the famous Gregory the Great, then a monk in the monastery of St. Andrew on the Cœlian mount at Rome, was one day passing through the market-place, when he noticed several gangs of slaves exposed for sale.[1] Amongst them three boys, distinguished for their fair complexion, the beautiful expression of their faces,[2] and their light flaxen hair, especially arrested his attention. Struck with pity, he inquired from what part of the world they had come, and was answered, " From Britain, where all the inhabitants

---

[1] On the traffic in slaves see above, pp. 38, 39.
[2] See Bede, "II. E." ii. 1.

have the same fair complexion." He next proceeded
to inquire whether the people of this strange country
were Christians or pagans, and hearing that they
were pagans, he heaved a deep sigh, and answered
that it was sad to think "that beings so full of light
and brightness should be in the power of the prince
of darkness."

He next asked the name of their nation. "Angles,"
was the reply; whereupon, as was his manner, playing on the word, he answered, "Rightly are they
called 'Angles,' for their faces are as the faces of
angels, and they ought to be fellow-heirs with the
angels of heaven." Once more he asked, "And from
what province do they come?" He was told that
they came from Deira.[1] "Rightly," he replied, "are
they named Deirans. From the ire of God are they
plucked, and to the mercy of God are they called.
And who is the king of this province?" he proceeded.
"Ælla," was the reply. The word reminded him of
the Hebrew expression of praise, and he answered,
"Allelujah! the praise of God shall be chanted in
that clime."

Then the abbot went his way, but he could not
forget the sight of those fair-haired Yorkshire boys.
He immediately conceived the idea of proceeding as a
missionary to England, and, having obtained the permission of the Pope, had actually accomplished three
days' journey thither, when he was overtaken by the
messengers, whom a furious mob had compelled the

---

[1] The country between the Tyne and the Humber, including Durham
and Yorkshire.

Pontiff to send and recall him to their city. Five years, however, after his own elevation to the Papal chair, A.D. 595, an opportunity occurred of carrying out by another the work he had been prevented executing in person.

In the year A.D. 568 Ethelbert succeeded to the kingdom of Kent, and soon became lord over all the kings south of the Humber. The proximity of Kent to the Continent had favoured the maintenance of the old connexion between Britain and France, and Ethelbert had married a Christian princess, Bertha, the daughter of Charibert, king of Paris. As one of the conditions of the marriage it had been agreed that the queen should be allowed to enjoy the free exercise of her religion, and she had been attended to the Kentish court by a French bishop named Luidhard, who was permitted by Ethelbert to celebrate the worship of the Christians' God in the little church of St. Martin, a relic of Roman-British times, outside the walls of Canterbury.

It is only probable that Bertha should have endeavoured, during a union of twenty years, to influence her husband on the side of Christianity, and it is not surprising that many of the people of Kent, whose own heathen hierarchy had sunk into insignificance, should have been anxious to receive some instruction in the religion of their queen. Accordingly they made application to the Frankish bishops for Christian teachers, and it was probably intelligence of this which determined Gregory to make another attempt to evangelize the country. He wrote, there-

fore, to Candidus,[1] who administered the patrimony
of the Roman Church in Gaul, directing him to
buy up English youths from seventeen to twenty
years of age, that they might be trained in different monasteries, and become missionaries in their
native land. At length, in the sixth year of his
pontificate, A.D. 596, he selected from his own monastery on the Cœlian hill a band of forty monks,
whom he placed under their prior, Augustine, and
enjoined them to commence a direct mission in
England.

Accordingly, in the summer of that year, Augustine and his companions set out, traversed rapidly
the north of Italy, and crossing the Gallic Alps reached
the neighbourhood of Aix in Provence. Here the
courage of the little band began to fail, and they
sighed for the security of their cells on the Cœlian
hill. The accounts they received of the savage
character of the Saxons filled them with alarm, and
they prevailed on Augustine to return to Rome, and
obtain for himself and his companions a release from
their arduous enterprise.

But Augustine had to deal, in Gregory, with one
who lived up to the stern rule of the Benedictine
order, who had learnt to crush all human weakness,
and to recognise no call but that of duty. He was
forthwith sent back with a letter to his timid brethren,
wherein they were enjoined to suffer nothing to deter
them from carrying out the work they had undertaken, and bidden to remember that the more

---

[1] See Greg. Epp. viii. 7.

arduous the labour, the greater would be their eternal reward.

Thus urged by an authority they dared not resist, the missionaries slowly bent their steps from Aix to Arles, thence to Vienne, and so through Tours and Anjou to the sea-coast. There they provided themselves with interpreters from among the Franks, and setting sail, landed at some point on the Isle of Thanet.[1]

Once safely on shore, they sent messengers to Ethelbert to announce that they had come from Rome, that they were the bearers of joyful tidings, and could promise him glory in heaven and an everlasting kingdom with the living and true God. Ethelbert received the messengers in a friendly spirit, but with characteristic caution begged that for the present they would remain on the other side of the Stour, and would abstain from entering Canterbury; and stipulated further that their first interview should not take place under a roof, but in the open air, for fear of the charms and spells which he fancied they might exercise upon him.

Accordingly the Saxon king repaired to the Isle of Thanet, and there under an ancient oak awaited the coming of Augustine. To make a deeper impression on the monarch's mind, Augustine, following probably advice he had received from Gregory, advanced in solemn procession, preceded by a verger carrying a

[1] Either at (1) Ebbe's Fleet, or (2) at a spot called the Boarded Groin, or (3) at Stonar near Sandwich, or (4) at Richborough. See Stanley's "Memorials of Canterbury," pp. 34, 35.

silver cross, and followed by another bearing aloft on a board, painted and gilded, a representation of the Saviour. Then came the rest of the brethren, and the choir headed by Laurence and the deacon Peter, who chanted a solemn litany.

Arrived in the king's presence, they were bidden to seat themselves upon the ground. Ethelbert could not understand Latin, and Augustine could not speak Anglo-Saxon; so the Frankish priests interpreted while the missionary explained the meaning of the picture which was borne aloft, and told the king how the merciful One there depicted had left his throne in heaven, died for the sins of a guilty world, and opened the kingdom of heaven to all believers.

Ethelbert listened attentively, and then, in a manner at once politic and courteous, replied that the promises of the strangers were fair, but the tidings they had announced new and full of a meaning he did not understand. He promised them, however, kindness and hospitality, together with liberty to celebrate their sacred services, and undertook that none of his subjects, who might be so disposed, should be prohibited from espousing their religion. Thus successful beyond their utmost expectations, Augustine and his companions again formed a procession; and crossing the ferry to Richborough, advanced into the rude city of Canterbury, then embosomed in thickets, chanting as they went along one of the solemn litanies they had learned from Gregory, and took up their abode in the Stable-gate, till the king should finally make up his mind.

Admitted into the city, the missionaries devoted themselves to prayer and holy exercises, and winning the regard of all the people were next allowed to worship with the queen in the church of St. Martin, and devoted themselves to their great work with renewed zeal. At last Ethelbert avowed his willingness to embrace the faith, and to the great joy, we need not doubt, of Bertha, was baptized in all probability at St. Martin's church, on the 2d of June, being the feast of Whitsunday, A.D. 597. The conversion of the sovereign was the signal for the baptism of the people also, many of whom, it is not improbable, had intermarried with their British subjects; and on the next Christmas Day upwards of ten thousand were baptized in the waters of the Swale, at the mouth of the Medway, and thus sealed their acceptance of the new faith.

Augustine's next step was to repair to France, where, in accordance with the plans of Gregory, he received consecration to the episcopal office at the hands of the Archbishop of Arles. On his return he took up his abode in the wooden palace of the king, who retired to Reculver. Hard by the residence of the bishop, shrouded in a grove of oaks, was an old British or Roman church. This Ethelbert had converted into a temple wherein to worship his Saxon gods. Augustine did not destroy it, but dedicated it to St. Pancras,[1] and it became the nucleus of his first monastery.

[1] Thus recalling to mind the monastery on the Cœlian hill, which had been built on the property belonging to the family of St. Pancras. See Stanley's "Memorials of Canterbury," p. 38.

Now also Laurence and Peter were entrusted with the task of returning to Gregory at Rome, and recounting to him the success of the mission. They were to tell him how the country of the fair-haired slaves he had pitied in the Forum had received the faith, and how Augustine himself, in conformity with his instructions, had been raised to the episcopate. Moreover, they were to beg for answers to certain questions which caused the new bishop some anxiety. These related to the establishment of the revenues of Canterbury, various points of discipline, and especially the differences between the Roman and the Gallican liturgies, with which Augustine had become acquainted during his passage through France, and which in the face of the British clergy in the island might cause trouble.

After some time the messengers returned with the replies of the Pope. Respecting the liturgies, Augustine was directed to select either from the Roman or the Gallican uses whatever appeared to him pious, religious, and right, to collect it into a volume, and establish it as the liturgy of the Anglo-Saxon Church, ever remembering as a guiding principle that "things were not to be loved for the sake of places, but places for the sake of good things." With these directions were others respecting the way in which the missionary was to deal with the monuments of heathenism. Gregory had written to Ethelbert requesting him to destroy the heathen temples in his dominions. But he was not satisfied as to the expediency of such a course, and now, after much consideration, he wrote to Augustine, directing him not to destroy the temples, but only the idols that might be therein. As to the structures themselves, if well built, they were to be purified with holy water and converted into Christian churches. The heathen festivals might, instead of being rudely abolished, be similarly consecrated by Christian associations and the celebration of the birthdays of the saints.

The bearers of these letters were accompanied by fresh labourers as a reinforcement to the mission, and they brought with them ecclesiastical vestments, sacred vessels, some relics of apostles and martyrs, a present of books, including a Bible in two volumes, two Psalters, two copies of the Four Gospels, and expositions of certain Epistles. They were further charged with the pall of a metropolitan for Augustine himself, which made him independent of the bishops of France, and with a letter explaining the course which the archbishop was to take in developing his work. London was to be his metropolitan see, and he was to consecrate twelve bishops under him; and whenever Christianity had extended to York, he was to place there also a metropolitan, with a like number of suffragans.

The course he was to pursue being thus defined, Augustine invited the old British or Welsh clergy to a conference at a spot on the Severn, in Gloucestershire, which was for a long time afterwards called "Augustine's Oak." Prepared to make considerable concessions, he yet felt that three points did not admit of being sacrificed. He proposed, therefore, that the British Church should conform to the Roman usage in the celebration of Easter and the sacrament of baptism, and that they should aid him in evangelizing the heathen Saxons. After a long and fruitless discussion on the first day, during which the British clergy clung as pertinaciously to their traditions as Columbanus at Luxeuil, he proposed that an appeal should be made to the Divine judgment. A blind Saxon was brought in, whom the British Christians were unable to cure. Augustine supplicated the Divine aid, and the man, we are told, forthwith recovered his sight.

Convinced, but unwilling to alter their old customs, the vanquished party proposed another meeting. Seven British bishops assembled on this occasion, together with Dinoth, abbot of the great monastery of Bangor in Flintshire. Before the synod met, they proposed to ask the advice of an aged hermit whether they ought to change the traditions of their fathers. "Yes," replied the old man, "if the new-comer be a man of God." "But how are we to know whether he be a man of God?" they asked. "The Lord saith," was the reply, "'Take my yoke upon you, and learn of me, for I am meek and lowly.' Now if this Augustine is meek and lowly, be assured that he beareth the yoke of Christ." "Nay, but how are we to know this?" they asked again. "If he rises to meet you, when ye approach," answered the hermit, "hear and follow him; but if he despises you, and fails to rise from his place, let him also be despised by you."

The synod met, and Augustine remained seated,

nor rose at their approach to receive them. It was enough. It was plain that he had not the spirit of Christ, and no efforts of the archbishop could induce the British clergy to yield one of his demands. " If he will not so much as rise up to greet us," said his opposers, " how much more will he contemn us if we submit ourselves to him ?" Thereupon Augustine broke up the conference, with an angry threat that, if the British clergy would not accept peace with their brethren, they must look for war with their foes, and if they would not proclaim the way of life to the Saxons, they would suffer deadly vengeance at their hands.

Thus unsuccessful in winning over the British clergy to conformity, Augustine returned to Canterbury. And now, as all Kent had espoused the faith, Justus was consecrated to the see of Rochester, and at the same time, through the connexion of Ethelbert with the King of Essex, that kingdom was opened to ecclesiastical supervision, and Mellitus was advanced to the bishopric of London. This was the limit of Augustine's success. It fell, indeed, far short of Gregory's design, but that design had been formed on a very imperfect acquaintance either with the condition of the island, the strong national prejudices of the British Christians, or the relations which subsisted between the Anglo-Saxon kingdoms. In the following year, May 26, A.D. 605, the first Archbishop of Canterbury died,[1] having already consecrated Laurence as his successor, and was laid in a grave by the Roman road outside the city walls.

[1] Stanley's "Memorials of Canterbury," p. 44 *n.*

After his death the work of evangelization still went on. It was the work, however, not of one, but of two parties; the Roman, aided by their converts and some teachers out of France, and the Irish, whom Augustine had vainly endeavoured to persuade to join him in the work of proclaiming the faith to the Saxons.

The first party sent Paulinus to Northumbria, Felix to East Anglia, Birinus to Wessex, and Wilfrid to Sussex; the latter sent Fursey to East Anglia, Aidan from the monastery of Hy to Northumbria,[1] Finan to Essex, Cedd, Atta, Diuma, and Cellach into Mercia. Though the labourers could not agree together on several points of ritual and discipline, the work nevertheless prospered, and at length the missionary stations dotted over the island were replaced by a regularly established Church, and our forefathers, once notorious for their fierceness and barbarity, were so far softened by Christian influences, that in no country was the new faith more manifestly the parent of progress and civilization, and, as will be seen in the next chapter, of an ardent missionary zeal, eager to transmit the light of truth to kindred Teutonic tribes in their native Germanic forests.

[1] See "The Hermits," by Professor Kingsley, pp. 289—291.

CHAPTER VII.

ST. WILLIBRORD.

IT was from Northumbria that the first of the numerous Anglo-Saxon missionaries went forth to proclaim
the word to their Teutonic brethren.

About the year A.D. 690, Ecgbert, a Northumbrian
of noble birth, left his native land, like many of his
fellow-countrymen, to study in retirement amongst the
famous schools of Ireland. Taking up his abode in a
monastery in Connaught, he became eminent for his
piety and learning, but was before long prostrated by
a severe illness. Recovering, contrary to all expecta-
tion, he made a vow that, instead of returning to his
country, he would devote himself to the service of
the Lord.

The condition of the heathen tribes in Northern
Germany, and along the Frisian coast, was at this
time a subject of deep solicitude in many of the Irish
monasteries. Ecgbert was filled with a desire to proceed thither, and proclaim the message of the Cross.
Selecting, therefore, the most zealous of his brethren,
he made every preparation for the voyage. But on
the very eve of their embarkation a storm shattered

the vessel which was to have conveyed him and his companions.

Though thus discouraged, Ecgbert was not willing to give up his project altogether. A vision bade him remain himself in Ireland, and "instruct the monasteries of Columba," and he began to look out for other labourers, who would carry on the work.

At last his eye rested on a Northumbrian countryman of his own, named Willibrord, whose education, commenced in the monastery of Ripon, had for twelve years been carried on under his own direction in Ireland. He was now thirty-two years of age, and in Ecgbert's opinion possessed many qualifications for such an undertaking.[1]

Yielding to the solicitations of his abbot, Willibrord agreed to select twelve companions, and enter upon the arduous undertaking. The vessel in which he sailed bore him in safety to the Frisian shores, where he was heartily welcomed by Pepin l'Heristal, who had been lately successful in several engagements against Radbod, a powerful native prince, and an energetic supporter of heathenism.

Commencing his labours in that part of Frisia which Pepin had wrested from his adversary, Willibrord showed such zeal and devotion, and attained such satisfactory results, that at the expiration of four years Pepin sent him to Rome, with the request that he might be elevated to the episcopal rank.

Sergius, the Pope, willingly complied, and in the

---

[1] "Vita S. Willibrordi," "Acta SS. Bened." sæc. iii. p. 564; Bede, "H. E." v. 10.

year A.D. 696 he was consecrated under the name of Clemens, and his seat as archbishop was fixed at Utrecht. Here Willibrord established himself, and succeeded in evangelizing a considerable portion of Frankish Frisia, and in building several churches and monasteries, being assisted by the brethren he had brought over from Ireland, and by others, who came out as soon as they heard of the opening in the Frisian territory.

In the following year the archbishop resolved to sail to Denmark, and plant there the Christian faith. The terror, however, inspired by Ongend, a ferocious Dane, rendered his efforts utterly useless, and he was fain to content himself with finding thirty boys, whom he resolved to take back with him to Utrecht, and educate as future missionaries.

On his return a severe storm drove him for shelter to the shores of Heligoland. This island was then of much greater extent than it is now, and was known by the name of *Fositesland*, from the Teutonic deity Fosite,[1] son of Baldr, to whom it was dedicated. So sacred indeed was it accounted, that it was deemed unlawful to touch any animal living there, or, except in solemn silence, to drink of its holy well. The archbishop, however, having to wait some time for a fair wind, killed several of the sacred cattle to provide food for his crew, and baptized three of his companions in a sacred spring.

[1] Son of Baldr and Nanna, who "settles all quarrels, and neither gods nor men know any better judgments than his."—Thorpe's "Northern Mythology," p. 30.

The natives, horrorstruck at his audacity, expected
the god would instantly vindicate his power by striking
him down with immediate death. Nothing, however,
occurred, and they deemed it right then to send messengers and recount the affair to Radbod, who was
then in the island. That chief instantly summoned
Willibrord into his presence, and decided that one of
the offenders must die. Thrice were the lots cast
before the victim could be determined. At last one
was taken and put to death to appease the wrath of
the insulted Fosite. Then Radbod asked the archbishop to explain his conduct, on which the latter
replied, in terms which certainly were explicit.

"It is not a god, O king," said he, "whom thou
worshippest, but a demon, who has seduced thee into
fatal error. For there is no other god but One, who
made the heaven, the earth, the sea, and all things
that are therein. He who worships this God with
true faith shall receive eternal life. I am his servant,
and I testify unto thee this day that thou must abandon these dumb idols which thy fathers worshipped,
and believe in one God Almighty, and be baptized
in the Fount of life, and wash away thy sins. If thou
followest my words, thou shalt enjoy eternal life with
God and his saints ; but if thou despisest me and the
way of salvation, know assuredly that thou shalt suffer
eternal punishment with the Wicked One whom thou
obeyest." Radbod marvelled at the boldness of the
speech, but acknowledged that the missionary's deeds
at least corresponded with his words, and sent him
back with an honourable escort to Pepin.

Encouraged by the protection of the latter and of his successor, Charles Martel, Willibrord now pushed forward his spiritual conquests, visited all parts of his diocese, and preached the word in every town and village whose inhabitants professed to have received the faith, adjuring them to stand fast and to glorify God by a consistent life.

Before long the news of his success reached England, and many Anglo-Saxons left their native land and eagerly associated themselves in his labours. Thus Adelbert came and laboured in the north of Holland, Werenfrid in the neighbourhood of Elste, Plechelm, Otger, and Wiro amongst the people of Gueldres. Two brothers also named Ewald joined the noble band, and selecting the territory of the Old Saxons as the scene of their labours, made their way thither, and in the first village they entered met with a hospitable reception.[1] Encouraged by this, they announced to their host that they wished to be led into the presence of their chief, for whom they had a message of the utmost importance. The introduction was promised, and they remained with their entertainer for some days. Meanwhile their daily prayers, Psalmody, and mysterious rites provoked the suspicions of the Saxons, and they began to fear lest, if introduced to their chief, the strangers might prevail upon him to forsake his ancestral faith, and so draw away the whole tribe into apostasy. They therefore fell upon them one day unexpectedly, and having decapitated one of the brothers, and hacked the other to pieces, flung their

[1] Bede, " H. E." v. 10.

bodies into the Rhine. The chief, however, of the
country, on hearing of what had taken place, did not
approve of this cold-blooded murder. Considering
that an insult had been offered to his authority, he
slew all the inhabitants of the village and laid it in
ashes. The bodies of the martyrs were afterwards
dragged from the river and buried with much pomp
at Cologne.

Another coadjutor who came to take part in the
work was Wulfram, bishop of Sens.[1] The exact date
when he appeared in the Frisian mission field is somewhat doubtful,[2] but it was the fame of the archbishop's
success which induced him to apply to the abbot of
Fontenelle for monks to accompany him to Frisia.
The abbot complied with his wishes, and on his
arrival amongst the Frisians Wulfram preached the
word with no little success.

Several incidents which occurred during his sojourn
in the country tended to make a considerable impression on the minds of the people. Wulfram found
them addicted to the custom of immolating human
beings in sacrifice to their gods. Some were hanged
on gibbets, others were strangled, others were drowned
in the sea or some river. Once, on the occasion of
a great festival, the bishop beheld a boy being led
forth to suffer. The gibbet had been erected, and
a vast crowd was collected to feast their eyes on the
cruel sight. Amongst those present was Radbod,
and with him Wulfram pleaded earnestly that the

---

[1] "Vita S. Wulframmi," "Acta SS. Bened." sæc. iii. p. 342.
[2] Döllinger fixes the date at about A.D. 712.

boy's life might be spared. This the Frisian chief
said could not be. The sacred lot had marked
him out as the destined victim, and he must die.
Still the bishop persisted in entreating for his life, and
at last the chief said, " If your Christ can rescue this
boy from death, he may be his servant and yours
for ever." Thereupon the victim was placed under the
beam, the rope fastened, and he was thrown off. Meanwhile Wulfram had flung himself on his knees and
prayed earnestly that, if it was God's will, he would
glorify his name by saving the boy's life. His prayer
was no sooner ended than the rope broke, and the
victim fell to the ground. Wulfram hurried to the
spot, and finding life not yet extinct took measures
for recovering him from the swoon into which he had
fallen, and then sent him, with others whom he had
similarly saved from a cruel death, to the monastery
of Fontenelle.

On another occasion the two sons of a widow
woman, one seven, the other five years of age, were
selected for sacrifice. A stake was erected on the
sea-shore, to which the boys were fastened, and they
were left to the mercy of the rising tide in a spot
where two seas met. As the waves crept nearer, the
elder of the two children tried to support the other
on his shoulders, and so save him for a little time at
least from his too certain doom. The crowd was
watching anxiously for the end, when Wulfram again
went to Radbod and begged the life of the children,
declaring it monstrous that beings made in the image
of God should be exposed to the sport of demons.

"If your God Christ," Radbod replied, "will deliver them from their peril, you may have them for your own." Thereupon the bishop prayed earnestly to God, and the waves, suddenly gathering into a heap, seemed to leave the spot where the children stood, so that it became as dry land. Then the bishop flung himself into the water, and seizing one of the children in his right hand and the other in his left, conveyed them safely home and restored them to their mother.

It is easy to imagine that incidents like these would make a strong impression on the people, and it is not surprising that Wulfram's expostulations won the sympathy of many who in their inmost hearts must have revolted from such cruel scenes. Even Radbod's son consented to be baptized, and that chief himself is said to have entertained at one period serious thoughts of following his example. He actually approached the baptismal font, but stopped on the way to ask the bishop, adjuring him to tell the truth, whether, if he received the rite, he might hope to meet in heaven his Frisian ancestors, or whether they were in that place of torment of which he had been told. "Do not deceive thyself," was the prelate's uncompromising reply. "In the presence of God assuredly is the ordained number of his elect ; as for thy ancestors, the chiefs of Frisia, who have departed this life without baptism, it is certain that they have received the just sentence of damnation." Thereupon Radbod drew back from the font, preferring, he said, to join his own people, wherever they might be, rather than sit down in the kingdom of heaven with a handful of beggars.

The obstinacy of the chief perplexed the bishop not a little. A last effort to overcome his scruples appears to have been made while he was confined to his bed by the disease which eventually terminated in his death. But this also was frustrated by an incident which is too curiously illustrative of the ideas of the times to be omitted.

"One day," writes the biographer of Wulfram, "while Radbod was lying sick, the Evil One, who is sometimes permitted to transform himself into an angel of light, appeared to him, crowned with a golden diadem, studded with brilliant gems, and arrayed in a robe spangled with gold. While the chief trembled with astonishment, his visitor asked him reproachfully, 'Tell me, who has so seduced thee, that thou wishest to give up the worship of thy gods, and the religion of thy ancestors? Be not deceived, continue constant to the faith thou hast been taught, and thou shalt assuredly sit down in the golden mansions of bliss, which I have appointed for thee in the world to come. And now that thou mayest know the truth of my words, go to-morrow to that Bishop Wulfram, and ask of him where is that mansion of eternal splendour which he promises thee if thou wilt receive the Christian faith, and when he fails to show it thee, then let two messengers, one of each faith, be sent, and I will lead the way, and show them the mansion of eternal glory, which I am about to give thee hereafter.'

"In the morning Radbod did as he was bid, and told Wulfram of the vision. But the latter was not to be duped. 'This is an illusion of the devil,' said he, 'who wishes all men to perish, and none to be saved. But be not thou deceived, hasten to the font, believe in Christ, and receive the remission of thy sins. As for the golden mansions which thy visitor has promised thee, believe him not, for he it is that seduceth the whole world ; by his pride he fell from his place in heaven, and from a beneficent angel became the enemy of mankind.' Radbod replied that he was willing to be baptized, but he should like first to see the mansion which his own deity had promised him. Thereupon Wulfram sent the messengers, his own deacon and a heathen Frisian. They had not gone far before they met one in human form, who said to them, 'Make haste, for I am about to show you the glorious abode which his god has prepared for Prince Radbod.'

" The messengers followed their guide, and after a long journey they came to a street paved with different kinds of marble, at the end of which was a golden house of marvellous beauty and splendour : entering it, they beheld a throne of immense size, and their guide addressing them, said, 'This is the mansion, and glorious palace, which his god has promised to bestow on Prince Radbod after his death.' The deacon, astonished at the sight, made the sign of the Cross, and replied, ' If these things have been made by Almighty God, they will remain for ever; but if they be the work of the devil, they will speedily vanish.' He had no sooner spoken these words, than their guide was instantly changed into the form of the

Prince of Darkness, and the golden palace into mud, and the messengers found themselves in the midst of a huge morass, filled with reeds and rushes. A tedious journey of three days brought them back to Wulfram, and they recounted to him what had befallen them."[1]

But they returned too late for their intelligence to be of any avail to the pagan chief, by assuring him that he had been deceived by the Prince of Darkness, for before their arrival he had paid the debt of nature. But the news of this marvellous occurrence made a deep impression on the Frisians. Multitudes of them agreed to receive the rite which their chief had scorned, and gladdened the heart of Wulfram by, at least, a nominal profession of Christianity, before his death in the following year, A.D. 720.

On the decease of Radbod, Charles Martel once more reduced the Frisians to a state of nominal subjection, and Willibrord was enabled to push forward his missionary operations with greater hope of permanent success. But he had been already joined by a still more eminent fellow-labourer, whose success speedily eclipsed his own, who won for himself the name of the "apostle of Germany," and whose labours must form the subject of our next chapter.

[1] " Vita S. Wulframmi," " Acta SS. Bened." sæc. iii. p. 348.

CHAPTER VIII.

ABOUT the year A.D. 680 there was living at Crediton, or Kirton, about eight miles north-west of Exeter, a noble family, amongst whose children was a boy named Winfrid. At an early period the boy betrayed much promise, and was designed by his parents for a secular career. But the visit of some monastic brothers to his father's house quickened a desire in his heart to embrace the monastic life. His father strongly opposed such a step, till at length alarmed by a dangerous illness he relented, and at seven years of age Winfrid was removed to a conventual school at Exeter under Abbot Wolfard, and thence to Nutescelle in Hampshire, in the diocese of Winchester.[1]

Here, under Abbot Winberct, he took the name of Boniface, and became eminent for his diligence and devotion, for his deep acquaintance with the Scriptures and his skill in preaching. At the age of thirty he received ordination, and his well-known talents procured for him on several occasions high ecclesiastical employments. King Ina honoured him with his confidence, and the united recommendations of

[1] "Vita S. Bonifacii," Pertz, "Mon. Germ." vol. ii. p. 336.

his brethren led to his being sent, on more than one occasion, on a confidential mission to Archbishop Brihtwald. He might therefore have risen to an honourable position in his native land, but other aspirations had now taken possession of his soul.

No stories were listened to at this time in the Anglo Saxon monasteries with greater avidity than those connected with the adventurous mission of Archbishop Willibrord among the heathen tribes of Frisia, and Boniface longed to join the noble band beyond the sea. On communicating his design to his abbot, the latter would have dissuaded him from the arduous enterprise, but he remained firm, and with three of the brethren, whom he had persuaded to accompany him, left Nutescelle for London. There he took ship, and crossing the sea, landed at Doerstadt, then a flourishing emporium, now almost obliterated from historical memory. But the time of his coming, A.D. 716, was unpropitious. Radbod was engaged in a furious conflict with Charles Martel, a fierce persecution of the Christians had broken out, and Boniface was fain to return to his cloister at Nutescelle.

During the ensuing winter Abbot Winberct died, and Boniface, had he listened to the earnest solicitations of his brethren, might have been cordially welcomed as his successor. But the old missionary ardour still burned brightly, and with the return of spring he had made up his mind to make another effort in Frisia. Daniel, bishop of Winchester, strongly favoured his designs, and gave him commendatory letters to the

Pope, whose consent and patronage he was anxious
to secure before entering a second time on his difficult
enterprise. Accordingly, the year A.D. 717 saw him
again in London, where he embarked and sailed to
Etaples, on the coast of Normandy. In the autumn
he set out through France with a large body of
pilgrims, and, crossing the Alps, reached Rome in
safety, and delivered the letters of his diocesan to
Gregory II. That Pontiff gave the ardent monk
a hearty welcome, and during the winter discussed
with him in frequent interviews the prospects of the
mission, and finally presented him with a letter
authorizing him to preach the Gospel in Germany
whenever he might find an opportunity.

In the following spring, therefore, armed with this
commission, he set out, and, crossing the Alps, first
commenced labouring in Thuringia. While thus employed he received intelligence of the death of Radbod,
and immediately repaired to the country of that chieftain. The recent successes of Charles Martel had
opened a way for Christianity in the Frisian kingdom, and for three years Boniface united himself with
the missionary band under Willibrord at Utrecht, and
in the destruction of many heathen temples and the
rise of Christian churches saw his labours crowned
with no little success. Feeling the advance of age,
Willibrord was now anxious that his friend from
Nutescelle should succeed him in the see of Utrecht,
but Boniface firmly declined the honour, and left him
to plunge into the wilds of Hesse. Two native chiefs
were attracted by his preaching, and submitted to

baptism. At Amöneburg, near the Ohm, a monastery speedily arose, and the energetic missionary found that the protection of the converted chief, and his own acquaintance with the native language, gained for him such an access to the hearts of the people, that multitudes, both in Hesse and on the borders of Saxony, accepted baptism at his hands.

A faithful brother, Binna, was now deputed to announce to Gregory these gratifying results ; and the Pope, who could not fail to foresee the issue of labours so auspiciously begun, summoned him once more to Rome. Thither Boniface obediently went, escorted by a numerous retinue of Franks and Burgundians, and in reply to the Pope's questions respecting the faith which he preached, handed him a copy of his creed. Gregory duly examined it, and, after an interval of five days, again admitted him to an audience, and announced that, in consideration of the success he had already achieved, he was ready to confer upon him the episcopal dignity. Accordingly, on the Feast of St. Andrew, A.D. 723, he was consecrated regionary bishop, without any particular diocese, but with a general jurisdiction over all whom he might win over from paganism to the Christian fold. Thus elevated to the episcopal dignity, with letters of commendation to Charles Martel, to the bishops of Bavaria and Alemannia, and the native chiefs of the countries where he was about to labour, Boniface recrossed the Alps, and, with the permission and pro-tection of Charles Martel, recommenced operations in Hesse.

He found that matters had not improved during his absence. Some of his converts had remained firm in the faith, but the majority, still fascinated by the spell of their old superstitions, had blended their new and old creed in a wild confusion. They still worshipped groves and fountains, still consulted augurs and cast lots, still offered sacrifice on the old altars. Boniface saw that he must take strenuous measures to convince them of the vanity of their old belief. A letter he received about this time from the Bishop of Winchester, now blind and far advanced in years, suggested caution in dealing with the primitive superstitions of the people. A Teuton himself, and writing to a Teutonic missionary, he would have him scrupulously avoid all contemptuous and violent language, and advised that he should try, above all things, to cultivate a spirit of patience and moderation. In preference to open controversy, he suggested that he should rather put such questions from time to time as would tend to rouse the people to a sense of the contradictions which their superstitions involved, especially in relation to the genealogy of their gods.

"They will admit," he writes, "that the gods they worship had a beginning, that there was a time when they were not. Ask them, then, whether they consider the world also to have had a beginning, or whether it has always existed from the first commencement of things. Again, inquire who governed and sustained the world before the birth of those gods whom they adore? By what means were they able to gain a supremacy of power over a universe which

had existed from all time? Whence, how, and when
was the first god or goddess born? Are more deities
still in process of generation? If not, why and when
did the law of celestial increase come to an end?
Ask them, again, whether, amidst such a multitude
of powerful deities as they acknowledge, there is
not danger of failing to discover *the most powerful*,
and thus offending him? Why, in fact, are these
gods worshipped? For the sake of present and temporal, or for the sake of future and eternal happiness?
What, again, is the import of their sacrifices? If the
gods are all-powerful, what do they gain by them?
If they do not need them, why attempt to appease
them with such costly offerings? Such questions I
would have thee put to them, not in the way of taunt
or mockery, which will only irritate, but kindly and
gently. Then, after a while, compare their superstitions with the Christian doctrines, and touch upon
the latter judiciously, that thy people may not be
exasperated against thee, but ashamed of their foolish
errors."[1]

Useful and wise as was such advice in reference to
his general conduct, Boniface deemed that the present juncture required sterner and more uncompromising measures. Near Geismar, in Upper Hesse,
stood an ancient oak, sacred for ages to Donar, or
Thor, the god of thunder. By the people it was
regarded with peculiar reverence, and was the rally-
ing-point of the assemblies of all the tribes. Again
and again had Boniface declaimed against such sense-

[1] Migne's "Script. Eccles." sæc. viii. p. 707.

less worship of the stock of a tree, but his sermons
had fallen dead on the ears of his hearers. He determined, therefore, to remove an object of such superstitious reverence from the midst of his converts.
One day, axe in hand, and accompanied by all his
clergy, he advanced to cut down the offending monarch
of the forest. The people assembled in thousands;
many enraged at his interference with their traditions,
many more confident, like the natives of Fositesland,
that an instant judgment would certainly strike down
so daring an offender. But stroke after stroke of the
axe fell, and it became clear that Thor could not
defend his own. In vain his votaries supplicated his
vengeance, and besought him to vindicate his power.
Before long a crashing was heard in the topmost
boughs, and then the leafy idol came down to the
ground, and split asunder into four quarters. Unable
to gainsay the reality of his victory, the people acknowledged that the missionary had prevailed, nor
did they interfere when he directed that an oratory in
honour of St. Peter should be constructed out of the
remains of their old divinity.

This stumbling-block having been removed out of
the midst of his people, Boniface found the work
of evangelization materially facilitated. Throughout
Hesse and Thuringia the word had free course;
heathen temples disappeared; humble churches rose
amidst the forest glades; monastic buildings sprung up
wherever salubrity of soil and the presence of running
water suggested an inviting site; the land was cleared
and brought under the plough; and the sound of prayer

and praise in humble churches awoke unwonted echoes in the forests. *The harvest truly was plenteous, but the labourers were few.*[1] Boniface determined, therefore, to invite assistance from his native land. In a circular letter addressed, in the year A.D. 733, to the bishops, clergy, and principal abbots in England, he pointed, in moving words, to the wants of his German converts. " We beseech you," he writes, "that ye will remember us in your prayers to God and our Lord Jesus Christ, who would have all men to be saved and come to a knowledge of the truth, that he will vouchsafe to convert to the true faith the hearts of the heathen Saxons, that they may be delivered from the snares of the Evil One, wherewith they are now held captive. Have compassion on them, brethren. They often say, ' We are of one blood with our brothers in England.' Remember they are your kinsmen according to the flesh. Remember that the time for working is short, for the end of all things is at hand, and death cannot praise God, nor can any give him thanks in the pit.[2] Aid us, then, while yet it is day." [3]

In other letters he begs for copies of different portions of the Divine Word. Thus to the abbess Eadburga he writes, to request her to send him the Epistles of St. Peter inscribed in gilded letters, that he might use them in preaching ; to another he writes for copies of the Gospels, written in a good, clear hand, suitable

---

[1] St. Matt. ix. 37, 38.
[2] Ps. vi. 5. ; Isa. xxxviii. 18.
[3] Migne, " Script. Eccles." sæc. viii. p. 739.

for his weak eyes, as also for commentaries, among
which he particularly specifies those of the venerable
Bede. His appeals were not ineffectual. Not a few
flocked from England to rally round him, and even
devout women were found willing to sacrifice the
pleasures and comforts of home, and go forth to
superintend the convents which the missionary had
inaugurated. As iron sharpeneth iron, so the coun-
tenances of friends from the old country refreshed
and invigorated the spirits of the good bishop.

Meanwhile news arrived of the death of Pope
Gregory II. Still anxious to maintain his connexion
with the Holy See, Boniface wrote to his successor
and besought his blessing on his labours, and in the
pall of a metropolitan received a marked recognition
of his work. But not content with a distant correspondence, he once more, A.D. 738, crossed the Alps
and sought a personal interview with Gregory III.
The latter received him with more than ordinary
respect. He invested him with plenary power as
legate of the Apostolic See, and authorized him
to visit and organize the Bavarian churches.

With letters accrediting him in his new capacity,
Boniface returned, in the spring of A.D. 739, and after
a short stay at Pavia with Liutprand, king of the
Lombards, commenced a thorough visitation of the
diocese of Bavaria, and added to the solitary see of
Passau those of Salzburg, Freisingen, and Ratisbon.
While at Rome, the archbishop had learnt that his
kinsman Wunibald had come thither from England,
and that another, Willibald, had just returned from

the Holy Land and entered the monastery of
Monte Cassino. He persuaded both of them, however, to join him in Germany ; placed Wunibald
in charge of seven churches in the newly-converted
Thuringia, and stationed Willibald at Eichstadt, then
a waste forest-land, which Count Suiger of Hirsberg
had bestowed upon the Church. He then wrote to
Tetta, abbess of Winburn, in Dorsetshire, requesting
that Walpurga, a sister of Wunibald, as well as any
other of his countrywomen who might be willing,
should be sent out to share the work in Germany.

Walpurga did not shrink from the perils of the
journey ; with thirty companions she crossed the sea,
and after a joyful meeting with the archbishop, proceeded to join her brother in Thuringia, and settled
for a time in a convent beside him there. Afterwards
she accompanied him to Heidenheim, in the wilds of
Suevia, where they built a church, and, after much
difficulty, a double monastery for monks and nuns.
The companions also of Walpurga before long presided
over similar sisterhoods. Thus Lioba, afterwards the
friend of Hildegard, consort of Charlemagne, was
stationed at Bischofsheim on the Tuber; Chunichild,
another devout sister, in Thuringia ; and Chunitrude
in Bavaria. It was not always easy to reconcile the
natives to the erection of these outposts of civilization in their midst. Many deemed it a profanation
of the awful silence of the old oak-groves, and an
insult to the elves and fairies who for untold ages had
haunted the primeval solitudes. Many more regarded
with much suspicion this intrusion on their old hunting-

grounds, and would have preferred that the peace
of the wolf and the bear should not be disturbed.
But as years rolled on, the peaceful lives of the missionaries won their respect and reverence, and the
sight of waving cornfields reconciled them to the
violation of their forest sanctuaries.

In the year A.D. 741 Charles Martel died, and
Boniface saw fresh opportunities opened up for carrying on and consolidating the labours of the various
missionary bands. It is true that the great Mayor of
the Palace never thwarted his operations, or declined
to recognise his authority, but he tolerated many of the
clergy whose lives by no means corresponded with
their sacred profession, and the gratitude due to the
conqueror of the Saracens was considerably marred
by his practice of pillaging churches and monasteries
from time to time, when he wanted money for his
numerous wars. Now that he was dead, the archbishop's course was more clear, and by reason of his
great influence over Carloman and Pepin he could
develope his plans for a systematic organization of the
German churches. He began by founding four new
bishoprics, Würzburg, Eichstädt, Bamberg, and Erfurt,
and in the following year proceeded to call a council
of ecclesiastics and the national estates to make pro-
vision for the moral and spiritual superintendence of
the newly-formed churches.

Three years afterwards the Bishop of Cologne died,
and the idea occurred to Boniface of elevating that
place to be his metropolitan see, especially as it was
suitable for a basis of more extended missions in

Friesland, where, since the death of Willibrord, the
work had somewhat retrograded. While corresponding on the subject with the Pope, an event occurred which gave an entirely different turn to the
negotiations. In the same year that the Bishop of
Cologne died, Gerold, bishop of Mayence, was slain
in a warlike expedition against the Saxons. To
console his son Gewillieb for the loss of his father,
he was consecrated as his successor, though until now
he had been only a layman in Carloman's court, and
had displayed more than ordinary fondness for the
chase. In the following year Carloman headed
another expedition against the Saxons, and Gewillieb
followed in his train. The armies encamped on either
side of a river, and, unmindful of his sacred office,
Gewillieb sent a page to inquire the name of the chief
who had slain his father. Ascertaining it, he sent the
same messenger a second time to request the chief to
meet him in friendly conference in the middle of the
stream. The latter complied, and the two rode into
the water, and during the conference the bishop
stabbed the Saxon to the heart.

This act of treachery was the signal for a general
engagement, in which Carloman gained a decisive
victory over the Saxons. Gewillieb returned to his
diocese. But Boniface could not allow so flagrant an
infraction of the canons enacted in the recent synod
to pass unrebuked. In the Council, therefore, of the
following year, he made a formal charge against the
blood-stained bishop. Unable to struggle against his
authority, Gewillieb was obliged to vacate his see, and

Mayence became the seat of Boniface as metropolitan, where he exercised jurisdiction over the dioceses of Mayence, Worms, Spires, Tongres, Cologne, Utrecht, as well as the newly-evangelized tribes whom he had won over to the Christian faith.

In the letter wherein Boniface communicated to the Pope this alteration in his plans he made a request more nearly relating to himself. He was now verging on threescore years and ten, and his long and incessant labours had begun to tell upon his constitution. Weighed down with the care of all the churches in Germany, he longed for some diminution of the burdens which pressed upon him, and had already requested to be allowed to nominate his successor. This the Pope declined to allow, but conceded to his age and infirmities the permission to select a priest as his special assistant, who might share a portion of his episcopal duties. Increasing weakness now induced him to reiterate his request, and the Pope, while reminding him of the words, *He that shall endure unto the end, the same shall be saved*,[1] agreed that if he could find amongst his clergy one in whom he could place implicit confidence, he might elevate him to the post, and receive his assistance as his coadjutor and representative. Upon this Boniface nominated his fellow-countryman and disciple, Lullus, and proposed to retire himself to the monastery now rising on the banks of the river Fulda, where he might spend the autumn of his life in watching the beneficial results of the labours of the brethren amidst the surrounding tribes.

[1] St. Matt. xxiv. 13.

But while thus toiling in the land of his adoption, he was not unmindful of his old friends in England. Pleasant memories of Crediton and Nutescelle still lay near his heart; and though unable to revisit these familiar scenes, he yet maintained a constant correspondence with friends in the old country, and rejoiced to receive tidings of the welfare of the Anglo-Saxon churches, just as he was pained to the heart when he heard of any moral or spiritual declension. Thus, hearing that Ethelbald, king of Mercia, was living in gross immorality, he wrote to him in earnest terms, and endeavoured to shame him into a more consistent life by contrasting his conduct with that of the still heathen Saxons in the forests of Germany, who, though they had not the law of Christianity, yet did by nature the things contained in the law, and testified by severe punishments their abhorrence of impurity. He also wrote to Archbishop Cuthbert, informing him of the regulations made in the recent synods, and urging him to use every endeavour to maintain the vitality of the Church of their native land.

Thus, amidst increasing infirmities and many causes for anxiety, he yet found time to remember old scenes and old friends. But very soon the conviction was deepened in his own mind that the day of his departure was at hand. Lullus had, indeed, been appointed his coadjutor in the see of Mayence, but his appointment had not yet received the royal sanction, and till this was secured Boniface could not feel free from anxiety for the welfare of his flock. One of his latest letters, therefore, was addressed to Fuldrad, Pepin's arch-chaplain, soliciting his protection and that of his royal master in behalf of his clergy and his many ecclesiastical foundations.   In this very year he had been called upon to restore upwards of thirty churches in his extensive diocese, which had been swept away during an invasion of the heathen Frisians, and it was with gloomy forebodings that he contemplated the fate of the German Church, if it was not shielded by royal protection.

" Nearly all my companions," he writes to Fuldrad, "are strangers in this land.   Some are priests distributed in various places to celebrate the offices of the Church and minister to the people.   Some are monks living in different monasteries, and engaged in teaching the young.   Some are aged men, who have long borne with me the burden and the heat of the day.   For all these I am full of anxiety, lest after my death they should be scattered as sheep having no shepherd.   Let them have a share of your countenance and protection, that they may not be dispersed abroad, and that the people dwelling on the heathen borders may not lose the law of Christ.   Suffer also Lullus, my son and coadjutor, to preside over the churches, that both priests and people may find in him a teacher and a guide ; and may God grant that he may prove a faithful pastor to the flock.   I have many reasons for making these requests.   My clergy on the heathen borders are in deep poverty.   Bread they can obtain for themselves, but clothing they cannot find here, unless they receive aid from some other quarter to enable them to persevere and endure their hardships. Let me know, either by the bearers of this letter or under thine own hand, whether thou canst promise the granting of my request, that, whether I live or die, I may have some assurance for the future."[1] The royal permission that Lullus should succeed him arrived, and his mind was relieved of its load of anxiety. But again the old missionary ardour burnt up as brightly as in earlier years. Though upwards of seventy-five years of age he determined to make one last effort to win over the still pagan portion of Friesland, and to accomplish what Willibrord had begun. Bidding, therefore, his successor a solemn farewell, he ordered preparations to be made for the journey. Something told him he should never return, and therefore he desired that with his books, amongst which was a treatise of St. Ambrose on "The Advantage of Death," his shroud also might be put up. Then, with a retinue of three priests, three deacons, four monks, and forty-one laymen, he embarked on board a vessel, A.D. 755, and sailed down the Rhine. At Utrecht he was joined by Eoban, an old pupil whom he had placed in charge of the see, and then together they advanced into the eastern part of Frisia, and commenced their labours.

For a time all went well. The missionaries were welcomed by several of the tribes, and were enabled to lay the foundation of several churches. Gladdened by the accession of many converts, they at length reached the banks of the river Burde, not far from

[1] Migne, "Script. Eccles." sæc. viii. p. 779.

Dockum. It was the month of June, and the festival of Whitsunday drew near. Boniface had dismissed many who had been baptized, bidding them return on the eve of Whitsunday to receive the further rite of confirmation. On the morning of the appointed day, June 5, the noise could be plainly heard of an advancing multitude, and the brandishing of spears and the clang of arms told only too plainly on what errand they were bound. The heathen party, enraged at the success of the daring missionary, had selected this day for a signal act of vengeance. Some of the archbishop's retinue counselled resistance, and were already preparing to defend themselves, when he stepped forth from his tent, and gave orders that no weapon should be lifted, but that all should await the crown of martyrdom. "Let us not return evil for evil," said he; "the long-expected day has come, and the time of our departure is at hand. Strengthen ye yourselves in the Lord, and he will redeem your souls. Be not afraid of those who can only kill the body, but put all your trust in God, who will speedily give you an eternal reward, and an entrance into his heavenly kingdom."

Calmed by his words, his followers bravely awaited the onset of their enemies, who rushed upon them, and quickly despatched them. The archbishop himself, we are told,[1] when he saw that his hour was come, took a volume of the Gospels, and making it a pillow for his head, stretched forth his neck for the blow, and in a few moments received his release.

[1] "Vita S. Bonifacii," Pertz, "Mon. Germ." vol. ii. p. 351 *n.*

The heathens speedily ransacked the tents of the
missionaries; but instead of the treasures they had
expected, found only the bookcases which Boniface
had brought with him. These they rifled, scattering
some of the volumes over the plain, and hiding others
among the marshes, where they remained till they
were afterwards picked up and reverently removed to
the monastery of Fulda, together with the remains of
the great missionary.

Thus died the father of German Christian civilization. A Teuton by language and kindred, he had
been the apostle of Teutons. Combining singular
conscientiousness with earnest piety, dauntless zeal
with practical energy, he had been enabled to consolidate the work of earlier Irish and Anglo-Saxon
missionaries; he had revived the decaying energies of
the Frankish Church; he had restored to her the
long dormant activity of the Ecclesiastical Council;
he had covered central and western Germany with
the first necessary elements of civilization. Monastic
seminaries, as Amöneburg and Ohrdruf, Fritzlar and
Fulda, had risen amidst the Teutonic forests. The
sees of Salzburg and Freisingen, of Regensburg and
Passau, testified to his care of the Church of Bavaria;
the see of Erfurt told of labours in Thuringia; that of
Buraburg, in Hesse; that of Wurzburg, in Franconia;
while his metropolitan see at Mayence, having jurisdiction over Worms and Spires, Tongres, Cologne, and
Utrecht, was a sign that even before his death the
German Church had already advanced beyond its
first missionary stage.

Well may Germany look back with gratitude to the holy Benedictine, and tell with joy the story of the monk of Nutescelle.   The roll of missionary heroes, since the days of the Apostles, can point to few more glorious names, to none, perhaps, that has added to the dominion of the Gospel regions of greater extent or value, or that has exerted a more powerful influence on the history of the human race.   In the monastery of Fulda was exposed for ages, to hosts of pilgrims, the blood-stained copy of St. Ambrose on " The Advantage of Death," which the archbishop had brought with his shroud to the shore of the Zuyder Zee, and the long-continued labours of many of his loving pupils and associates will prove that in his case, as in so many others, " The blood of the martyrs is the seed of the Church."

CHAPTER IX.

DURING one of his earlier missionary journeys in Hesse, Archbishop Boniface arrived on one occasion, about the year A.D. 719, at a nunnery in the district of Trier, on the banks of the Moselle, presided over by the abbess Addula.[1] After service the abbess and her guest repaired to the common hall, and, as was customary, a portion of Scripture was read during meal-time.

The reader was Gregory, a nephew of the abbess, a lad of fifteen, who had lately returned from school. Boniface was pleased with the way in which the boy read his Latin Vulgate, and proceeded to inquire whether he understood the passage he had been reading. The boy, misunderstanding his question, read the words a second time. "Nay, my son," replied the missionary, "that is not what I meant. I know you can read well enough, but can you translate the passage into your own mother-tongue?" The other confessed he was unable, and thereupon Boniface himself translated it into German, and having done so, proceeded to make the passage the

---

[1] "Vita S. Gregorii," "Acta SS. Bolland." Aug. 25.

ground of a few words of exhortation to the whole company.

We know neither what the passage was, nor what the missionary said, but we know what was uppermost in his mind, and may be quite certain he did not lose the opportunity of exhorting the inmates of the secluded cloister to prize the blessings they enjoyed, and of telling them of the many thousands in northern and western Germany, bone of their bone and flesh of their flesh, who knew not the truth, and to whom it was his privilege to proclaim the word of life. Of one other thing also we are certain; and that is, the effect of his earnest words. So deep was the impression they made on the mind of the listening youth, that he was seized with an unconquerable desire to accompany the preacher in his arduous work. In vain the abbess tried to dissuade him from intrusting himself to an entire stranger. The boy persisted in his request, and at length the abbess was fain to yield; and supplying him with horses and attendants, she suffered him to depart and accompany his new-found friend.

That friend he never forsook. He shared with him all his trials and dangers, and, in spite of many privations and frequent poverty, continued his constant companion wherever he went. He was with him during his journeys to Rome, and brought back many copies of the Scriptures, in which, as his master's chief assistant, he taught the numerous candidates for missionary work, whom Boniface had in training in his different monasteries. He was with

him also during his last journey to Frisia ; and on
the death of Bishop Eoban determined to take upon
himself the direction of the mission in that country.

Under his superintendence as abbot, the monastery
of Utrecht became an important missionary college,
where assembled youths from England, France, Friesland, Saxony, Suabia, and Bavaria, whom he diligently trained to emulate the zeal of his deceased
master. In preparing them for their high duties, he
was instant in season and out of season. Early in
the morning he might be found sitting in his cell
writing for such of his pupils as sought his counsel
or encouragement. One by one they would come to
him, and received suitable advice according to their
individual wants and peculiarities.

A pleasing instance of the way in which he was
enabled to adorn the doctrine of a merciful and
crucified Redeemer amongst the heathen population
is recorded by his biographer. Two of his brothers
were journeying into France, when they were waylaid
by robbers and murdered. A pursuit was set on foot,
and on the capture of the murderers they were dragged
into the presence of the abbot, and it was thought
likely to soothe the pang of sorrow, if he should be
allowed to select the kind of death by which they
should die. But Gregory persuaded the captors to
suffer the men to be released, and furnishing them
with clothes and food, dismissed them with a suitable
admonition.

In labours of love like these, teaching and preaching, he persevered till he had reached his seventieth

year. He was then seized with paralysis of the left side, which continued for three years. During this period he still strove to exhort his scholars, dividing amongst them presents of books, one of which, the "Enchiridion" of St. Augustine, his biographer affectionately mentions as having been bestowed upon himself, and bidding all, amidst the toils and privations of their daily life, to think of those encouraging words of the Apostle, *Eye hath not seen, nor ear heard, neither hath it entered into the heart of man to conceive the things that God hath prepared for them that love him.*[1] At last his sufferings became so severe he could bear up no longer. Having bidden his successor Albric a final farewell, he ordered that he should be carried to the church, and placed at the door, and in full view of the altar. There he prayed; and, having received the Holy Eucharist, died in the midst of his disciples, who had gathered round his bed, uttering as his last words, " To-day I have my release."

Another eminent pupil of the great apostle of Germany was the abbot Sturmi.[2] His parents, who were of noble descent and natives of Bavaria, committed him to the care of Boniface, at the period that he was engaged in organizing the Church in that country. Boniface accepted the boy with joy, and on his arrival at Fritzlar placed him in a monastery there, under the care of the abbot Wigbert. The latter undertook his education with alacrity, taught

[1] Isa. lxiv. 4 ; 1 Cor. ii. 9.
[2] " Vita S. Sturmi Abbatis," Pertz, " Mon. Germ." vol. ii. p. 366.

him to repeat by heart the Psalms, then opened up
to him the four Gospels, and bade him commit to
memory large portions of the Epistles, and also of the
Old Testament.

The period of instruction completed, Sturmi was
consecrated priest, and for three years continued to
assist Boniface in missionary work. He was then
seized with an eager desire to found a monastery in
the awful forest of Burchwald, which then covered a
great portion of Hessia. Such a desire was no sooner
communicated to Boniface than it met with his most
cordial approval; and he saw that an opening was
now possible towards converting that impassable forest
into a cultivated country, and establishing another of
his numerous monastic colonies in its midst. Two
companions were assigned to Sturmi; and before the
three set out, Boniface solemnly commended them to
the Lord, and prayed that he who made heaven and
earth, from whom every good thing proceeded, and
without whom all the efforts of human weakness were
vain, would enable them to find a suitable habitation
in the wilderness, and lead to a good issue the journey
on which they were setting out.

The three then started on their way, and after some
days reached a spot now called Hersfelt, which seemed
well adapted to their purpose. A portion of ground
was cleared, a few small huts were constructed of the
bark of trees, and their new abode was consecrated
with fasting and prayer. Sturmi, after a short stay,
determined to return and recount to the archbishop
all that had befallen them. He told him exactly every

particular respecting the situation, soil, watershed, and salubrity of their new abode. The prudent Boniface would not immediately discourage his zealous disciple by telling him the spot was not suitable. He bade him stay and refresh himself awhile, and cheered his spirits by reminding him of the consolatory promises of Scripture, and the enduring reward promised to perseverance. At length he told him plainly the situation was not advantageous; it was too near the pagan Saxons, and might suffer from their wild incursions : he bade him, therefore, renew the search for some locality more suitable and more secure.

Again Sturmi set out, rejoined his associates at Hersfelt, and informed them of the decision of Boniface. A second journey was accordingly undertaken amidst the trackless forest, but was scarcely more successful. In a boat the little band sailed up the river Fulda, and observed several spots which seemed adapted to their purpose, but none combined the precise qualifications which Boniface required. To Hersfelt, therefore, they returned, and there found a messenger from the archbishop, summoning Sturmi to meet him at Fritzlar. The faithful monk straightway obeyed, and recounted to him the bootless result of the second expedition. But Boniface still encouraged him to make another attempt. " A place," he said, " is prepared for us in the forest. Whenever it is the will of Christ, he will show it to his servants. Therefore desist thou not from thy efforts, but be assured that without doubt thou wilt discover it there."

After a short interval of refreshment and repose,

Sturmi, undeterred by previous failures, again determined to prosecute the search. This time he proceeded alone, under the huge oak-groves where the
foot of man had never trod. Against the wild beasts
he protected himself in the day-time by chanting
hymns and prayers, and in the night-time he cut down
branches from the trees, kindled a fire, signed himself
with the sign of the cross, and commended himself to
the divine protection.

On the fourth day, guided by a forester, he reached
a spot on the banks of the Fulda which seemed
to combine all the advantages of situation, salubrity,
and seclusion which Boniface required. Carefully
he examined and re-examined the spot. Every hill,
every valley, every spring was duly noted, and then
he went back; and after communicating the joyful
news to the brethren, who were praying for his
success at Hersfelt, passed on and sought out the
archbishop, and declared his belief that the long-
desired locality had at last been found. Boniface,
overjoyed, listened eagerly to every detail, and then
announced that he was satisfied. Shortly afterwards
he repaired to the court of Carloman, and prevailed
upon him to grant him the spot with a demesne
extending four miles each way. Sturmi then set out,
and with seven companions commenced the foundation of the monastery. Thither also Boniface himself
repaired with several of the brethren, and watched the
felling of the trees and the clearing of the ground
with the utmost interest.

Thus was founded the great monastery of Fulda.

No other of his many conventual houses did Boniface regard with such deep affection. Appointing Sturmi its first abbot, he despatched him into Italy to inspect all the monastic houses, especially that of the Benedictines at Monte Cassino, that they might be reproduced at Fulda. So popular did the new establishment become, especially after the remains of the great apostle of Germany had been transferred thither from the Frisian plain where he fell a martyr, that numbers, even more than it could hold, sought to be received within its walls. Sturmi is said to have directed the labours of upwards of four thousand monks, who gladly submitted to his paternal rule, and employed themselves in clearing the waste, felling the trees, reducing the wilderness to cultivation, and preparing themselves for missionary labours amongst their Teutonic brethren.

In the year A.D. 768 Charlemagne ascended the throne, and four years afterwards had commenced the first of his eighteen campaigns against the Saxons, and slowly but steadily extended his conquests from the Drimel to the Lippe, from the Weser to the Elbe, and thence to the Baltic Sea. In the year A.D. 772 he captured Eresburg, a strong fortress on the Drimel, and thence advanced to the neighbourhood of the source of the Lippe, where was the celebrated idol called the Irminsaule, which has been already described.[1] This he destroyed, and then devoted himself to the task of penetrating the bleak and unknown Saxon world, seeking out the native tribes amidst

[1] See above, pp. 20, 21.

their endless swamps, their trackless forests, and wide heaths, and erecting everywhere the Christian church and the monastic seminary.

Sturmi now found full employment for all his energies. The greater part of the conquered races which had felt the conqueror's sword, and witnessed the destruction of the Irminsaule, were committed to his care. Aided by numerous helpers from Fulda, he busied himself with exhorting them to destroy their temples, cut down their groves, and embrace the faith. His exertions were crowned with no inconsiderable success. But before long a rebellion broke out. The Saxons burst in vast numbers into the territory of Fulda, determined to destroy the monastery, and crush the foes of their national faith. The abbot was informed of their design, and determined to seek safety in flight. The coffin of the apostle of Germany was hastily exhumed, and the brethren set forth from their retreat. But they had not proceeded far before they heard that the tide had turned, and the Saxons had been driven back. Charlemagne, informed of the irruption, had flown to the rescue, and advanced with his forces as far as the Weser.

But Sturmi, who had been far from well when obliged to fly, sickened rapidly after his return to the monastery. In vain Charlemagne sent his own physician, Wintar, to minister to him. A mistake was made in the prescription, and the sufferings of the patient were only aggravated. Perceiving that his end was nigh, the abbot ordered all the bells to be rung, and when the brethren had assembled round his bed, he begged them all to forgive him if any had aught against him. The next day he sank rapidly, and, as the brethren stood round his bed, " Father," said one, " we doubt not thou art about to depart hence and to be with the Lord ; we beseech thee therefore that in the kingdom of heaven thou wilt remember us, and pray unto the Lord in behalf of thy servants, for sure we are that the prayers of such an advocate will avail us much." " Show yourselves worthy that I should pray for you," said the dying abbot, " and I will do as ye require;" and with these words he expired, on the 27th December, A.D. 779.

While Sturmi was thus breathing forth his life in the seclusion of the monastery of Fulda, the storm of war was raging without. Throughout the length and breadth of the Saxon territory troops were marching and countermarching, and Charlemagne was pushing on his conquests. In the midst of the din of arms it is not surprising that even missionaries were tempted to forget that the weapons of their warfare were not carnal, and to appeal at times to other feelings than those of faith and love. One of these, Lebuin,[1] a man of intrepid zeal, had come over from England, and built an oratory on the banks of the Ysell. Here, encouraged by the advice and countenance of Gregory, the abbot of Utrecht, he continued to exhort the heathen Saxons to forsake their idolatries, and by the ruggedness of his life succeeded in awing many even of the martial chiefs.

But at length the wrath of the Saxons was kindled;

[1] "Vita S. Lebuini," Pertz, " Mon. Germ." vol. ii. p. 361.

they rose in arms and burnt his oratory to the ground. Nothing daunted, Lebuin resolved to go forth and confront an enormous gathering of the tribe at their approaching assembly on the banks of the Weser. Arrayed in full canonicals, with an uplifted cross in one hand and a volume of the Gospels in the other, he presented himself to the astonished Saxons, as they were engaged in solemn sacrifice to their national gods. " Hearken unto me," he thundered forth ; "and yet not to me, but unto him that speaketh by me. I declare unto you the commands of him, whom all things serve and obey."

Struck dumb with astonishment, the warriors listened as he went on, " Hearken, all ye, and know that God is the Creator of heaven and earth, the sea and all things that are therein. He is the one only true God. He made us, and not we ourselves. The images, which ye call gods, and which, beguiled by the Evil One, ye worship, what are they but gold, or silver, or brass, or stone, or wood? They neither live, nor move, nor feel. They are but the work of men's hands, and can neither help themselves nor any one else. God, the only good and righteous Being, whose mercy and truth remain for ever, moved with pity that ye should be thus seduced by doctrines of demons, has charged me, his ambassador, to beseech you to lay aside your present errors, and to turn with sincere and true faith to him, by whose goodness ye were created, and in whom *we live and move and have our being.*[1] If ye will acknowledge him, and

[1] Acts xvii. 28.

repent and be baptized in the name of the Father, and of the Son, and of the Holy Ghost, and will keep his commandments, then will he preserve you from all evil, he will vouchsafe unto you the blessings of peace, and in the world to come life everlasting.

"But if ye despise and reject his counsels, and persist in your present errors, know that ye shall suffer terrible punishment for scorning his most merciful warning. Behold I, his ambassador, declare unto you the sentence which has gone forth from his mouth, and which cannot change. If ye do not obey his commands, then will sudden destruction come upon you. For the King of kings and Lord of lords hath appointed a brave, prudent, and terrible prince, who is not afar off but near at hand. He like a swift and roaring torrent will burst upon you and subdue the ferocity of your hearts and crush your stiff-necked obstinacy. He will invade your land with a mighty host, and ravage it with fire and sword, with desolation and destruction. As the avenging wrath of that God, whom ye have ever provoked, he will slay some of you with the sword, others he will cause to waste away in poverty and want, others he will lead into perpetual captivity. Your wives and children he will sell into slavery, and the residue of you he will reduce to ignominious subjection, that in you may be justly fulfilled what has been long ago predicted, ' They were made a handful, and scattered and tormented with the tribulation and anguish of the wicked.' "[1]

[1] "Vita S. Lebuini," Pertz, "Mon. Germ." vol. ii. p. 363.

The effect of these words can easily be imagined. The warriors, who had listened at first with awe-struck reverence, were seized with ungovernable fury. "Here is that seducer," they cried, "that enemy of our sacred rites and of our country. Away with him from the earth, and let him suffer the just penalty of his crimes." Thereupon the whole assembly was in a ferment. Stakes were cut from the adjoining thickets, stones were taken up, and Lebuin would have atoned for his temerity with his life had it not been for the intervention of an aged chief named Buto, who, standing on an eminence, thus addressed the excited throng :

"Men and heroes all, listen to my words. Many a time have ambassadors come to us from the Normans, Sclaves, and Frisons. As is ever our custom, we have listened attentively to their words, received them peaceably, and dismissed them to their homes loaded with suitable presents. But now an ambassador from a powerful deity hath not only been despised, but struck and stoned, and almost deprived of life. That the God, whose messenger he is, hath power and majesty, is plain from the fact that he has delivered his servant out of our hands. Be assured, then, that what he has threatened will surely come to pass, and those judgments he has denounced will be fulfilled by a deity whom we know and see to be great, powerful, and mighty."

With these words the old chief calmed the storm, and so Lebuin escaped. The spirit, however, which breathes through his address illustrates the spirit of the times. The Saxons were regarded as barbarians and heathens, with whom no promises were to be kept, no treaties maintained. While Charlemagne's soldiers fought against their idolatrous foes, threw down their temples, and cut down their groves, the priests followed in their wake. The reception of baptism was regarded as the symbol of peace; refusal of the sacrament the symptom of disaffection and the signal for war.

In vain men like Alcuin protested against the monarch's plan for securing at once the subjection and the conversion of the Saxons. In vain the emperor was exhorted to remember the example of the Apostles and their Divine Master in the propagation of the Gospel. Charlemagne persisted in his policy. Death was denounced as the penalty for neglecting baptism, or resorting to secret idolatry. The same penalty was threatened for burning churches, neglecting fasts, burying the dead according to heathen customs, or offering human sacrifices, and at last, wearied with the ceaseless din of war, the Saxons were fain to lay down their arms, and to acknowledge that they were conquered.

Still side by side with this short-sighted policy, which could not fail to promote the commingling of Christian and heathen elements, other and better agencies were at work. The disciples whom Boniface had trained did not fail to walk in the steps of their master, and laboured not only to uproot idolatry, but to plant the truth which should absorb heathen error, building schools and monasteries, erecting churches, and thus laying the best and surest foundations for the future.

The abbey of Utrecht, under the presidency of the devoted Gregory, had sent forth many noble labourers into the mission-field, and many more had come over from England to take their share in the good work, and to spread the knowledge of the truth. One of the most eminent of these was Liudger, the grandson of Wursing, a Frisian chief, and a firm friend of Willibrord. The seeds of early piety had been quickened within him in the school of Utrecht, and his knowledge had been still further extended in that of Alcuin at York, whither Gregory had sent him with his coadjutor Alubert. He returned after an interval of three years and six months, and being well supplied with books, and well instructed, commenced his missionary labours in the region where Boniface had met with his death, assisting Albric, the successor of Gregory, who was consecrated bishop of Cologne.

His exertions, however, had not continued more than seven years, when they were rudely cut short by a rebellion of the Saxons, who rose in A.D. 780, under their leader Widikind, and ravaged the country from Cologne to Coblentz. Albric died, and from the sight of burning churches and exiled clergy Liudger betook himself, with two companions, to Rome, and thence to the abbey of Monte Cassino, to study the monastic rule of St. Benedict. Returning after the lapse of five years he found that peace had been restored, and that the Saxon chief Widikind had submitted to baptism ; and his arrival becoming known to the emperor, the latter assigned him a sphere of labour among the Frisians in the neighbourhood of Gröningen and Norden.[1]

Not content with the area marked out for him, Liudger extended his labours to Heligoland, or Fositesland, famous, as we have seen,[2] in the life of Willibrord. His biographer tells us that, as he sailed to the island, holding the cross in his hand, a dark mist appeared to the sailors to roll off the shore, followed by a bright calm. Interpreting this as an omen of good success, Liudger landed, preached the word, and destroyed the temples, erecting churches in their stead. Many listened to his message, and were baptized in the waters of the very fountain in which Willibrord, at so much risk, had baptized three of the islanders on a former occasion. A son also of one of the chiefs embraced the faith, was baptized, and became a teacher of the Frisians and the founder of a monastery.

After the complete subjugation of the Saxons, Liudger was directed by the emperor to repair to the district of Munster. Here he erected a monastery, travelled over the district with unflagging energy, instructed the barbarous tribes, and appointed priests to take charge of them. After many refusals he was at last induced by Hildebold, archbishop of Cologne, to accept the episcopal dignity ; but he did not cease to carry on as strenuously as ever his missionary work, and even longed to undertake a mission to the wild Normans. This, however, the emperor would

[1] "Vita S. Liudgeri," Pertz, "Mon. Germ." vol. vii. p. 410.
[2] See above, pp. 101, 102.

not allow, and he was fain to remain in his own
diocese, where he did not cease to labour till the day
of his death. On this day, after preaching to two
different congregations in the morning at Cosfeld, and
celebrating the sacrament of the Lord's Supper in the
afternoon at Billerbeck, he bade farewell to the sheep
for whom he had so long laboured, and entered into
his rest, A.D. 809.[1]

Another eminent missionary, and during part of his
life a contemporary of Liudger, was Willehad, a native
of Northumbria,[2] who was induced to leave his country
and join the band of missionaries, commencing, like
Liudger, in the district where Boniface suffered. Re-
moving thence to the district of Gröningen, he found
himself in the midst of a population still fanatically
addicted to paganism. Undeterred by the enmity he
was too likely to arouse, he persevered in delivering
his message, declaimed against the futility of the
national worship, and urged his hearers to embrace
the true faith.

Thereupon the wrath of the people burst forth;
they gnashed with their teeth at the contemner of
their gods, and declared him worthy of death. One
of the chiefs urged caution before proceeding to such
an extremity. "This faith," said he, "is new to us,
and as yet we know not whether it be offered to us
by some deity; the preacher is not guilty of any
crime; let him not, then, be put to death, but let us
cast lots, and ascertain what is the will of heaven

---

[1] "Vita S. Liudgeri," Pertz, vol. ii. p. 414.
[2] "Vita S. Willehadi," Pertz, vol. ii. p. 380.

respecting him, whether he ought to live or die." The people consented, and the lóts were cast. The decision was in his favour, and he was sent away in safety, and was enabled to prosecute his labours in the region of Drenthe.

There, for some time, all went well; the people listened to the intrepid preacher; and not a few embraced the doctrines he taught them. At last some of his companions began to attack the objects of native worship. A riot ensued, and Willehad was set upon with clubs and severely wounded. One of his assailants drew his sword, but the blow, which was intended to have cleft his skull, only severed the thong which fastened the box of relics that he carried. Even the pagans interpreted this as a favourable omen, and he was suffered to depart.

Charlemagne, who had just returned from an expedition against his old enemies the Saxons, now proposed that he should labour amongst the people in the district of Wigmodia, and raise up amongst them an outpost of Christian civilization. The intrepid man eagerly accepted the arduous task, settled down amongst the people, and, for a space of two years, saw in the adhesion, whether feigned or real, of the natives to the new faith, some reward of his labours. But the rebellion of Wittekind in A.D. 782 roused all the old animosity, the churches fell, several of the clergy were murdered,[1] and Willehad was constrained to flee for his life.

An interval of rest was now afforded him, and he

---

[1] "Vita S. Willehadi," cap. vi.

turned it to account by visiting Rome, and obtained
an interview with the Pope. Returning through
France, he took up his abode in a convent founded by
Willibrord at Epternach. Here he gathered together
his scattered scholars, and spent two years in the
quiet study of the Scriptures, edifying many by the
consistency and holiness of his life and conversation. Again, however, he was called forth from his
seclusion by the emperor, and bidden to revisit his
former sphere of labour. The churches which had
been destroyed during the Saxon rising were rebuilt,
and approved clergy stationed in all places where the
people appeared willing to receive the word. The
land enjoyed a still longer period of rest on the
baptism of Wittekind, and Charlemagne, judging it a
fit opportunity to found an episcopal diocese, caused
Willehad to be consecrated the first bishop of Eastern
Frisia and Saxony.[1]

He had no sooner been raised to this new dignity
than he commenced a general visitation of his diocese,
preaching the word where as yet it had not been
heard, and confirming all that had been baptized.
He also erected and consecrated with no little pomp
a cathedral church at Bremen. But he had presided
over his diocese little more than two years, when a
fever, caught during one of his numerous visitation-
journeys, laid him on his deathbed near Blexem on
the Weser. Round his bed gathered the many
scholars he had trained, and with whom he had shared
so many perils. To their mournful regrets at the

---

[1] "Vita S. Willehadi," cap. viii.

prospect of being so soon parted from their master and friend[1] he replied in words which expressed not only his own feelings, but those, doubtless, of many then toiling in the arduous Saxon mission-field.

"O seek not," said he, "to detain me any longer from the presence of my Lord; suffer me to be released from the trials of this troublesome world. I have no desire to live any longer, and I fear not to die. I will only beseech my Lord, whom I have striven to love with my whole heart, that he will deign to give me such a reward for my labour as he in his mercy may see fit. The sheep which he entrusted to me, I again commit to his care. If I have done anything that is good, it has been done through his strength. His goodness will never fail you, for the whole earth is full of his mercy."[2] With these words he expired on the 8th of November, A.D. 789, and was buried in his own cathedral at Bremen.

Three years after his death the long struggle between Charlemagne and the Saxons, between civilization and heathenism, came to a close. For thirty-one years that monarch had persevered in his policy of subjugating his restless foes, and now he had his reward. Slowly but steadily the wave of conquest had extended into the unknown Saxon world, from the Drimel to the Lippe, from the Weser to the Elbe, and thence to the sea, the limit of the Saxon dominion. Peace and rebellion, the reception of baptism and the burning of Christian churches, had

[1] "Vita S. Willehadi," cap. 9.
[2] "Vita S. Willehadi," Pertz, vol. ii. p. 384.

marked the successive alternations of the bloody strife, and at last, wearied with the ceaseless din of war, the Saxons were fain to acknowledge that civilization had conquered. Cruel as may have been some of the expedients to which the victor resorted in gaining his end, he followed up his conquests by measures which command our respect.

His eight bishoprics[1] of Osnaburg, Bremen, Münster, Minden, Halberstadt, Paderborn, Verden, and Hildesheim, with many monasteries, which he richly endowed, were so many great religious colonies, whence the blessings of Christianity and civilization spread abroad in ever-widening circles.

It may, indeed, be said that he exalted the Church to a dangerous elevation ; but while she possessed a monopoly of the knowledge of the age, it was inevitable. Nowhere else could either the means or the men be found to exert a beneficial influence on the half-civilized masses he had subdued, and it is difficult to see how the wild world of the ninth century could have been lifted out of the slough of barbarism, or how the isolated efforts of a Sturmi, a Willehad, a Liudger, could have brought forth any fruit to perfection, had it had not been for the rare energy and skill of this great monarch.

For the dark shadow of his private life, and the cruelty of many of his campaigns,[2] may be pleaded as some atonement the huge Dom-Minsters which

---

[1] Milman, ii. 287.
[2] Palgrave's "Normandy," vol. i. p. 26 ; Sir J. Stephen's "Lectures," vol. i. p. 96.

look into the waters of the Rhine, and the schools
where Alcuin from England, and Clement[1] from Ireland, and Peter of Pisa, and Paulinus of Aquitaine,
and many others, kept alive the torch of learning, and
handed it on to others.

[1] Lanigan's "Ecclesiastical History of Ireland," vol. iii. p. 208.

CHAPTER X.

THOUGH the victories which Charlemagne now gained over the Saxons were thus decisive, he yet lived to see that the tide of barbaric invasion had been thrown back only to be poured upon Europe by a different channel.

He was once, we are told,[1] at Narbonne, when, in the midst of the banquet, some swift barks were seen putting into the harbour. The company started up, and while some pronounced the crew to be Jewish, others African, others British traders, the keen eye of the great emperor discerned that they were bound on no peaceful errand. "It is not with merchandise," said he, "that yonder barks are laden; they are manned by most terrible enemies." And then he advanced to the window, and stood there a long while in tears. No one dared to ask him the cause of his grief, but at length he explained it himself. "It is not for myself," said he, "that I am weeping, or for any harm that yon barks can do to me. But truly I am pained to think that

[1] Pertz, "Mon. Germ." vol. ii. p. 757.

even while I am yet alive they have dared to approach this shore; and still greater is my grief when I reflect on the evils they will bring on my successors."

His words were only too truly fulfilled. The sight of those piratical banners told its own tale. The fleets he had built, the strong forts and towns he had erected at the mouths of the various rivers throughout his empire, were neglected by his successors, and what he foresaw came to pass. Year after year, during the ninth century, the children of the North burst forth from their pine forests, their creeks, their fiords, and icebound lakes, and prowled along the defenceless shores of Germany, France, and England. They laughed at the fiercest storms, landed on the most inaccessible coasts, and pushed up the shallowest rivers, while Charlemagne's degenerate successors, bowed down by a wretched fatalism, scarcely dared to lift a hand, and tamely beheld the fairest towns in their dominions sacked and burnt by the terrible crews of those terrible barks.

"Take a map," writes Sir Francis Palgrave, "and colour with vermilion the provinces, districts, and shores which the Northmen visited, as the record of each invasion. The colouring will have to be repeated more than ninety times successively before you arrive at the conclusion of the Carlovingian dynasty. Furthermore, mark by the usual symbol of war, two crossed swords, the localities where battles were fought by or against the pirates; where they were defeated or triumphant, or where they

pillaged, burned, destroyed; and the valleys and
banks of the Elbe, Rhine, and Moselle, Scheldt,
Meuse, Somme, and Seine, Loire, Garonne, and
Adour, the inland Allier, and all the coasts and
coastlands between estuary and estuary, and the
countries between the river-streams, will appear
bristling as with *chevaux-de-frise.* The strongly-
fenced Roman cities, the venerated abbeys, and their
dependent *bourgades*, often more flourishing and
extensive than the ancient seats of government, the
opulent sea-ports and trading-towns, were all equally
exposed to the Danish attacks, stunned by the
Northmen's approach, subjugated by their fury."[1]

But while the mind faintly strives to conceive the
misery and desolation thus inflicted on well-nigh every
town and village of Germany and France, it finds
satisfaction in the thought that even now missionary
zeal did not falter; that while every estuary and river
darkened under the dark sails of the Northmen's
barks, there were not lacking those who had the
Christian bravery to penetrate into the dreary
regions whence they issued forth, to seek them out
amidst their pine forests and icebound lakes, and
to plant amongst them the first germs of Christian
civilization.

The first mission in Denmark was organized in the
year A.D. 826, when Harold, king of Jutland, his queen,
and a large retinue of Danes, were baptized with
great pomp in the vast Dom of Mayence. On this
occasion, Harold solemnly did homage to Louis le

[1] Palgrave's "Normandy and England," vol. i. p. 419.

Débonnaire, and agreed to hold the Danish kingdom as a feudatory of the Carlovingian crown. On this occasion, also, Ebbo, the primate of France, determined to seek out a monk who would be willing to accompany the newly-baptized king on his return to Denmark, and remain at his court as a priest and teacher. But the well-known ferocity of the Northmen long deterred any one from offering himself for such a duty. At length the abbot of Corbey, near Amiens, announced that one of his monks was not unwilling to undertake the arduous task.

The intrepid volunteer was Anskar,[1] a native of a village not far from Corbey. Born in the year A.D. 801, and early devoted by his parents to the monastic life, he had always evinced the deepest religious enthusiasm, and his ardent imagination taught him to believe that he often saw visions and heard voices from another world. When he was only five years of age, he lost his mother; and a dream, in which he saw her surrounded by a majestic choir of virgins, the fairest of whom bade him, if he would join his mother in bliss, flee the pomps and vanities of the world, exerted a profound impression upon him, and induced him to devote himself more than ever to prayer and meditation.

But when he was thirteen years of age, A.D. 814, an event occurred which exercised a still deeper influence over his susceptible mind. News reached the monastery that Charlemagne was dead. The greatest of great emperors had passed away, and now, in the sepulchre

[1] "Vita S. Anskarii," Pertz, "Mon. Germ." vol. ii. p. 690.

which he had made for himself, "he was sitting on
his curule chair, clad in his silken robes, ponderous
with broidery, pearls, and orfray, the imperial diadem
on his head, his closed eyelids covered, his face
swathed in the dead-clothes, girt with his baldric, the
ivory horn slung in his scarf, his good sword 'Joyeuse'
by his side, the Gospel-book open on his lap, musk
and amber and sweet spices poured around."[1]

Great were the searchings of the heart in the silent
cloisters when the tale of the mighty monarch's death
and strange entombment was repeated from lip to lip.
Dread were the misgivings in the hearts of many
respecting the great emperor's eternal state, and some
even told how in dreams they had seen him punished
in the fire of a purgatorial Phlegethon.

Anskar at this time had relaxed somewhat of his
usual austerities, and now the thought that even that
mighty prince, whom he himself had seen in all the
plenitude of his power, could not escape the hand of
death, filled him with awe and horror, and he gave
himself up more unreservedly than ever to the severest
discipline. Meanwhile his talents had brought him into
general notice, and when his abbot founded another
monastic outpost in Westphalia, in a beautiful valley
on the west bank of the Weser, and called it New
Corbey, Anskar was removed to the new foundation,
and at the age of twenty-five was elected, with the
common consent of all, to superintend its conventual
school, and to preach to the neighbouring population.

He was on a visit to Old Corbey, when the news

[1] Palgrave's "Normandy and England," vol. i. p. 158.

arrived that a monk was much needed to accompany
the Danish Harold to his native land, and that the
abbot Wala had nominated him to the emperor as a
fit person to be entrusted with the arduous mission.
Summoned to the court, Anskar calmly but resolutely
announced his willingness to go. In dreams and
visions, he said, he had heard the voice of Christ
himself bidding him preach the word to the heathen
tribes; and nothing could induce him to shrink from
the plain path of duty. In vain, therefore, on his
return to the monastery, the brethren learning that
he was about to resign all his hopes and prospects
to preach amongst heathens and barbarians, warned,
protested, and even mocked at him for his madness.
Immovable in his resolution to brave all risks, he
began to prepare himself for his great enterprise by
prayer and the study of the Scriptures; and so deep
was the impression made by his evident sincerity and
self-devotion that Autbert, steward of the monastery,
and a man of noble birth, when every one else hung
back, declared that he could not find it in his heart to
desert his friend, and was resolved to become his
companion.

A foretaste of the difficulties that awaited them was
experienced at the very outset. No one could possibly be prevailed on to accompany them as an
attendant. The abbot himself shrank from interpo-
sing his authority, and they were fain to set out alone.
Before starting they had an interview with Louis, and
received from him everything they were likely to
need for their undertaking in the shape of church

vessels, tents, and books. From Harold, however, they met with but little encouragement, and neither he nor his nobles cared much for their company.

On their arrival at Cologne, whence they were to sail up the Rhine to Holland, and so to Denmark, Bishop Hadebold bestowed upon them a ship with two cabins. The better accommodation promised in such a vessel induced Harold to share it with Anskar; and the engaging manners of the missionary gradually won his respect, and inspired him with an interest in his undertaking.

On landing, Anskar fixed his head-quarters at Schleswig, and commenced the foundation of a school, purchasing or receiving from Harold Danish boys, whom he tried to train so as to form the nucleus of a native ministry. Two years thus passed away, and some impression seemed to have been made upon the people, when Autbert sickened, and was obliged to return to Corbey, where he died. Meanwhile the baptism of Harold, and still more his destruction of the native temples, was bitterly resented by his subjects. Before long a rebellion broke out, and the king was obliged to fly for refuge to a spot within the ancient Frisian territory, while Anskar finding it necessary to leave Schleswig, was consoled by an unexpected opportunity of commencing a similar work in Sweden.

In the year A.D. 829 ambassadors from Sweden presented themselves at the court of Louis, and after arranging the political object of their mission, announced that many of their countrymen were favourably disposed towards Christianity.[1] The commerce carried on at this period between Sweden and the port of Doerstadt, combined with the teaching of some Christian captives whom the Swedes had carried off in their piratical excursions, had predisposed not a few towards lending a favourable ear to Christian teachers. The emperor gladly embraced the opportunity thus afforded, and summoned Anskar to the palace, who, after an interview, declared his entire willingness to undertake the enterprise.

A monk named Gislema was therefore left with Harold, and Anskar having found a new companion in Witmar, a brother monk of Corbey, set out in the year A.D. 831 with presents from Louis to the King of Sweden.

But the voyage was most disastrous. The missionaries had not proceeded far when they were attacked by pirates. A fierce battle ensued, and their crew, though first victorious, were overpowered in a second engagement, and barely escaped to land. The pirates plundered them of everything, the presents for the king, their sacred books, and all their ecclesiastical vestments. In this forlorn and destitute condition they reached Birka, a haven and village on the Mälar lake, not far from the ancient capital Sigtuna, the residence of rich merchants, and the centre of the northern trade. Here they were hospitably welcomed by the king, Biorn "of the Hill," and received full permission to preach and baptize. The nucleus of a church was found already existing in the persons of

[1] "Vita S. Anskarii," cap. ix.

many Christian captives, who had long been deprived
of.the consolation of Christian ordinances. The work,
therefore, of the missionaries commenced under fair
auspices, and before long Herigar, the king's counsellor, announced himself a convert, and erected a
church on his estate.

A year and a half was thus employed, and then
Anskar returned to the court of Louis with a letter
from the King of Sweden, and an account of all that
had befallen him. Thereupon Louis resolved without
delay to give effect to the ecclesiastical plans of his
father, and to make Hamburg an archiepiscopal see,
and the centre of operations for the northern missions.
accordingly Anskar was elevated to the archiepiscopal
dignity, and was consecrated at Ingelheim by Drogo,
archbishop of Mayence, and other prelates. At the
same time, because of the poverty of the diocese and
the dangers to which the mission would be inevitably
exposed, the monastery of Turholt in Flanders, between
Bruges and Ypres, was assigned to him as a place of
refuge and a source of revenue. Then he was directed
to repair to Rome, where he received the pall from
Gregory IV. and was regularly authorized to preach
the Gospel to the nations of the North.

These arrangements made, Anskar returned from
Rome. Ebbo, who had been associated with him
in the commission to evangelize the northern tribes,
deputed his missionary duties to his nephew Gauzbert,
who was raised to the episcopal dignity, and entrusted
with the special care of the Swedish mission. Thither,
accordingly, Gauzbert set out, received a hearty wel-

come from Biorn and his people, and laid the foundation of a church at Sigtuna. Meanwhile Anskar had proceeded to Hamburg, and, in pursuance of his former plan, bought or redeemed from slavery a number of Danish youths, whom he either educated himself or sent for that purpose to the monastery of Turholt.

But the times were hardly ripe for successful operations. Three years had barely elapsed when an enormous army of Northmen, led by Eric, king of Jutland, attacked Hamburg, and before relief could arrive, sacked and burned it, together with the church and monastery which Anskar had erected with great trouble. He himself had barely time to save the sacred vessels, and, before the sun went down, every external memorial of his mission was reduced to ashes. *The Lord gave, and the Lord hath taken away, and blessed be the name of the Lord,*[1] was the exclamation of the archbishop, as he surveyed the scene. Driven from Hamburg, he now wandered for a long time over his devastated diocese, followed by a few of his clergy and scholars, and at length sought refuge at Bremen. But the envious Bishop Leutbert refusing to receive him, he was fain to avail himself of the hospitality of a noble lady in the district of Holstein. And as if this was not enough, he now received intelligence that, owing to similar risings of the Northmen, the hopes of the Swedish mission were utterly crushed.

The pagan party had conspired against Bishop Gauzbert, expelled him from the country, and murdered his nephew Nithard. But divine vengeance, so

[1] Job i. 21.

we are assured, did not fail to pursue the conspirators. One of them had carried home some of the property of the missionaries. Before long he died, together with his mother and sister, and his father found his own property wasting from day to day. Alarmed at this sudden reverse of fortune, he began to consider what god he could have offended to bring all these troubles on his house. Unable to solve the difficulty himself, he had recourse to a soothsayer. The lots were cast, and it was found that none of the native deities bore him any ill will. At length the soothsayer explained the cause. "It is the God of the Christians," said he, "who is the author of thy ruin. There is something dedicated to him concealed in thy house, and therefore all these evils have come upon thee, nor canst thou hope to prosper till the sacred thing is restored."

After vainly trying for some time to comprehend what this could mean, he suddenly recollected the day when his son had brought home from the spoil of the missionaries' dwellings one of their sacred books. Stricken with alarm, he immediately called together the inhabitants of the place, told them all that had occurred, and prayed their advice in the emergency. Every one declined to receive the terrible relic, and at last, fearful of further vengeance if he retained it any longer in his house, the man covered it carefully, and then fastened it to a stake on the public road, with a notice that any one who wished might take it down, and that for the crime he had unwittingly been guilty of against the Christians' God he was ready to offer any satisfaction that might be required. One of the native Christians took it down, and the man's terrors were appeased.[1]

Anskar meanwhile was still wandering over his desolated diocese. Even the monastery of Turholt, which Louis had bestowed upon him for the very purpose of being a covert from such storms as these, was closed against him, having been bestowed upon a layman by Charles the Bald. Under such accumulated misfortunes most men would have sunk, but Anskar waited patiently in the hope of some change, and comforted himself with the words of Archbishop Ebbo before his death: "Be assured, brother," said that prelate, "that what we have striven to accomplish for the glory of Christ will yet, by God's help, bring forth fruit. For it is my firm and settled belief, nay, I know of a surety, that though the work we have undertaken among these nations is for a time subject to obstacles and difficulties on account of our sins, yet it will not be lost or perish altogether, but will, by God's grace, thrive and prosper, until the name of the Lord is made known to the uttermost ends of the earth."[2]

Before long events occurred which seemed to promise that the clouds would roll away, and a brighter era be inaugurated. Mindful of the converted chief, Anskar sent to Sigtuna an anchoret named Ardgar, with directions to see how he fared, and to strengthen him against falling back into heathenism. Thither Ardgar set out, and was rejoiced to find Herigar

[1] "Vita S. Anskarii," cap. xviii.
[2] Ibid. cap. xxxiv.

still remaining faithful to the faith he had embraced. The recollection of the Divine vengeance, which was deemed to have attended the previous outbreak, protected the missionary from injury, and the new king who had succeeded Biorn was persuaded by Herigar to permit Ardgar to preach the Gospel without fear of molestation.

That chief was no half-hearted believer, and openly confronted the malice of the pagan party. On one occasion, as they were boasting of the power of their gods, and of the many blessings they had received by remaining faithful to their worship, and were reviling him as a traitor and apostate, he bade them put the matter to an open and decisive proof. "If there be so much doubt," said he, "concerning the superior might of our respective gods, let us see whose power is greatest; whether that of the many whom ye call gods, or that of my one omnipotent Lord, Jesus Christ. Lo! the season of rain is at hand. Do ye call upon the names of your gods that the rain may be restrained from falling upon you, and I will call upon the name of my Lord Jesus Christ that no drop may fall on me; and the god that answereth our prayers, let him be God."

The heathen party agreed, and repairing to a neighbouring field, took their seats in great numbers on one side, while Herigar, attended only by a little child, sat on the other. In a few moments the rain descended in torrents, drenched the heathens to the skin, and swept away their tents; while on Herigar and the little child, we are assured by Anskar's biographer, no drop fell, and even the ground around them remained dry. "Ye see," he cried, "which is the true God; bid me not, then, desert the faith I have adopted, but rather lay aside your errors, and come to a knowledge of the truth."

On another occasion the town of Birka was attacked by a piratical expedition of Danes and Swedes, under the command of a king of Sweden who had been expelled from his realm. The place was closely invested, and there seemed to be no prospect of a successful defence. In their alarm the townspeople offered numerous sacrifices to their gods, and when all other means failed, collected such treasures as they possessed, together with a hundred pounds of silver, and succeeded in coming to terms with the hostile chiefs. But their followers, not satisfied with the amount, prepared to storm the town. Again the gods were consulted, the altars raised, the victims offered, but with results equally unpromising. Herigar now interposed, rebuked the people for their obstinate adherence to the worship of gods that could not profit them or give any aid in their trouble, and when they bade him suggest some device, and promised to follow his counsel, he urged them to make a solemn vow of obedience to the Lord of the Christians, assured that, if they turned to him, he, at any rate, would not fail them in the hour of danger. The people took his advice, went forth to an open plain, and there solemnly vowed to keep a fast in honour of the God of the Christians, if he would rescue them from their enemies.

Help came in an unexpected fashion. The Swedish king, while the army was clamouring for the signal to attack, suggested that the gods should be consulted by lot, whether it was their will that Birka should be destroyed. "There are many great and powerful deities there," said he ; "there also formerly a church was built, and even now the worship of the great Christ is observed by many, and he is more powerful than any other of the gods, and is ever ready to aid those that put their trust in him. We ought, then, to inquire first whether it is the divine will that we attack the place." Accordingly the lots were cast, and it was discovered that the auspices were not favourable for the assault ; and thus Birka was spared. The arrival, therefore, of Ardgar was well timed, and he was not only welcomed by Herigar, but the Christians were strengthened by his coming in their adherence to the faith.

Nor was it in Sweden only that the prospects of the missionaries brightened. In A.D. 847, Leutbert, the bishop of Bremen, died. Anskar's own see of Hamburg was now reduced by the desolating inroads of the Northmen to four baptismal churches.[1] It was therefore proposed that the see of Bremen should be annexed to the archbishopric of Hamburg, and after some difficulty the plan was matured, and Anskar no longer found himself hampered by want of means from devoting all his energies to the wider planting of the faith. At the same time he was enabled to appoint a priest over the church at Schleswig, and from Horik, king of Jutland, he no longer experienced opposition in preaching the word amongst the people. This

[1] "Vita S. Anskarii," cap. xxii.

encouraged many who had been baptized at Hamburg
and Doerstadt, but who had secretly conformed to
idolatrous practices, to publicly profess their adhesion
to the Christian faith, and they rejoiced in the opportunity of joining in Christian fellowship. The trade
also of Doerstadt prospered by the change; Christian
merchants flocked thither in greater numbers and
with greater confidence, and thus helped forward the
work of Anskar and his colleagues.

At this juncture the hermit Ardgar returned from
Sweden. Anskar, more than ever unwilling that the
mission there should be allowed to drop, tried to prevail on Gauzbert to revisit the scene of his former
labours. But the latter, discouraged by his previous
failure, declined, and Anskar finding no one else willing to undertake the work, once more girded up his
loins, and encouraged by Horik, who gave him letters
to Olaf, king of Sweden, set out for Birka. The
time of his landing was unfortunate. The heathen
party had been roused by the native priests, and a
crusade was proclaimed against the strange doctrines.
Suborning a man who pretended to have received a
message from the native deities, the priests announced
it to be the will of heaven that, if the people wished
for new gods, they should admit into their company
the late king, Eric, and allow divine honours to be
paid to him. This wrought up the feelings of the
populace to such a pitch that the retinue of the
archbishop pronounced it absolute madness to persevere in his undertaking.

But Anskar was not thus to be thwarted. He

invited Olaf to a feast, set before him the presents
sent by the King of Jutland, and announced the
object of his visit.   Olaf on his part was not indis-
posed to make the concessions he desired, but as
former missionaries had been expelled from the
country, he suggested that it would be well to submit
the affair once for all to the solemn decision of the
sacred lots, and consult in an open council the feelings
of the people.   Anskar agreed, and a day was fixed
for deciding the question.

First, the council of the chiefs was formally asked,
and their opinion requested.   They craved the casting of the sacred lots.   The lots were accordingly
cast, and the result was declared to be favourable
to the admission of the archbishop and his retinue.
Then the general assembly of the people of Birka
was convened, and at the command of the king a
herald proclaimed aloud the purport of the archbishop's visit.   This was the signal for a great tumult,
in the midst of which an aged chief arose, and thus
addressed the assembly :

" Hear me, O king and people.   The God whom
we are invited to worship is not unknown to us, nor the
aid he can render to those that put their trust in him.
Many of us have already proved this by experience,
and have felt his assistance in many perils, and especially on the sea.   Why, then, reject what we know to
be useful and necessary for us ?   Not long ago some
of us went to Doerstadt, and believing that this new
religion could profit us much, willingly professed ourselves its disciples.   Now the voyage thither is beset

with dangers, and pirates abound on every shore. Why, then, reject a religion thus brought to our very doors, which before we went a long way to seek? Why not permit the servants of God, whose protecting aid we have already experienced, to abide amongst us? Listen to my counsel, then, O king and people, and reject not what is plainly for our advantage. We see our own deities failing us, and unable to aid us in time of danger. Surely it is a good thing to obtain the favour of a god who always can and will aid those that call upon him."

His words found favour with the people, and it was unanimously resolved that the archbishop should be permitted to take up his abode in the country, and should not be hindered in disseminating the Christian faith. This resolution was announced to Anskar in person by the king, who further conceded a grant of land for building a church, and welcomed Erimbert, a colleague of the archbishop, whom he presented as the new director of the Swedish mission.

Meanwhile matters had not been so prosperous in Denmark. Eric "the Red," though not professedly a Christian, had, as we have seen, aided the archbishop materially in the introduction of Christianity. His apostasy provoked the inveterate hostility of the Northmen, and the sea-kings determined to avenge the insult offered to the national gods.

Rallying from all quarters under the banner of Guthrun, the nephew of Eric, they attacked the apostate king near Flensburgh, in Jutland. The battle raged for three days, and at its close Eric and

Guthrun, and a host of kings and jarls, lay dead upon
the field ; and so tremendous had been the slaughter,
that the entire Viking nobility seemed to have been
utterly exterminated.[1]

The new king, Eric II., easily persuaded that the
recent reverses were entirely due to the apostasy
of his predecessor, ordered one of Anskar's churches
to be closed, and forbade all further missionary operations. After a while, however, he was induced to
change his policy, and Anskar, on his return from
Sweden, was reinstated in the royal favour, and received a grant of land for the erection of a second
church at Ripa, in Jutland, over which he placed
Rimbert, a native, charging him to win the hearts of
his barbarous flock by the sincerity and devotion of
his life.

Anskar now returned to Hamburg, and devoted
himself to the administration of his diocese. One of
the latest acts of his life was a noble effort to check
the infamous practice of kidnapping and trading in
slaves. A number of native Christians had been
carried off by the northern pirates, and reduced to
slavery. Effecting their escape, they sought refuge
in the territory of Northalbingia. Instead of shelter-
ing the fugitives, some of the chiefs retained a portion
of them as their own slaves, and sold others to heathen
and even professedly Christian tribes around. News
of this reached Anskar, and at the risk of his life he
sternly rebuked the chiefs, and succeeded in inducing

---

[1] "Vita S. Anskarii," cap. xxxi.; Palgrave's "Normandy and
England," vol. i. p. 449.

them to set the captives free, and to ransom as many as possible from the bondage into which they had sold them.

This noble act formed an appropriate conclusion of his life. He was now more than sixty-four years of age, and during more than half that period had laboured unremittingly in the mission-field. His biographer expatiates eloquently on his character as exhibiting the perfect model of ascetic perfection. Even when elevated to the episcopal dignity he never exempted himself from the rigid discipline of the cloister. He wore a haircloth shirt by night as well as by day. He measured out, at least in his earlier days, his food and drink by an exact rule. He chanted a fixed number of Psalms, alike when he arose in the morning and when he retired to rest at night. His charity knew no bounds. Not only did he erect a hospital at Bremen for the sick and needy, distribute a tenth of his income among the poor, and divide amongst them any presents he might receive, but every five years he tithed his income afresh that he might be quite sure the poor had their proper share. Whenever he went on a tour of visitation through his diocese, he would never sit down to dinner without first ordering some of the poor to be brought in, and he himself would sometimes wash their feet, and distribute amongst them bread and meat.

Such a practical exhibition of Christian love could not fail to exercise a gradual influence even over the rough pirates of the North, and they testified their sense of the power he wielded over them by ascribing to him many miraculous cures. But he was not one to seek a questionable distinction of this kind. " One miracle," he once said to a friend, " I would, if worthy, ask the Lord to grant me ; and that is, that by his grace he would make me a good man."

A single source, however, of disquietude troubled his last hours. In vision he believed it had been intimated to him that he might hope to win the martyr's crown. What sin of his had deprived him of this honour ? In vain one of his most attached companions pointed out that it had not been told him distinctly by what death he was to die, whether by fire, or the sword, or shipwreck. In vain he recalled the hardships the archbishop had undergone, and the perils which had made his life a continual martyrdom. At length, his biographer tells us, another and a last vision assured him that his fears were groundless, that no sin of his had robbed him of his crown. Thus comforted, he employed his last days in arranging the affairs of his diocese, and of his various mission-stations, and calmly expired on the 3d of February, A.D. 865.

CHAPTER XI.

UNTIL the ninth century Norway was divided into numerous petty principalities, and was little known to the rest of Europe, except as the hive whence issued numberless hordes of pirates who devastated her shores. Up to the same period the political power in the country had been shared by a host of petty princes, who, true to the motto of the Norsemen, "a man for himself," gratified their love of war by constant contentions with one another.

But about the year A.D. 860 there arose a king who had very different ideas respecting royal power than those he had received from his fathers. Harold, son of Halfdan "the Black," having conquered many of the petty kings of the country, sought, we are told, the hand of Gyda, most beautiful of all the maidens in Norway.[1] But his suit was rejected with scorn. Gyda would never marry the lord of a few thinly-peopled kingdoms. He who had the courage and power to win for himself the mastery over the whole country, he, and he alone, should gain her hand. Harold heard her reply, and swore he would never comb his

[1] Snorro Sturleson's "Heimskringla," translated by Laing, i. 273.

beautiful hair till he had become absolute monarch, like Eric of Sweden, or Gorm of Denmark.

Assembling a crowd of youthful warriors, he quickly fought his way with his terrible sword, and wherever he went, broke up the little separate clans, abolished the allodial laws of inheritance, and made every land a fief to be held directly from himself. Furthermore, he insisted that all rents should be paid in kind, that the Northman should be his, not only in time of war, but at all times, that he should submit to the jarl appointed by the king, and do him the same suit and service that the Franks rendered to the great counts set over them by Charlemagne. It was a long struggle, but his undaunted courage and perseverance carried him through, and then, mindful of his vow, he cut and combed his hair, and exchanged his name Harold Lufa, or Harold "of the horrid hair," for Haarfager or "Fair-hair," and sent for and married Gyda, by whom he had one daughter and four sons.

But the change was utterly repugnant to his sturdy and independent subjects, and he saw them leave the land in numbers, to colonize the Orkneys, the Hebrides, the Faroes, and Iceland, to invade Russia and Normandy, and become the terror of the coasts of England, Ireland, and Spain. He retained, however, his supremacy, till the year A.D. 938, when he resigned in favour of his son Eric Blodoxe. The new king became involved in perpetual wars with his surviving brothers, and the people, groaning under his rule, began to sigh for a deliverer.

At length news of Eric's cruelties reached the court

of our Anglo-Saxon king Athelstan, where Hacon, the youngest son of Harold, was at this time residing. His protector had taken care that the young prince should be baptized and "brought up in the right faith, and in good habits, and all sorts of exercises," and now strongly favoured his design of offering himself to his countrymen as their deliverer. Furnished with ships and men, Hacon sailed to Drontheim, and was straightway joined by Sigurd, earl of Lade, who espoused his cause, and recommended him to the Thing. The people welcomed their deliverer with shouts of applause, and listened with delight while he promised to secure to the bonders their full udal rights, and restore the old customs. One by one the jarls gave in their adhesion to his cause, and when Eric, convinced of the disaffection of his people, left the country, they gladly made Hacon sole king in his stead.

During his residence in England the new king had, as we have said, been baptized, and he now determined to expel the native heathenism, and plant in its stead his newly-adopted faith. Such a design, however, was fraught with peril, and Hacon could not fail to foresee the storm of opposition he would encounter. Resolved to proceed by degrees, he contented himself, for the present, with a secret conformity to his new creed, and kept holy the Sundays and the Friday fasts. As a first step, however, in the proposed direction, he contrived to persuade his people to keep the great festival of Yule[1] at the same time

1 "Yule, or the midwinter feast, was the greatest festival in the countries of Scandinavia. Yule bonfires blazed to scare witches and

that Christian people celebrated the Saviour's nativity. His next step was to entice over to the new faith such of the courtiers as were dearest to him, and sending to England for a bishop and priests, he persuaded some of them to receive baptism, and lay aside their heathen rites. He even succeeded in building a few churches in the Drontheim district, and at last determined to propose to the people, at the next Froste-Thing, that all, great and small, should be baptized, "believe in one God, and Christ the son of Mary, abstain from all heathen sacrifices, keep holy the seventh day, and refrain from all work thereon."

The Thing accordingly was summoned, and after the usual solemn sacrifices, and great feastings, Hacon made his formal proposition. It was received with universal surprise. The masters were entirely opposed to such a frequent cessation from labour, the slaves were equally opposed to the imposition of repeated fasts, and the heathen faction mustered so strong that the king's proposition was rejected with general indignation.

"We bonders," said one, speaking for the rest, "do not know whether we have really got back our freedom, or whether thou wishest to make vassals of us again by this extraordinary proposal that we should abandon the ancient faith, which our fathers and fore-

wizards; offerings were made to the gods; the boar dedicated to Freÿr was placed on the table, and over it the warriors vowed to perform great deeds. Pork, mead, and ale abounded, and the Yuletide passed merrily away with games, gymnastics, and mirth of all kinds."— Worsae's "Danes and Northmen," p. 83.

fathers have held from the oldest times, in the days
when the dead were burned, as well as since they
were laid under mounds, and which, though they were
braver than the people of our days, has served us as
a faith to the present time. Thou, king, must use
some moderation towards us, and only require from
us such things as we can obey thee in, and are not
impossible for us. If, however, thou wilt take up this
matter with a high hand, and wilt try thy power and
strength against us, we bonders have resolved, among
ourselves, to part with thee, and to take to ourselves
some other chief, who will so conduct himself towards
us, that we can freely and safely enjoy that faith
which suits our own inclinations."

Great applause followed this independent speech,
and Earl Sigurd, who presided over the sacrifices, was
fain to intimate to the people the king's acquiescence
with their wishes, and to advise him to postpone his
religious reforms to a more convenient season. But
the suspicions of the people were now excited, and
Earl Sigurd's promises did not satisfy them. At
the next harvest festival, therefore, they demanded
that Hacon should openly avow his attachment to
the national faith by drinking, as heretofore, in
honour of the gods. Earl Sigurd promised that he
should do so, and persuaded the king, who had
hitherto been wont on such occasions to take his
meals in a little house by himself, to present himself
on his throne before his people, and quiet their
suspicions. The first goblet went round, and was
blessed in Odin's name. The earl drank first, and

then handed it to Hacon, who took it, and made the sign of the Cross over it. "What does the king mean by doing so?" said one of the bonders; "will he not sacrifice?" "He is blessing the goblet in honour of Thor," replied the earl, "by making the sign of his hammer over it when he drinks it." This quieted the people.

But, on the next day, they resolved to put Hacon's sincerity to a severer test, and therefore pressed him to eat of the horseflesh slain in the sacrifices. This was one of the distinguishing marks of heathenism, and had been solemnly forbidden by the Church ever since the days of Archbishop Boniface. Hacon, therefore, positively refused to comply with the demand. Thereupon the bonders offered him the broth; and when he also declined this, they declared he should at least taste the gravy; and when he refused this too, they were going to lay hands on him, when Earl Sigurd interposed, and so far prevailed with the king that he consented to hold his mouth over "the handle of the kettle, upon which the fat smoke of the boiled horseflesh had settled itself; and the king first laid a linen cloth over the handle, and then gaped over it, and returned to the throne; but neither party was satisfied with this."[1]

In the following winter the popular feeling expressed itself still more plainly against Hacon's religious reforms. Four chiefs bound themselves by an oath to root out Christianity in Norway, while four others resolved to force the king to offer sacrifice to

[1] Snorro, i. 331.

the gods. Three churches were burnt and three priests
killed at Mære, and when Hacon came thither with
Earl Sigurd to hold the Yule feast, the bonders
insisted that the king should offer sacrifice. The
tumult could only be appeased by some show of
compliance, and at Earl Sigurd's intercession Hacon
consented at last to taste some of the horse-liver,
and to empty such goblets as the bonders filled for
him. This determined opposition to his plans roused
the king's anger, and he was meditating a violent
revenge, when the news arrived of the invasion of
his kingdom by the sons of his brother Eric. A
battle ensued, and the invaders were forced to retire.
Henceforth Hacon is said to have become more
tolerant of heathen rites, and finding it impossible
to stem the torrent of opposition, consented to forego
his designs.

In the year A.D. 963 his kingdom was again invaded by his nephews, and in a great battle he
himself was mortally wounded. Perceiving that his
end drew near, he called together his friends, and after
arranging the affairs of his kingdom, began to feel
the pangs of remorse on account of his guilty concession at the Drontheim feast. "If Fate," said he,
"should prolong my life, I will at any rate leave this
country, and go to a Christian land, and do penance
for what I have done against God; but should I die
in a heathen land, give me any burial you may think
fit." Shortly afterwards he expired, and was buried
"under a great mound in North Hordaland, in full
armour, and in his best clothes." Though he had

incurred much enmity from his determination to impose Christianity on his people, all was now forgotten; friends and enemies alike bewailed his death, and solaced themselves for his apostasy by believing that because he had spared the temples of Odin he had now found a place in Valhalla, "in the blessed abodes of the bright gods."

On the death of Hacon, the sons of Eric, of whom Harold was the eldest, assumed the supreme authority, and having been baptized in England, thought it their duty to pull down the heathen temples, and forbid the sacrifices in all places where they had the power. Great opposition was roused, which was not appeased by the badness of the seasons during their reign, and the harshness they displayed towards the bonders. "In Halogaland," says the Saga, "there was the greatest famine and distress; for scarcely any corn grew, and even snow was lying, and the cattle were bound in the byres all over the country, until midsummer."[1]

In the midst of the commotions that now ensued, Harold Blaatand, king of Denmark, conquered the country, and placed over his new territory the jarl Hacon as his viceroy. Hacon allied himself with the heathen party, and did all in his power to re-establish paganism, in direct contravention of the wishes of Harold Blaatand, who, on the occasion of his baptism, had given him priests and other learned men, and commanded him to make all the people in Norway be baptized. Hacon's crowning act of apostasy was

[1] Snorro, i. 365.

N 2

the sacrifice of one of his sons in honour of Thor,
in the great battle with the Jomsburg pirates. His
rule was offensive and unpopular, and he was de-
posed in A.D. 995 by Olaf, the son of Tryggve, a
petty prince, whom the oppressed Norsemen welcomed
as their deliverer.

The history of the new king is a remarkable illus-
tration of the times in which he lived, as the transition
period between Odinism and Christianity. He is
represented in the Sagas as one of the handsomest
men, excelling in all bodily exercises. He was, withal,
a great traveller, and had visited not only England
and the Hebrides, but northern Germany, Greece,
Russia, and Constantinople. In Germany he had become acquainted with a certain ecclesiastic of Bremen,
named Thangbrand, a son of Willebald, count of
Saxony. Thangbrand is described " as a tall man
and strong, skilful of speech, a good clerk, and a good
warrior, albeit a teacher of the faith; not provoking
others, but once angered, and he would yield to no
man in deeds or in words." Olaf was attracted by a
large shield which the martial ecclesiastic was wont to
carry. On it was embossed in gold the figure of Christ
on the Cross. Olaf asked the meaning of the symbol,
and was told the story of Christ and of his death.
Observing how greatly he was taken with it, Thangbrand offered him the shield as a present, which was
gratefully accepted, and preserved with diligent care.
The rude Viking carried it about with him wherever
he went, and ascribed to it his deliverance from many
dangers both by sea and land.

Thangbrand gives his shield to Olaf.—P. 180.

During one of his many piratical voyages, Olaf touched at the Scilly Islands,[1] where he heard of the fame of a great seer. Having made trial of his skill, he repaired to his cell, and asked him who he was, and whence he had this knowledge of the future. The man told him he was a hermit, and that the Christians' God revealed to him the secrets of the future. Thereupon Olaf resolved to be baptized with all his followers, and going thence to England, was confirmed by Elphege, bishop of Winchester, in the presence of the Saxon king Ethelred. Repairing afterwards to Dublin,[2] he married Gyda, sister of King Olaf Kvaran, and during his stay in Ireland received a visit from one of the northern Vikings, who persuaded him to revisit his native land, and assured him that one of Harold Haarfager's race would be welcomed by the people. Adopting his advice, Olaf sailed to Norway, where he was welcomed as a deliverer from the oppressive cruelty of Hacon the Bad, and at a general Thing held at Drontheim was unanimously chosen to be king

[1] Snorro, i. 397 ; Lappenberg, ii. 158 ; Dasent's "Burnt Njal," ii. 360. Worsae, however, holds that the Isles where Olaf landed were "not the Scilly Isles near England, but the Skellig Isles on the southwest coast of Ireland, on one of which there was at that time a celebrated abbey."—"Danes and Northmen," p. 333.

[2] Dublin was the central point of the Norwegian power in Ireland, though the Ost-men also settled in considerable numbers at Waterford Limerick, Wexford, and Cork. The Norwegians and Danes settled in Ireland, were soon converted from heathenism by Irish monks and priests. and through these converts Christianity was communicated to many of their Scandinavian fellow-countrymen.—Worsae's "Danes," p. 315.

over the whole country, as Harold Haarfager had been.

No sooner had Olaf strengthened himself on the throne than he resolved on the extermination of heathenism. His long abode with his brother-in-law, King Olaf Kvaran, in Dublin, where he had been in constant intercourse with the Irish Christians, could not fail to have strengthened him in this determination. The means he resorted to were such as might have been expected from a northern Viking, with an ecclesiastic like Thangbrand at his side. He began by destroying the heathen idols and temples, wherever it was practicable, and then, summoning his relatives, declared he would either bring it to pass that all Norway should be Christian, or die. "I shall make you all," he said, "great and mighty men in promoting this work, for I trust to you most as blood-relations and brothers-in-law." They agreeing to do as he desired, he made a public proclamation to all the people of Norway, declaring it to be his will and pleasure that Christianity should be adopted as the national faith. Those who had already pledged their assistance straightway gave in their adhesion, and being very powerful and influential, speedily induced others to follow their example, till at last the inhabitants of the eastern part of Viken allowed themselves to be baptized. Proceeding thence to the northern part of the same district, he invited every man to accept the new faith, and punished severely all who opposed him, killing some, mutilating others, and driving the rest into banishment.

Successful in his own kingdom, and in that of his relative Harold Greenske, he next proceeded to Hordaland and Rogaland, summoned the people to a Thing, and proposed the same terms. Here, however, he encountered more active opposition. The bonders no sooner received the message-token for the Thing, than they assembled in great numbers and in arms, and selecting three men who were regarded as the best spokesmen, they bade them argue with the king, and answer him, and especially decline anything against the old customs, even if the king demanded it.

"When the bonders came to the Thing," we read in the quaint language of the Saga, "and the Thing was formed, King Olaf rose, and at first spake good-humouredly to the people ; but they observed he wanted them to accept Christianity, with all his fine words ; and in conclusion he let them know that those who should speak against him, and not submit to his proposal, must expect his displeasure and punishment and all the ill it was in his power to inflict. When he had ended his speech, one of the bonders stood up, who was considered the most eloquent, and who had been chosen as the first to reply to King Olaf. But when he would begin to speak, such a cough seized him, and such a difficulty of breathing, that he could not bring out a word, and was obliged to sit down again.

"Then another bonder stood up, resolved not to let an answer be wanting, although it had gone so ill with the former ; but he became so confused, that he could not find a word to say, and all present set up a laughter, amid which the bonder sat down again. And now the third stood up to make a speech ; but when he began, he became so hoarse and husky in his throat that nobody could hear a word he said, and he also had to sit down again. There were now none of the bonders to speak against the king, and as nobody answered him, there was no opposition; and it came to this, that all agreed to what the king had proposed. Accordingly all the people were baptized before the Thing was dissolved."[1]

Shortly afterwards, the king summoned the bonders of the Fiord district, South Möre, and Raumsdal, and offered them two conditions, either to accept Christianity, or to fight. Unable to cope with the forces the monarch had brought with him, they too made a virtue of necessity, and agreed to be baptized. Sailing next to Lade, in Drontheim, Olaf destroyed the temple, despoiled it of its ornaments and property, and, amongst the rest, of the great gold ring which the apostate Hacon had ordered to be made and caused to be hung in the door of the temple. Then at a Thing held in Viken he denounced terrible penalties against all who dealt with evil spirits, or were addicted to sorcery and witchcraft.

Summer came round, and Olaf, collecting a large army, sailed northwards to Nidaros, in the Drontheim district, where he summoned the people of eight districts round to a Thing. The bonders, however, changed the Thing-token into a war-token, and called together all men, free and unfree, to resist

[1] Snorro, i. 429.

the king. Remembering how they had succeeded in forcing Hacon into some sort of submission, they interrupted Olaf's proposals by threatening him with violence. Perceiving that this time he was numerically weaker, Olaf feigned to give way, and expressed a desire to go to their temples, and see their customs, and decide which to hold by. A midsummer sacrifice was fixed to take place at Mære, the site of an ancient temple in the Drontheim district, and thither all the great chiefs and bonders were invited to repair. As the day approached, Olaf ordered that a great feast should be prepared at Lade, at which the mead-cup went round freely.

Next morning he ordered early mass to be sung before him, and then summoned a House-Thing, to which the bonders repaired. "We held a Thing at Froste," said he, when they were all seated, "and I proposed to the bonders that they should allow themselves to be baptized. But they invited me to offer sacrifices, as Hacon had done. So we agreed to meet at Mære, and make a great sacrifice. Now if I, along with you, shall turn again to making sacrifice, then will I make the greatest of sacrifices that are in use ; and I will sacrifice men. But I will not select slaves or malefactors for this, but will take the greatest men only to be offered." Thereupon he nominated eleven principal chiefs, whom he proposed to sacrifice to the gods for peace and a fruitful season, and he ordered them to be seized forthwith.

So unexpected a proposal utterly confounded the bonders, and they were fain to be baptized, and to remain as hostages until the arrival of their relatives. Having taken these precautions, Olaf set out for the great sacrifice at Mære. Here the whole heathen party had assembled in great force, determined to make the king comply with the national customs. Olaf proposed his usual terms, and the bonders demanded that he should offer sacrifice to the gods. Mindful of his former promise, Olaf then consented to go to their temple and watch the ceremonies, and entered it with a great number of his men. As the sacrifice proceeded, the king suddenly struck the image of Thor with his ˊgold-inlaid axe, so that it rolled down at his feet, and at this signal his men struck down the rest of the images from their seats. Then coming forth, he proposed his usual conditions, and the bonders, after this manifest proof of the powerlessness of their deities, surrendered to his will, and gave hostages that they would remain true to Christianity, and "took baptism."

Shortly afterwards Olaf made him a great long ship, which he called the *Crane*, and sailed northwards to Halogaland, imposing Christianity wherever he went. But at Godö Isle in Salten Fiord he encountered great opposition. There dwelt here, the Saga tells us, a chief of great power, but a great idolater, and very skilful in witchcraft, named Raud the Strong. Hearing that Olaf was coming, he went to meet him in his own great ship the *Dragon*. A fight ensued, in which Raud was vanquished, and forced to retreat to his island. Olaf followed, but when he reached Salten Fiord, which is more dreaded even than the famous Maelstrom, such a storm was raging that for a whole week he could not make the land. In this difficulty he applied for counsel to Bishop Sigurd, who accompanied him on this occasion, and whom he had placed over the Drontheim district. Sigurd promised to try if " God would give him power to conquer these arts of the devil."

Accordingly, arrayed in all his mass-robes, he went to the bows of the *Crane*, lit many tapers, kindled incense, set the crucifix at the stern, read the Evangelist, offered many prayers, and finally sprinkled the whole ship with holy water. Then, declaring that the charm could not fail to be efficacious, he bade Olaf row into the fiord. Thus encouraged, the king, followed by his other long ships, rowed boldly up the throat of the fiord : and so efficacious had been the bishop's prayers, that " the sea was curled about their keel-track like as in a calm, so quiet and still was the water ; yet on each side of them the waves were lashing up so high that they hid the sight of the mountains."

After a day and a night's rowing, Godö Isle was reached, and an attack was immediately made on Raud, as he was sleeping. After many of his servants had been killed, the chief was dragged into the presence of Olaf. " I will not take thy property from thee," said the king, " but will rather be thy friend, if thou wilt make thyself worthy to be so, and be baptized." Raud exclaimed he would never believe in Christ, and made his scoff of God. Thereupon Olaf was wroth, and ordered him to be put to death amidst

revolting tortures,[1] and having carried off all his effects
and his fine dragon-ship, he made all his men receive
baptism, and imposed Christianity on all the people
of the fiord, and then returned southward to Nidaros.

Thus did Olaf "bend his whole mind" to uprooting
heathenism and old customs which he deemed contrary to Christianity.   Iceland, also, did not escape
his attentions.   He had sent Thangbrand thither on
account of his misdeeds, to bring it over to the faith.
But that rough ecclesiastic found this no easy matter.
Some of the chiefs submitted to baptism, while others
not only refused, but composed lampoons upon him ;
whereupon Thangbrand slew two of them outright.

About this time some of the Icelandic chiefs paid a
visit to Nidaros, and stayed there during the winter,
where they encountered Olaf, and were obliged, much
against their will, to answer him many questions
about Iceland.   The following Michaelmas the king
had high mass celebrated with great splendour, and
the Icelanders came, and listened to the singing and
the sound of the bells, and on the following day were
baptized and treated with much kindness.   At this
juncture Thangbrand returned, and informed the king
of his ill success, and how the Icelanders made lampoons upon him, and threatened to kill him.   Olaf
was so enraged that he ordered a horn to be blown
and all the Icelanders in Nidaros to be summoned,
and would have put them all to death, had not one
of them reminded him of his promise to forgive all

[1] According to the Saga, a serpent was forced down his throat, which
ate its way through his body (!) and caused his death.   Snorro, i. 448.

who turned from heathenism and became Christians, and declared that Thangbrand's ill success was the result of his own violence and bloodshed. It was owing to the influence of these Icelandic chiefs on their return, that the lawman Thorgeir proposed to the Icelandic national council that Christianity should be introduced, which resolution was supplemented afterwards by another, that all the islanders should be baptized, the temples destroyed, and at least the public ceremonies of paganism abolished.[1]

In the same year, however, that this resolution was passed in Iceland, Olaf's violent efforts to uproot heathenism in Norway were brought to a close. Worsted in a tremendous engagement with the united forces of Denmark and Sweden, rather than yield to his enemies, he flung himself from the deck of Raud's ship into the sea, and sank beneath the waters. He was the type of a northern Viking. The Sagas delight to record instances of his strength and agility : how he climbed the Smalsor Horn, an inaccessible peak of a mountain in Bremager, and fixed his shield upon it ; how he could run across the oars of the *Serpent*, while his men were rowing; how he could cast two spears at once, and strike and cut equally

---

[1] It was at this Thing that Snorri made his famous speech. " Then came a man running, and said that a stream of lava (earth-fire) had burst out at Olfus, and would run over the homestead of Thorod the priest. Then the heathen men began to say, ' No wonder that the gods are wroth at such speeches as we have heard.' Then Snorri the priest spoke and said, ' At what, then, were the gods wroth, when this lava was molten, and ran over the spot on which we now stand?'"— Dasent's "Burnt Njal," vol. i. p. xci. *n.*

with both hands. In private life, they tell us, he was gay, social, and generous ; and though, when enraged, he was distinguished for cruelty, burning some of his enemies, tearing others to pieces by mad dogs, and mutilating or casting down others from high precipices, yet he was as dear to his subjects as Ivan the Terrible to the Russian people of Moscow ; nay, many of them are said to have died of grief for him, and after his death exalted him to the dignity of a saint.

During the fifteen years which succeeded the death of Olaf Christianity made but slow progress in Norway, though its followers were not persecuted by the sons of Earl Hacon, whom the conquerors at the great battle of·Svöldr had set over the country. At length, about the year A.D. 1015, a descendant of Harold Haarfager, Olaf Haraldson, better known as Olaf the Saint, gathered a party, put an end to the domination of the Swedes and Danes in Norway, and became Overking. His youth had been spent in piratical expeditions, and he had shared in the invasions of England. Seated on the throne, he invited a considerable number of clergy from that country,[1] at

---

1 " The English missionaries with Scandinavian names," who went over to Scandinavia in the tenth century, for the purpose of converting the heathens, were, as their names show, of Danish origin, and undoubtedly natives of the Danish part of England. Sprung from Scandinavian families, which, though settled in a foreign land, could scarcely have so soon forgotten their mother-tongue, or the customs which they had inherited, they could enter with greater safety than other priests on their dangerous proselytizing travels in the heathen North ; where, also, from their familiarity with the Scandinavian language, they were manifestly best suited successfully to prepare the entrance of Christianity."—Worsae's "Danes and Northmen," p. 135.

whose head was Bishop Grimkil, who composed a
system of ecclesiastical law for the Norsemen. Olaf
also wrote to the Archbishop of Bremen, and requested his aid in evangelizing his people. His own
measures savoured too much of the example set by
Olaf Tryggveson. Accompanied by Bishop Grimkil,
" the horned man," as the people called him from the
shape of his mitre, he made frequent journeys through
his kingdom, summoned the Things, and read the
laws which commanded the observance of Christianity;
all who refused to obey them he threatened with con-
fiscation of property, maiming of the body, or death.

At length, having discovered that the old heathen
sacrifices were still secretly offered in divers places,
he determined to ascertain the truth of these reports.
Summoning his bailiff in the Drontheim district,
he desired to know whether the proscribed rites
were still celebrated there. Under a promise of
personal security, the man confessed that the old
autumn, winter, and summer sacrifices were still
secretly offered, and presided over by twelve of the
principal bonders. Thereupon Olaf equipped a fleet
of five vessels and three hundred men, and sailed for
Mære Fiord, where, in the middle of the night, he
surprised the guilty parties, put their leader to death,
and divided their property amongst his men-at-arms.
Then, having taken many of the chief bonders as
hostages, he summoned a Thing, and obliged the
people to submit to the erection of several churches,
and the location amongst them of several clergy.[1]

[1] Snorro, ii. 152.

Proceeding afterwards to the Uplands, he summoned a Thing for the districts of Loar and Hedal,
and made his usual requisition. Not far from Loar
dwelt a powerful chief named Gudbrand, who, hearing of Olaf's arrival, sent a message-token calling
together the peasantry far and wide, to resist these
encroachments on the national faith. " This Olaf,"
said he in the Thing, "will force upon us another
faith, and will break in pieces all our gods. He says
he has a much greater and more powerful god ; and
it is wonderful that the earth does not burst asunder
beneath him, or that our god lets him go about
unpunished when he dares to talk such things. I
know this for certain, that if we carry Thor, who
has always stood by us, out of our temple that is
standing on this farm, Olaf's god will melt away,
and he and his men be made nothing, so soon as
Thor looks upon them."

The bonders shouted applause, and Gudbrand's
son was directed to repair northwards to Breeden,
and watch the movements of Olaf, who, with Bishop
Sigurd, was busy in fixing teachers in various places.
Hearing rumours of opposition, Olaf hurried to
Breeden, and in a battle which ensued utterly
routed the rude peasantry, and captured Gudbrand's son, whom he sent to his father with the
news of his own speedy approach. Gudbrand, in
his alarm, consulted the neighbouring chiefs, and it
was resolved to send an embassy to Olaf to propose
that a Thing should be summoned to decide whether
there was any truth in this "new teaching," and that

during it a strict truce should be maintained on both sides.

Olaf consented, and the bonders met to decide the question between the rival creeds. The king rose first, and informed the assembly how the people of the neighbouring districts had received Christianity, broken down their houses of sacrifice, and now believed in the true God, "who made heaven and earth, and knows all things." "And where is thy god?" asked Gudbrand. "Neither thou nor any one else can see him. We have a god who can be seen day by day. He is not here, indeed, to-day, because the weather is wet; but he will appear to thee, and I expect fear will mix with thy very blood when he comes into the Thing. But since, as thou sayest, thy god is so great, let him send us to-morrow a cloudy day, without rain, and then let us meet again."[1]

His counsel was adopted, and Olaf returned to his lodging accompanied by Gudbrand's son, whom he retained as a hostage. As the evening drew on, the king inquired of the youth what the god was like of which his father had spoken. Thereupon he learnt that the image was one of Thor, that he held a hammer in his hand, was of great size but hollow within, that he lacked neither gold nor silver about him, and every day received four cakes of bread, besides meat.

Thereupon, while the rest retired to bed, the king spent the night in prayer, and in the morning rose, heard mass, and after service proceeded to the

[1] Snorro, ii. 157.

Thing, the weather being such as Gudbrand had
desired. The first speaker was Bishop Sigurd, who,
arrayed in all his robes, with his mitre on his head
and his pastoral staff in his hand, spake to the
bonders about the true faith, and the wonderful
works of God.

To this one of the bonders replied, "Many things
are we told of by this horned man with the staff in
his hand crooked at the top like a ram's horn; but
since ye say, comrades, that your God is so powerful, and can do so many wonders, tell him to make it
clear sunshine to-morrow forenoon, and then we shall
meet here again, and do one of two things, either
agree with you about this business, or fight you."

Then they separated. One of the king's retinue
on this occasion was Kolbein the Strong, a chief
of high birth, who usually carried, besides his sword,
a great club. Olaf begged him to keep close to
him next morning, and meanwhile sent men to bore
holes in the bonders' ships, and loose their horses
on the farms. This done, he again spent the night
in prayer, and in the grey of the morning, as soon
as he had heard mass, proceeded to the Thing-field,
he and his party ranging themselves on one side,
Gudbrand and his faction on the other.

Before long a great crowd appeared carrying "a
great man's image" glittering all over with gold and
silver. The bonders rose, says the Saga, and did
obeisance to the "ugly idol," while Gudbrand cried
aloud to the king, "Where is now thy God? I think
neither thou nor that horned man yonder will lift your

heads so high as in former days. See how our idol looks upon you." Olaf, thereupon, whispered to Kolbein, " If, while I am speaking, the bonders look elsewhere than towards their idol, see that thou strike him as hard as thou canst with thy club." Then turning to the bonders, he said, " Dale Gudbrand would frighten us with his god that can neither hear, nor see, nor save himself, nor even move without being carried. Ye say our God is invisible; but turn your eyes to the east, and see him advancing in great splendour."

At that moment the sun rose, and all turned to look. Kolbein was duly on the alert, and immediately struck the image with all his might, so that it burst asunder and disclosed a number of mice and other vermin which had hitherto fattened on the sacrifices offered to the idol. The bonders, terrified at this unexpected result, fled in alarm to their ships, which soon filled with water, while others ran for their horses, and could not find them.

Retreat being thus cut off, they returned once more to the Thing-field. " I cannot understand," said Olaf when they were seated, "what this noise and uproar means. There is the idol, which ye adorned with gold and silver, and supplied with meat and provisions. Ye see for yourselves what he can do for you, and for all who trust to such folly. Take now your gold and ornaments that are lying strewn about on the grass, and give them to your wives and daughters; but never hang them hereafter upon stock or stone. Here are now two conditions between us to choose upon,—either accept

Christianity, or fight this very day; and the victory
be to them to whom the God we worship gives it."

Even Gudbrand could do nothing. "Our god,"
he said to the king, "will not help us, so we will
believe in the God thou believest in;" and he and
all present were baptized, and received the teachers
whom Olaf and Bishop Sigurd set over them, and
Gudbrand himself built a church in the valley.[1]

This story, told with all the quaintness of the
Saga, illustrates sufficiently the contest which was
now going on throughout the length and breadth of
the land between Christianity and expiring Odinism.
Wherever Olaf went, accompanied by his bishops, the
same scenes were constantly enacted. He even extended his care to Greenland and the Orkneys, and sent
to Iceland a quantity of timber for building a church,
and a bell to be suspended in it, and endeavoured at
the same time to introduce Grimkil's ecclesiastical
laws. The example which he himself set to his subjects
was more satisfactory than that of either of his predecessors. He was exemplary in observing the ordinances of religion. It was his custom, the Saga tells
us, to rise betimes in the morning, put on his clothes,
wash his hands, and then go to church and hear
matins. Thereafter he went to the Thing-meeting to
arrange quarrels or amend the laws, and settled all
matters of religion in concert with Bishop Grimkil
and other learned priests.

The impartial severity with which he administered
the laws, punishing equally both great and small, was

[1] Snorro, ii. 161.

one of the chief causes of the rebellion against his
rule which broke out about the year A.D. 1026, and
was greatly fomented by Canute, king of Denmark,
who sowed disaffection amongst the chiefs. At last
Olaf determined to leave his kingdom, and fled to
Russia, where he was honourably received by Yaros-
loff, and requested to settle in the country.

But, while doubting between accepting the offer of
a province and undertaking a pilgrimage to Jerusalem,
Olaf Tryggveson is said to have appeared to him in
vision, and bade him return to Norway and reclaim
his kingdom. Olaf therefore set out, and sailed to
Sweden, where the king, Onund, his brother-in-
law, welcomed him, and aided him in his plans for
recovering Norway.

He no sooner appeared in the latter country than
multitudes flocked to his standard, but he rejected all
who did not comply with the one condition of service,
—the reception of baptism. The helmets and shields
of all who fought on his side were distinguished by a
white cross, and on the eve of battle Olaf directed
many marks of silver to be given for the souls of his
enemies who should fall in the battle, esteeming the
salvation of his own men already secured. He also
directed that the war-shout should be, "Forward,
Christ's-men! cross-men! king's-men." The battle
was hot and bloody, and Olaf was defeated and
slain.

After his death his people repented of their rebellion. They found that, if Olaf had *chastised them
with whips*, the new ruler, Swend, son of Canute,

chastised them with scorpions; [1] and they groaned
under the taxes now imposed upon them. Meanwhile it began to be whispered that Olaf was a holy
man, and had worked miracles; and many began
to put up prayers to him as a powerful saint, and to
invoke his aid in dangers and difficulties.

News of this reached the ears of Bishop Grimkil,
who, during Olaf's absence in Russia, had remained
in Norway. He came to Nidaros, and obtained leave
from Swend to exhume the body of the departed
king.

On opening the coffin, the Saga tells us, "there was
a delightful and fresh smell, the king's face had undergone no change, but his hair and nails had grown as
though he had been alive." Alfifa, Swend's mother,
remarked sneeringly that "people buried in sand rot
very slowly, and it would not have been so if he had
been buried in earth." Grimkil bade her notice his
hair and beard. " I will believe in the sanctity of his
hair," replied Alfifa, "if it will not burn in the fire."
Thereupon the bishop put live coals in a pan, blessed
it, cast incense on it, and then laid thereon King
Olaf's hair. The incense caught fire, but the hair
remained unsinged.

Alfifa proposed it should be laid on unconsecrated
fire. But her unbelief shocked the bystanders ;
bishop, and king, and assembled people, all agreed
that Olaf should be regarded as a man "truly holy."
His body was, therefore, removed to St. Clement's
church, which he himself had built at Nidaros, and

---

[1] 1 Kings xii. 11.

enclosed in a shrine mounted with gold and silver, and studded with jewels.[1] And so Olaf became patron saint of Norway, pilgrims flocked to his tomb, and churches were dedicated to his name not only in his native land, but in England and Ireland, and even in distant Constantinople.

The story of Olaf the Saint may be taken as a sign of the change which was now coming over the Norseman. He was beginning to lay aside his old habits of lawless piracy, and to respect civilized institutions; the Viking was gradually settling down into the peaceful citizen. Expeditions to Christian lands, intermixture with the populations, admission to ecclesiastical offices, had gradually brought about very different feelings towards Christian institutions than those entertained by the Vikings of the eighth and ninth centuries.

We are not surprised, then, that when Canute had seated himself on the throne of England, and had espoused an English consort, he not only promulgated severe laws against heathenism,[2] and undertook a pilgrimage to Rome, but despatched missionaries to evangelize his Scandinavian subjects, and strengthen the cause of Christianity throughout the North. His influence in Denmark, combined with

---

[1] Snorro, ii. 350; Adam Brem. ii. 59. "St. Olave's church and Tooley Street in London are very remarkable memorials of the conversion of the Scandinavians on English soil."—Pauli's "England," p. 412.

[2] Amongst the objects of worship forbidden are, the sun and moon, fire and flood, fountains and stones, trees and logs; also witchcraft, framing death-spells, either by lot or by torch, or phantoms.

that of Olaf the Lap-king in Sweden, had an important influence on the progress of the Scandinavian churches. Schools and monasteries now gradually rose, bishoprics were founded, the rude Runic characters retired before the Latin alphabet, agriculture was encouraged by the Benedictine monks, and new kinds of corn were planted, mills were built, mines were opened, and before these civilizing agencies Odinism retired more and more from a useless contest, as surely as Brahmanism in India is yielding before European science and European literature, before the telegraph and the railway, the book and the newspaper.

CHAPTER XII.

ST. CYRIL AND METHODIUS.

AND now let us turn from the blue fiords and pine forests of Scandinavia to the great Sclavonian family of nations, whose wide territory extended eastward from the Elbe to the sluggish waters of the Don, and from the Baltic on the north to the Adriatic on the south.

While for upwards of three centuries the Teutonic tribes had been yielding to the influences of Christianity, scarcely any impression had been made on the vast population which clustered together on either side of the Danube, and thence spread onwards into the very heart of the modern Russian empire. They were still rude, warlike, and chiefly pastoral tribes, inaccessible alike to the civilization and the religion of Rome. The Eastern Empire had neither a Charlemagne to compel by force of arms, nor zealous missionaries like those of Germany to penetrate the vast plains and spreading morasses of the provinces on either side of the Danube, to found abbacies and bishoprics, to cultivate the soil and reclaim the people.[1]

[1] Milman's "Latin Christianity," vol. ii. p. 419.

1. With the death, however, of the great apostle of Denmark synchronizes one of the earliest missionary efforts made amongst any portion of this great family. A map of Europe in the sixth century discloses to us the Bulgarians established along the western shore of the Euxine, between the Danube and the Dnieper. About the year A.D. 680 they had moved in a southerly direction into the territory known in ancient times as Macedonia and Epirus. Here they bestowed their names on the Sclavonians, whom they conquered, gradually adopted their language and manners, and by intermarriage became entirely identified with them.

Unable to return either in a northerly or westerly direction, in consequence of the formidable barrier which the irruption of more powerful nations had interposed in their rear, they extended their conquests to the south of the Danube, and became involved in continual struggles with the Greek emperors. In the year A.D. 811 the Emperor Nicephorus advanced into the centre of their kingdom, and burnt their sovereign's palace. The insult was terribly avenged. Three days after his disastrous success, he was himself surrounded by the collected hordes of his barbarous foes, and fell ignominiously with the great officers of the empire. His head was exposed on a spear, and the savage warriors, true to the traditions of their Scythian wilderness, fashioned his skull into a drinking-cup, enchased it with gold, and used it at the celebrations of their victories.

But these border-wars were destined to produce

more beneficent results. In the early part of the ninth century, when Theodora was Empress of Byzantium, a monk named Cupharas fell into the hands of the Bulgarian prince Bogoris.[1] At the same time, a sister of the prince was in captivity at Constantinople, and it was proposed by the empress that the two captives should be exchanged. During the period of her captivity the princess had adopted the Christian faith, and on her return she laboured diligently to deepen in her brother's mind the impression which had already been made by the captive monk.

The prince long remained unmoved by her entreaties. At length a famine, during which he had vainly appealed to his native deities, induced him to have recourse to the God of his sister. The result was such as he desired, and he was baptized by Photius the patriarch of Constantinople, the emperor himself standing sponsor by proxy, and the Bulgarian prince adopting his name. A short time afterwards the prince requested the emperor to send him a painter for the decoration of his palace. A monk, named Methodius, was accordingly sent, and was desired by Bogoris to adorn his hall with paintings representing the perils of hunting. As he appeared anxious for terrible subjects, the monk employed himself in painting the scene of the "Last Judgment;" and so awful was the representation of the fate of obstinate heathens, that not only was Bogoris himself induced to put away the idols he had till

[1] Cedreni "Annales," p. 443.

now retained, but even many of the court were so
moved by the sight as to desire admission into the
Christian Church.

So averse, however, was the great bulk of the nation
to the conversion of their chief, that his baptism,
which was celebrated at midnight, was kept a profound secret, the disclosure of which was the signal
for a formidable rebellion in favour of the national
gods, and Bogoris could only put it down by resorting
to the severest measures. Photius had given to the
prince at his baptism a long letter, or rather a treatise
on Christian doctrine and practice, as also on the
duties of a sovereign. But its language was far too
refined for his comprehension ; and his difficulties
were further increased by the arrival of missionaries,
Greek, Roman, and Armenian, who all sought his
union with their respective Churches, and all pro-
pounded different doctrines. Thus perplexed by
their rival claims, and unwilling to involve himself
in more intimate relations with the Byzantine court,
Bogoris turned to the west for aid, and made an
application to Louis II. of Germany, and, at the
same time, to Nicholas the Pope, requesting from
both assistance in the conversion of his subjects, and
from the latter more intelligible advice than he had
received from the Patriarch of Constantinople.

The Pope replied by sending into Bulgaria Paul,
bishop of Populonia, and Formosus, bishop of Portus,
with Bibles and other books. At the same time he
also sent a long letter treating of the various subjects
on which Bogoris had requested advice, under one

hundred and six heads. Respecting the conversion
of his subjects, he advised the Bulgarian chief to
abjure all violent methods, and to appeal to the
weapons of reason only. Apostates, however, ought
to meet with no toleration, if they persisted in
refusing obedience to the monitions of their spiritual
fathers. As to objects of idolatrous worship, they
ought not to be treated with violence, but the company of idolaters ought to be avoided, while the
cross, he suggested, might well take the place of
the horse-tail as the national standard. All recourse
to divination, charms, and other superstitious practices, ought to be carefully abolished, as also poly-
gamy. As to prayer for their forefathers, who had
died in unbelief, in respect to which the simple prince
had requested advice, such a vain mark of filial
affection could not be allowed for a moment.

With these precepts bearing on their spiritual
welfare were mingled others designed to soften and
civilize their savage manners. The Pope exhorted
them to greater gentleness in the treatment of their
slaves, and protested against their barbarous code of
laws, their use of the rack in the case of suspected
criminals, and their too frequent employment of
capital punishment. Finally, as to the request of
the prince that a patriarch might be sent him, the
Pope could not take such an important step till he
had more accurate information as to the numbers
of the Bulgarian Church : meanwhile he sent a
bishop, who should be followed by others if it was
found necessary ; and as soon as the Church was

organized, one with the title of archbishop or patriarch was promised.

2. The reception of Christianity in Bulgaria paved the way for its admission in other quarters. The Chazars of the Crimea, the Sclaves in the interior of Greece, the Servians, who extended from the Danube to the Adriatic, and other tribes, were more or less affected by Christian influences, though in several cases they were weakened by the equally zealous efforts of Jewish and Mussulman propagandists.

But a more important portion of the South-Sclavonic area was now to be added to the Church. In the early part of the ninth century the kingdom of Moravia comprised a considerable territory, extending from the frontiers of Bavaria to the river Drina, and from the banks of the Danube to the river Styri in Southern Poland. Falling within the everwidening circle of the empire of Charlemagne, it had acknowledged that monarch, and afterwards his son Louis, as its suzerains. According to the settled policy of these princes, the conquered territory had received a compulsory form of Christianity, and a regionary bishop had endeavoured, under the auspices of the Archbishop of Passau, to bring about the conversion of the people. But these efforts had been productive of very partial results. Foreign priests, unacquainted with the Sclavonic language, were not likely to attract many to their Latin services, or to prevent the great bulk of the people relapsing into heathenism.

But in the year A.D. 863 Moravia made great efforts

to recover its independence, and Rostislav, its ruler, requested the Greek emperor Michael to send him learned men, who might translate the Scriptures into the Sclavonic tongue, and arrange the public worship upon a definite basis. "Our land is baptized," ran the message, "but we have no teachers to instruct us, or translate for us the sacred books. We do not understand the meaning of the Scriptures. Send us teachers who may explain them to us and tell us their meaning."

When the emperor Michael heard this, he called together his philosophers, and told them the message of the Sclavonic prince. The philosophers replied, "There is at Thessalonica a man named Leon. He has two sons, who both know well the Sclavonic tongue, and are both clever philosophers." On hearing this, the emperor sent to Leon at Thessalonica, saying, "Send to us thy sons Methodius and Constantine." Whereupon Leon straightway sent them; and when they came to the emperor, he said to them, "The Sclavonic lands have sent to me, requesting teachers, that they may translate for them the Holy Scriptures."[1]

Persuaded by the emperor, they therefore went into Moravia, and having arrived began to compose a Sclavonic alphabet, making use in the composition of it of Greek letters, with the addition of certain other characters, partly Armenian and Hebrew, and partly of their own invention; the whole number amounting to forty. They then translated the

[1] "Vita S. Constantini" (Cyrilli), "Acta SS. Bolland." March 2.

Gospels and Acts of the Apostles, the Psalter, and
other books, and this innovation on the methods
hitherto employed by western missionaries was
blessed with signal success. Many of the people
rejoiced to hear the word of God in their own
language, and several churches were erected.

For four years and a half their work went on in
peace; but soon they found no little opposition from
the neighbouring German clergy, who regarded their
translation of the Scriptures into the Sclavonic tongue
as little short of heresy. Intelligence of this strange
innovation even reached the ears of the Pope, who
summoned Cyril and Methodius to Rome. Admitted
to an audience with Adrian, they recounted the
method of their proceedings, and offered their creed
for examination. Adrian pronounced himself satisfied,
and appointed Methodius metropolitan of Moravia,
and Pannonia, but without any fixed see.

Thus armed with Papal authority, Methodius returned to the scene of his labours, and achieved still
greater success. But before long political troubles
arose ; Rostislav was betrayed into the hands of
Louis of Germany, dethroned, and blinded. Thus
deprived of the protection of his patron, Methodius
was constrained to retire from his dangerous post
into Pannonia. But even here he found himself
exposed to constant suspicions, owing to his Sclavonic
liturgy and Bible, and deemed it necessary to repair
a second time to Rome and defend his conduct before
Pope John VIII.

From this Pontiff, after much discussion, he succeeded in obtaining a qualified approval of his work. The Pope's scruples, we are told, were removed by remembering the verse in the Psalms, " *Praise the Lord, all ye nations.*" This verse appeared to him decisive. It could hardly mean that the Creator's praise was to be restricted to three languages, Hebrew, Greek, and Latin. He who formed these languages must have formed others for His own glory. One condition, however, was annexed to the concession. The mass must be celebrated in one at least of the languages of the Church, either Greek or Latin, and the Gospel must be read in Latin, and then if it was thought necessary translated into the Sclavonian tongue.

Once more, therefore, Methodius returned to Moravia, and in spite of much opposition adhered firmly to the great principle that the language of each separate nation is not to give place in public worship to a sacred language peculiar to the clergy, but is itself adapted alike for public instruction and for private reading. But after his death, about A.D. 885, the opposition of the German party increased greatly, and many of the Sclavonic clergy were driven out of Moravia.

Before long Moravia was invaded by the pagan Magyars or Hungarians, whose ravages at this period in Bavaria, Germany, and Southern France, presented one of the most serious obstacles to the establishment of Christianity. More terrible than the Saracen and the Northern viking, inexhaustible in number, superior to all the Scythian hordes in military prowess, they were identified by fear-stricken Christendom with Gog and Magog, the forerunners of the dissolution of the world. From their devastations the wretched people of Moravia suffered terribly, and on the restoration of order found themselves united to the kingdom of Bohemia.

3. From Moravia, therefore, let us turn in an easterly direction towards those Scythian wilds and level steppes, where, in A.D. 862, arose the Russian kingdom of Ruric the Norman ; and where, while the Western Church was contemplating with awe and terror the gradual approach of the Day of Doom, the Eastern Church " silently and almost unconsciously bore into the world her mightiest offspring."[1]

In A.D. 955 the Princess Olga, accompanied by a numerous retinue, left Kieff on a journey to the Byzantine capital. There she was induced to embrace Christianity, and returning to her native land exerted herself with exemplary diligence to instil the doctrines of her new creed into the mind of her son Swiatoslav. But on this prince her exhortations produced little or no effect. He was the very type of the rough Varangian warrior. " Wrapped in a bearskin," writes Gibbon, " he usually slept on the ground, his head reclining on a saddle. His diet was coarse and frugal, and, like the heroes of Homer, his meat (it was often horseflesh) was boiled or roasted on the coals."[2] For him the gods of his ancestors were sufficient, and the entreaties of his mother were entirely thrown away.

---

[1] Stanley's "Eastern Church," p. 294.
[2] Gibbon's "Decline and Fall," vol. vii. p. 92.

Her grandson Vladimir seemed likely to prove a more docile pupil, though the zeal he subsequently displayed for the savage idolatries of his countrymen was not for some time calculated to inspire much confidence. In his reign the only two Christian martyrs of the Russian chroniclers were put to death by the fury of the people, because one of them, from natural affection, had refused to give up his son, when he had been devoted by Vladimir to be offered as a sacrifice to Peroun.[1]

But before long the desire of converting so powerful a chief attracted missionaries from many quarters.

First, according to the Russian chronicler, came the Mahometan Bulgarians from the Volga, but " the mercy of Providence inspired Vladimir to give them a decided refusal."

Then appeared Jews from amongst the Chazars, priding themselves on their religion, and telling many stories of the ancient glories of Jerusalem. " But where is your country ? " said the prince. " It is ruined by the wrath of God for the sins of our fathers," was the reply. Thereupon the interview was cut short by the decisive answer, " How can I embrace the faith of a people whom their God has utterly abandoned ? "

Next appeared Western doctors from Germany, who would have had the prince embrace the creed of Western Christendom. But Vladimir knew of no form of Christianity save such as was taught at Byzantium.

[1] Mouravieff's "Church of Russia," translated by Blackmore, p. 10.

Last of all came a teacher from Greece. He reasoned with Vladimir long and earnestly, and learning that he had received emissaries from the Jews, who accused the Christians of worshipping a God who had been crucified, he took the opportunity of relating the true account from beginning to end. Then he went on to speak of judgment to come, and showed the prince on a tablet the scene of the Last Day. On the right were the good going into everlasting joy; on the left were the wicked departing into eternal fire. "Happy are those on the right," said Vladimir; "woe to the sinners who are on the left." "If thou wishest to enter into happiness with those on the right," replied the missionary, "consent to be baptized."[1]

The prince reflected in silence, but deferred his decision. Next year, however, he sent for certain of his nobles, and informed them of the different deputations he had received. "Every man praises his own religion," said they; "send, therefore, certain of thy court to visit the different churches, and bring back word."

Messengers were accordingly despatched to the Jews and Mahometans, as also to the German and Eastern churches. They returned a very unfavourable report of all, except only the Church of Constantinople. Of this they could not say enough. When they visited the Byzantine capital, they were conducted to the Church of St. Sophia, then perhaps one of the finest ecclesiastical structures in the world. The patriarch himself celebrated the Liturgy with

Mouravieff, p. 11.

the utmost pomp and magnificence. The gorgeous processions, the music, the chanting, the appearance of the deacons and sub-deacons with lighted torches and white linen wings on their shoulders, before whom the people prostrated themselves, crying, "Kyrie eleison,"—all this, so utterly different from anything they had ever witnessed amidst their own wild steppes, had such an overpowering effect on the Russian envoys, that on their return to Vladimir they spoke not a word in favour of the other religions, but of the Greek Church they could not say enough.

"When we stood in the temple," said they, "we did not know where we were, for there is nothing else like it upon earth. There in truth God has his dwelling with men, and we can never forget the beauty we saw there. No one who has once tasted sweets will afterwards take that which is bitter, nor can we any longer abide in heathenism." Thereupon the Boyars said to Vladimir, "If the religion of the Greeks had not been good, your grandmother Olga, who was the wisest of women, would not have embraced it." The weight of the name of Olga decided her grandson, and he said no more in answer than these words, " Where shall we be baptized ? "[1]

Still he hesitated before taking so important a step, and "led by a sense which had not yet been purged by grace," to adopt the words of the Russian chronicler, he thought fit to overawe the country where he intended to receive the new faith, and laid siege to Cherson in the Tauride. The siege was long

[1] Mouravieff, pp. 12 and 353.

and obstinate. At length, by means of an arrow
shot from the town, a priest informed the Russian
chief that its safety depended on cutting off the
supply of water from the aqueducts. Elated at the
prospect of success, Vladimir vowed to be baptized
as soon as he should be master of the place. His
wish was gratified, and forthwith he sent ambassadors
to Constantinople to demand the hand of Anne, sister
of the Emperor Basil.

Compliance was promised on condition of his accepting Christianity. Vladimir declared his consent,
and the sister of the emperor was constrained to go,
and she sailed from Cherson accompanied by a large
body of clergy. Her arrival hastened the baptism of
the prince, which, according to the Russian authority,
was not unaccompanied by miracle. Vladimir was
suffering from complaint of the eyes when his new
consort reached him, but no sooner had he risen from
the font cleansed of the leprosy of his heathenism,
than the bishop of Cherson laid his hands upon his
eyes, and his sight was restored, while the prince
exclaimed, " Now have I seen the true God."

Thereupon many of his suite consented to follow his
example; and shortly afterwards, accompanied by the
Greek clergy, he returned to Kieff, one of the great
centres of the Sclavonic religion, and forthwith ordered
that his twelve sons should be baptized, and proceeded
to destroy all the monuments of heathenism. The
huge idol Peroun was dragged from its temple at a
horse's tail, scourged by twelve mounted pursuers,
and then flung into the Dnieper. " The people," we

are told, " at first followed their idol down the stream, but were soon quieted when they saw it had no power to help itself."

Thus successful, Vladimir felt encouraged to take a further step, and gave orders for the immediate baptism of his people. "Whoever on the morrow," ran the proclamation, " shall not repair to the river, whether rich or poor, I shall hold him for my enemy." On the word all the inhabitants, with their wives and children, flocked in crowds to the Dnieper, and there, in the words of Nestor, " some stood in the water up to their necks, others up to their breasts, holding their young children in their arms, while the priests read the prayers from the shores, naming at once whole companies by the same name." Vladimir, transported at the sight, cried out, " O great God, who hast made heaven and earth, look down upon thy new people ; grant unto them, O Lord, to know thee the true God, as thou hast been made known to Christian lands, and confirm in them a true and unfailing faith ; and assist me, O Lord, against my enemy that opposes me, that, trusting in thee and in thy power, I may overcome all his wiles."

The spot where the temple of Peroun had stood now became the site of the Church of St. Basil, and the Greek priests were encouraged by Vladimir in erecting others throughout the towns and villages of his realm. The close of the tenth century saw Michael the first metropolitan travelling from place to place, baptizing and instructing the people. Churches were built, the choral music and service books of Constantinople were introduced, as also the Greek canon law. Before long schools also arose, and the people became familiar with the Sclavonic Scriptures and Liturgy, which the labours of Cyril and Methodius in Bulgaria and Moravia had made ready to their hands.

CHAPTER XIII.

THOUGH by his reception of Christianity Vladimir dealt a heavy blow to the supremacy of Sclavonic superstitions in Russia, they long continued to maintain their ascendency in other parts of Europe, and nowhere more persistently than in Poland, Pomerania, and Prussia. In these countries the Sclavonic hierarchy, who were as numerous and almost as potent as in the religious institutions of India and Egypt, presented a formidable obstacle to the labours of the Christian missionary. Not only had they their representatives in every town and village, but the higher members of the order wielded a power always equal, and often superior to that of the dukes or princes of the several tribes.[1]

About A.D. 1121 the eastern and western districts of Pomerania became, after ceaseless contests, tributary to the Polish duke, Boleslav III., who thereupon became anxious to extend amongst his new subjects some notions of Christianity. But so fanatical were they known to be that the Polish

[1] Helmold, "Chron. Slav." ii. 12; Peter de Dusburg, "Chronicon Prussiæ," p. 79.

bishops each and all declined the dangerous task of attempting their evangelization.

In A.D. 1122, however, a Spanish priest named Bernard, who had been elevated to a bishopric at Rome, appeared at his court, and requested permission to preach the word in Pomerania. The duke did not conceal from his visitor the difficulties of the undertaking ; but Bernard, though unacquainted with the Pomeranian language, resolved to make the attempt. Accompanied by his chaplain, and an interpreter supplied him by Boleslav, he repaired to the town of Julin, barefooted and in the garb of a mendicant.

The Pomeranians—an easy, merry, well-conditioned race[1]—accustomed to the splendid appearance of their own priests, regarded the missionary with profound disdain. When he asserted that he had come as the messenger of God, they asked how "it was possible to believe that the great Lord of the world, glorious in power and rich in all resources, would send as his messenger a man in such a despicable garb, without even shoes on his feet. If he had really desired their conversion, he would surely have sent a more suitable envoy and representative. As for Bernard, if he had any regard for his own safety, he had better straightway return whence he came, and not discredit the name of his God by pretending to have a mission from him, when in reality he only wanted relief amidst his destitution."

---

[1] Herbordi, "Vita Ottonis," ii. p. 40 ; Pertz, "Mon. Germ." vol. xii.

Bernard replied by proposing, if they would not believe his words, that a ruinous house should be set on fire, and he himself flung into the midst. "If, while the house is consumed, I come forth unscathed," said he, "then believe that I am sent unto you by Him whom fire and every other created thing obeys." The Pomeranians, convinced that he was mad, urged him to leave the place ; but, instead of heeding the advice, Bernard struck down one of the sacred images, on which a riot ensued and he was hurried from the place with the advice, since he was so eager to preach, to exercise his talents in addressing the fish of the sea and the fowls of the air.[1]

Bernard, seeing there was no hope of success, retired to Bamberg, and there met with Bishop Otho, a Suabian of noble family, who had lived in Poland as the chaplain of the Duke Wratislav. In his visitor Bernard felt he had found one peculiarly suited to carry out an enterprise which had so signally failed in his own hands, and he assured the bishop that he could not fail of success if he would consent to make his appearance amongst the Pomeranians with becoming pomp and circumstance, and attended by a numerous retinue. To the solicitations of Bernard were soon added those of Boleslav, who engaged to defray all the expenses of the mission, to provide an escort, a body of interpreters, and whatever else might be necessary. Thus pressed on all sides, Otho at length determined to comply ; and having received from the Pope, Callixtus II., the appointment of Papal legate,

<hr>

[1] "Vita Ottonis," ii. 1.

and collected a numerous body of clergy, ecclesiastical furniture for such churches as he might build, together with costly robes and other presents for the Pomeranian chiefs, he set out on the 25th of April, A.D. 1124.

Passing through the friendly territory of the Duke of Bohemia, he arrived at Breslau on the 2d of May, and, after a stay of two days at Posen, proceeded to Gnesen, where Boleslav was awaiting his arrival with several of the neighbouring chiefs. Otho's entrance into the town was welcomed by a crowd of spectators, who flung themselves at his feet and besought his blessing. Seven days were spent here, during which the legate discussed with Boleslav their future mode of operations, and was furnished with waggons to carry provisions and baggage, money, interpreters, and a protecting escort under the command of a captain named Paulicius.

On the eighth day Otho and his retinue bade farewell to their entertainer, and plunged into the vast forest which then formed the boundary between the Polish and Pomeranian provinces. As yet it had only once been traversed by the soldiers of Boleslav, and the trees they had felled marked the only practicable path. Into this the missionary party struck, and with the utmost difficulty, and no little danger from wild beasts and quaking morasses,[1] succeeded in making their way to the river Netze, where a Pomeranian chief met them at the head of five hundred soldiers.

[1] " Vita Ottonis," ii. 10.

While Otho and the chief conferred together in private, the ecclesiastics in his train were thrown into no little alarm by the terrible looks of the Pomeranian warriors, who, drawing their long knives, threatened to flay them alive and bury them in the ground up to their necks. These threats, and the uncertainty as to the intentions of the Pomeranian chief, added to the rapidly deepening shades of evening, threw a gloom over the whole party, which, however, was dispersed in the morning, when it was discovered that the chief's intentions were peaceful, and that his rude warriors shared his feelings.

Pyritz was their next destination, and the way thither lay through a district which had suffered severely during the late wars, and thirty scattered peasants were the sole representatives of many ruined villages. They were asked whether they were willing to be baptized, and, scared by the martial retinue of the legate, they flung themselves at his feet, and professed their entire willingness to submit to his wishes. Without more ado they were baptized, and the missionaries resumed their journey towards Pyritz, which was reached late in the evening. A great religious festival was going on at the time, and the town was crowded with a vast number of strangers who had assembled to join in the revels. It was thought prudent, therefore, to remain outside the walls ; and the night was spent in the open fields, the trembling missionaries scarcely daring to sleep, much less to kindle a fire or address one another in tones louder than a whisper.

As soon as it was day, Paulicius entered the
town, and convened an assembly of the principal
inhabitants. Reminding them that their promise to
accept Christianity was one of the conditions of
peace between them and their liege lord Boleslav,
he announced that the legate, a man of noble birth,
and no mendicant like Bernard, but rich and powerful,
was nigh at hand, and he warned them not to incur
the displeasure of his master by declining to receive
him.

Overawed by this threatening address, and deeming themselves deserted by their national gods,
the people of Pyritz agreed to admit the legate
within the town. Accordingly a procession was
formed, and Otho made his entrance with every
sign of pomp which a long train of baggage-wag-
gons, and his retinue of ecclesiastics and soldiers,
could inspire. At first the people misinterpreted
the meaning of this display, and thought they had
been deceived. But Otho quickly reassured them,
and after fixing his tent in one of the squares,
ascended an eminence, attired in his full pontifical
robes, and thus opened his commission :—

"The blessing of the Lord be upon you, people
of Pyritz. We return you many thanks for having
refreshed our hearts by your hearty and loving
reception. Doubtless ye have already heard what
is the object of our coming, but it will not be
amiss to remind you again. For the sake of your
salvation, happiness, and joy, we have come a long
and weary way, and assuredly ye will be happy and

blessed, if ye be willing to listen to our words, and to acknowledge the Lord your Creator, and to serve and worship him only."

Having thus announced the object of his coming, he and his attendant ecclesiastics appointed a fast of three days, and bade the people prepare themselves for baptism. Meanwhile large vessels were sunk in the ground, filled with warm water, and surrounded with curtains. Hither great numbers of candidates were led, and were solemnly addressed by Otho on the vows they were about to make. The usual questions were duly asked and answered, and then the bishop and the rest of the clergy baptized the different groups as they were successively led up.[1]

From Pyritz, where they spent twenty days, they next repaired to Cammin, where the missionaries stayed for forty days, instructing and baptizing the people, and laying the foundations of the Church. The waggons which had hitherto conveyed the baggage were now exchanged for boats, in which to navigate the inland rivers and lakes which lay between Cammin and Julin in the island of Wollin, the spot selected for their next visit.

Julin was a place strongly fortified and devoted to the Sclavonic superstitions. As they neared the town, therefore, the boatmen advised that they should cast anchor at some little distance till the evening, and thus avoid the tumult likely to be excited by entering the place in the broad daylight. Not far from the spot where they anchored was a fort, which had been

[1] " Vita Ottonis," ii. 15.

erected according to a custom common to all the
Pomeranian towns, as a sanctuary and place of
refuge for such as might fly thither when pursued
by an enemy, or in any sudden emergency. The
boatmen advised the bishop to steal into the sacred
inclosure under cover of the night, and assured him
that there he would be quite secure. The suggestion
was acted on, and the night was spent in safety.

But the morning had no sooner dawned than an
immense multitude of the townspeople surrounded
the fort, and threatened the legate and his retinue
with death if he did not instantly quit the place. In
vain the commander of the escort begged them to
respect the sanctity of the asylum; the excited
throng would pay no heed to his words, and with
the utmost difficulty the missionaries effected their
escape, and got safely to their boats, having broken
down the bridge in their rear.

It was now resolved to anchor for a week on the
other side of a neighbouring lake, and to wait any
change that might take place in the popular feeling,
and in the meantime communications were kept up
between the town and the military escort, who proclaimed the rank and style of the legate, and threatened the speedy vengeance of the duke for the insult
they had received. This alarmed the people. The
leading chiefs called together an assembly, and
after much discussion respecting the admission of the
legate, it was agreed to abide by the decision of the
people of Stettin, the oldest and wealthiest of the
Pomeranian towns. If Stettin was willing to receive

him, they would be also. A pilot was therefore procured, who escorted the boats of the missionaries till the Pomeranian capital was in sight, and then left them for fear of detection.

Night was setting in when they reached Stettin, and again Otho and his retinue sought security by taking refuge in a fort which had been erected by the duke. In the morning their landing was discovered, and they explained to the townspeople the purport of their visit, and the desire of the duke that they should embrace Christianity. But their overtures were rejected with scorn. "What have we to do with you?" was the universal cry. "We will not put away our national customs, and are well content with our present religion. Are there not thieves and robbers among you Christians, whom we have seen deprived of their feet and eyes? Keep your own faith for yourselves, and intermeddle not with us."[1]

After two months had been spent in fruitless efforts to induce the people to reconsider their resolution, Otho determined to send messengers to Boleslav, informing him of the obstinacy of the Pomeranians, and asking his advice as to the course that ought to be pursued. His intentions transpired, and the townspeople, filled with alarm, determined to send a counter-embassy, promising conformity to the duke's wishes, if he would promise them a permanent peace, and agree to reduce the heavy tribute hitherto exacted from them.

While the messengers went on their respective

[1] "Vita Ottonis," ii. 25.

errands, Otho and his companions paid frequent
visits to the town, set up a cross in the market-
place, and, in spite of much opposition, persevered
in preaching to the people and exhorting them to
abandon their errors. At length two young men,
sons of one of the principal chiefs, paid him a visit,
and requested information concerning the doctrines
which he preached. To them accordingly the legate
expounded the teaching of the Church respecting
the immortality of the soul, the resurrection of the
body, and the life of the world to come.

The visit was often repeated, and before long the
young men declared their willingness to be baptized.
Unknown to their parents they approached the font,
and during the eight days following remained with
the missionaries, who welcomed with joy these fruits
of their toil. Meanwhile news of what had occurred
reached their mother, and she immediately set out
to visit the legate and receive back her sons.

Knowing her influence in the place, Otho received
her seated on a bank of turf in the open air, surrounded
by his clergy, with the young men, arrayed in their
white baptismal robes, seated at his feet. As she
approached, they on a signal from the bishop rose and
went forth to meet her, when, to the surprise of all
present, she prostrated herself on her knees upon
the ground, and in a flood of tears gave glory to
God that she had lived to see the day of her sons'
baptism. Then turning to Otho she informed him
that she had long been secretly a Christian, and
now she was willing openly to avow the Faith which

she had learnt while a captive in a distant land.
The impression made upon the townspeople was
profound. The baptism of the entire household
speedily followed, and the young men, returning
with costly presents from the legate, were successful in inducing many to listen favourably to his
exhortations.

While the excitement caused by this incident was
at its height, the messengers returned from Gnesen,
with a letter from Boleslav, in which he informed
the townspeople that he could not understand their
behaviour towards his friend the legate. Had it not
been for the intercession of the latter, he would have
inflicted on them the severest punishment; as it was,
he had determined to forgive them, and was willing
to remit a considerable portion of the tribute, and
to guarantee a permanent peace, on condition that
they submitted to the instructions of their spiritual
teachers.

This letter Otho did not fail to read to the
people, exhorting them to embrace the terms proposed by the duke, and, by way of proving their
sincerity, to suffer the temples of their gods to be
destroyed. If they felt any scruples about doing this
themselves, he, with his clergy, would commence the
work of destruction; and if they escaped unhurt, this
should prove the worthlessness of the national faith.
Permission was at length given; and after mass had
been duly celebrated, Otho set out at the head of his
clergy, armed with clubs and axes, to commence the
work of demolition, while crowds of the townspeople

stood anxiously on the watch to see what their own
gods would do. One temple fell, and then another, and
still the bishop with his retinue were unharmed.
Thereupon the multitude cried out, "What power can
these gods have, who do not defend their own abodes?
If they cannot defend themselves, how can they defend
or advantage us?" Hundreds of willing hands now
joined in the work of destruction, and in a very short
time four of the largest temples were razed to the
ground, and the materials converted into fuel.[1]

One of these structures, dedicated to the triple-
headed Triglav, and adorned with the rarest carvings,
was stored with a vast number of votive offerings of
considerable value, consisting of the spoils taken in
battles, gold and silver beakers, bulls' horns tipped
with gold, swords, knives, and sacred vessels. These
the people freely offered to Otho, but he caused them
to be sprinkled with holy water, and then gave them
up for general distribution. All he reserved for himself was the triple head of Triglav, which he sent to
Pope Honorius II., as a memorial of his victory over
Sclavonic idolatry.

Other monuments of superstition now excited his
attention, among which were a gigantic oak, and a
sacred spring close by, which were regarded with peculiar reverence. The tree Otho consented to spare,
in compliance with the solicitations of the people,
on condition that they would agree to resort to it
for the future merely to enjoy its shade, and not to
perform any heathen ceremonies.[2] The like indul-

[1] "Herbordi Vita," ii. 31.   [2] *Ibid.* iii. 22.

gence, however, he would not extend to a black horse of great size, which was used for taking the spear-omens on going out to war.

When the emblems of heathen worship had thus been put away, the bishop exhorted the people to regard all Christian men as brethren, whom it was sinful to sell into slavery, maltreat, or torture; he warned them against piracy, robbery, and infanticide; and after instructing them in the first principles of the Christian Faith, admitted numbers to the baptismal font. The only man of influence who held out against his exhortations was the high priest, whose duty it was to wait upon the sacred horse. Nothing would induce him to forsake his old faith, and we are assured that his obduracy was punished by a sudden and awful death; and before Otho left, he could point to a tangible memorial of his victory over the national heathenism, in a church which was erected in the market-place of the town.

Meanwhile what had taken place was not unknown at Julin. The townspeople had sent messengers and spies to the Sclavonic capital, who narrowly watched and reported the bishop's proceedings, and the conduct of the people of Stettin. Consequently, when Otho again presented himself at Julin, he found the populace ready and eager to receive baptism. The sacrament was celebrated as in other places, and with the consent of the chiefs it was agreed that a bishopric should be established here, to which Boleslav subsequently nominated one of his chaplains, Adelbert, who had accompanied Otho on his tour. Having

consecrated the chancels of two churches, he left
Julin, and visited Clotkowe, Colberg, and Belgrade,
where he was equally successful in inducing many to
abandon idolatry.   But the approach of winter warned
him to bring his labours to a close, and after revisiting
the places where he had achieved such rapid success,
and exhorting the infant churches to constancy
in the faith and in a holy life, left the country for
his own diocese, where he arrived in the February
of A.D. 1125.

Though anxious to resume his labours in the
Pomeranian mission-field, Otho found the cares of his
own diocese sufficient to claim all his attention.   But,
in the spring of A.D. 1127, he determined to set out
again, and once more collected, as preliminary to his
journey, a number of costly presents.   On this occasion he selected a different route.   Passing through
Saxony, he laded his vessels at Halle, and dropping
down the Elbe, reached the town of Demmin.   Here
he met his old friend Wratislav, and agreed with him
that a diet should be assembled at Usedom, at which
the acceptance of Christianity should be formally
proposed to the neighbouring chiefs.

Whitsunday was the day fixed for the diet, and
on the arrival of the chiefs Wratislav addressed them
in the presence of the bishop, and urged that they
should lay aside their idolatrous rites, and follow the
example of their countrymen at Stettin and Pyritz.
Otho then came forward, and, basing his discourse on
the theme suggested by the day, preached on the
first Pentecostal effusion of the Holy Spirit, on the

various gifts then imparted to the early Church, on the remission of sins, and the divine mercy.

His words were not lost upon his hearers. Many who had relapsed into idolatry confessed their sins, and were reconciled to the Church ; others received instruction, and were then baptized. The diet ended, Wratislav suggested to the bishop, now that the reception of Christianity had been formally attested by a solemn assembly, that he should send forth his clergy, two and two, to the different towns and villages, and prepare the people for his own coming.

Accordingly two of his clergy, Ulric and Albin, set out for the town of Wolgast, and were hospitably welcomed by the wife of the burgomaster. No sooner, however, had they explained to her the object of their coming, than in great alarm she informed them that the people were in no friendly mood, that their priests had denounced death as the penalty if any emissaries of the hateful bishop entered the place.

The reason of this unusual hostility soon transpired. One of the chief priests in the town, enraged at the decree passed at Usedom, determined to defeat it by stratagem.[1] Clad in his white sacerdotal robes, he concealed himself in the night-time in a neighbouring wood, and remained there till dawn. As the day broke, a peasant journeying towards the town heard a voice calling to him from the sombre forest. Looking up, he could just discern, in the dim light, a white figure partially concealed by the brushwood. "Stand," said the voice, "and hearken to what I say. I am thy

[1] " Herbordia Vita," iii. 3.

god ; I am he that clothes the fields with grass, and
arrays the forest with leaves; without me the fruit-tree
cannot yield its fruit, or the field its corn, or the cattle
their increase. These blessings I bestow on them that
worship me, and from them that despise me I take
them away. Tell the people of Wolgast, therefore, that
they think not of serving any other god but me, for
no other can profit them, and warn them that they
suffer not those preachers who are coming to their
town to live." With these words the figure vanished
into the depths of the woods.

Trembling with alarm, the peasant staggered into
the town, and announced to the people what had
occurred. The excitement was intense. Again and
again he was constrained to tell the tale to eager
listeners, amongst whom at length stole in the priest
himself. Pretending to disbelieve the account, he bade
the man repeat afresh every detail ; and when he saw
the people were sufficiently moved, "Is not this," he
burst forth, "what I have been telling you all the
year long? What have we to do with any other god?
Is not our own god justly angry with us ? How can
we, after all his benefits, ungratefully desert him for
another? If we would not have him in righteous
anger strike us dead, let us put to death these men
who would seduce us from our faith."

Such was the tale which had roused all Wolgast
against the missionaries. The woman, however,
though at great risk, concealed her visitors for two
days, till Otho made his appearance with a large
body of troops, and some of the chiefs from Usedom.

Overawed by their appearance, the people did not venture to oppose his entrance, and he was enabled to open his mission as in other towns. But some of his clergy, ridiculing the alarming news of the hostility of the inhabitants which had been spread by Ulric, strayed carelessly into the town to view the idol temples, and were followed by a mob threatening vengeance if they proceeded further. Some, therefore, made their way back to the bishop's quarters, but one, undeterred by danger, rushed into a temple dedicated to Gerovit, the god of war, and, arming himself with the sacred shield which hung there, and which no one might touch on penalty of death, came forth amongst the people, who gave way on every side at this daring instance of impiety. A commotion ensued, but the heathen party found it useless to struggle against the well-known determination of the dukes, and, before he left, Otho laid the foundation of another church, and administered baptism to considerable numbers.

From Wolgast the bishop proceeded to Gützkow. This was the site of one of the most splendid of the Sclavonic temples, which Otho determined to raze to the ground, fearing to suffer so prominent a memorial of their old superstitions to remain. The people at length consented, and the bishop rewarded their obedience by commencing the erection of a church of unusual size and splendour.

The foundations were laid, and at the consecration he preached so eloquently on the duty of consecrating the heart to God, and the utter use-

lessness of temples of wood and stone, if men did
not devote themselves to works of mercy, forgiveness, and love, and avoid all rapine, fraud, and slave-
dealing, that Mizlav, the governor of the district,
who had been already baptized at Usedom, agreed
to release all those he held imprisoned for debt.
In reply to the bishop's exhortation to remember
the words of the Lord's Prayer, *Forgive us our
debts, as we forgive our debtors,* he exclaimed,
"Here, then, in the name of the Lord Jesus,
I give these men their liberty, that, according to
thy words, my sins may be forgiven me, and that
dedication of the heart, of which thou hast spoken,
may be fulfilled in me."

Shortly after an accident revealed the existence
of a noble Danish youth in one of his subterranean
cells, who was detained there as a security for a
debt of five hundred pounds, which his father owed
the governor. Otho hardly ventured openly to require another and so great a sacrifice from his new
convert, but suggested to some of his clergy that
they should intimate to him how acceptable to
the Lord would be such a proof of obedience and
mercy. It was a hard struggle, but at last the
governor consented; the young man, laden with
fetters, was brought forth from his cell, and in the
presence of large numbers, who could not restrain
their tears when they beheld his forlorn condition,
was led to the altar of the newly-erected church,
where the governor solemnly pronounced his freedom,
and expressed his own hope that, as he had forgiven

his father that debt, so his sins might be forgiven
him at the last day. The example of a man of so
much influence was not lost upon the people, and
many, according to their measure, strove to prove the
sincerity of their faith by works of mercy and justice.
Otho's influence with the Pomeranians was thus
greatly increased, and he had his reward in the peace
and prosperity of his newly-founded churches.

One place alone withstood all his efforts. The
island of Rugen, situated about a day's voyage from
Usedom, was, as we have said, the Mona of the Baltic
Sclavonians; and hither all the lingering fanaticism of
the native religion fled as to its last refuge. The
bishop, indeed, would have gladly flung himself upon
the island and perished, if need be, in preaching to its
benighted inhabitants; but only one of his clergy
was found willing to share with him the dangerous
enterprise, and repeated storms prevented their landing. At last the Pomeranian chiefs absolutely forbade his exposing himself to certain death, and, much
against his will, he was forced to comply.

He now determined to divide his followers, and
to send them into different parts of the Pomeranian
territory, while he himself selected Stettin for another
visit. Here the heathen faction had again acquired
their old ascendancy, and the uncertainty of their
reception so discouraged his clergy that none would
volunteer to follow him. He determined, therefore,
to set out alone, and stole away, after engaging in
earnest prayer, without disclosing his intentions to
any one. In the morning he was found missing, and

then some of his clergy, ashamed of their own cowardice, and alarmed for his safety, hurried in quest
of him, and persuaded him to enter the place with
them. Their presence was greatly needed to revive
the spirits of the new converts.

Irritated at the success which had attended the
bishop's efforts, the pagan party, whose influence
was unbounded with the lower orders, had succeeded
in rousing a great commotion. A pestilence had
broken out, and was readily interpreted by the priests
as a sign of the anger of the national gods. An
assault was commenced against the churches which
Otho had erected, when one of the ringleaders in
the, movement was struck by a sudden fit, his hand
stiffened, and his club fell. On his recovery he persuaded his fellow-townsmen, after this proof of the
power of the Christians' God, to spare the church,
and to erect an altar to one of the national deities
by the side of the Christian altar, that so the joint
protection of both might be secured.[1]

Such was the state of affairs when the bishop and
his party entered the town. The incident just related
had somewhat calmed the popular excitement, and
now aid came in another shape. During his previous
visit Otho had baptized an influential chief, who had
subsequently been captured by the Danes, and thrown
into prison. One night, so his story ran, having
fallen asleep after earnest prayer for release, he
dreamt that Bishop Otho appeared to him, and promised him speedy liberation. On awaking he found

[1] " Herbordi Vita," iii. 15.

the door of his cell unclosed, and taking advantage of this unlooked-for opportunity he darted forth, escaped to the shore, and, finding a boat, succeeded in reaching Stettin. He could only ascribe his deliverance to miraculous interposition, and therefore hung up the boat at the gates of the town, recounting to the people his dream and his escape. His tale, coming so soon after the late mysterious failure in the attack upon the church, made a deep impression on the people of Stettin in favour of the bishop, who had now entered the town.

But the heathen party determined to make one last effort to rouse the popular feeling, and, surrounding the church whither the bishop and his clergy had repaired, threatened them with instant death. Had the bishop's courage now failed him, he would in all probability have fallen a victim to their fury. But he ordered the cross to be uplifted, and went forth at the head of his clergy, chanting psalms, to meet his enemies. Half in awe, and half in admiration, the mob desisted from their attack. At the suggestion of Witstack—the chief who had just escaped from captivity—the bishop on the next Sunday repaired to the market-place, and there preached to the people.

He had just concluded his sermon, when a heathen priest, blowing a trumpet, called on the people to make an end of the enemy of their gods. This was the most critical moment in Otho's life. The lances were already poised to pierce him through, when again the undaunted composure with which he confronted his adversaries struck them with mysterious awe, and induced them to stay their hands. Otho seized the favourable moment, and advancing with his clergy to the church threw down the altar which the heathen party had erected, and commenced the immediate repair of the edifice. An assembly was then summoned, and the acceptance or rejection of the Christian faith was formally proposed. After a long discussion it was resolved to offer no further opposition to the establishment of Christianity. The bishop, overjoyed at the favourable turn affairs had taken, received back all who had apostatized from the faith, and baptized all who were willing to receive that rite. His uniformly kind and conciliating disposition, joined to the readiness he displayed in redeeming numerous captives from the horrors of slavery, won for him the popular respect, which was not lessened when he once more interceded for the people with Boleslav, and succeeded in averting another threatened invasion.

News of what occurred at Stettin soon reached Julin, and, on his second visit, Otho found himself able to consolidate his previous success, and secure the adherence of the wavering. From Julin he set out on a final visit to the churches he had founded in Pomerania, and in the following year returned to Germany to attend the imperial diet, and thence repaired to his diocese at Bamberg. Though unable to revisit the scene of his missionary labours, he did not forget the churches he had founded. One of the last acts of his life evinced the interest he took in his

converts. Hearing that a number of Pomeranian
Christians had been taken captives by a horde of
heathen invaders, he bought up a quantity of valuable
cloth at Halle, and sent it into Pomerania, with orders
that part should be distributed among the chiefs to
conciliate their goodwill in behalf of the native Christians, and part sold and applied to the ransom of the
captives. Thus, as well as in other ways, he continued, so far as he was able, to superintend the
Pomeranian Church till the year A.D. 1139, when he
departed this life amidst the universal regret of all
ranks in his diocese.[1]

[1] " Herbordi Vita," iii. 35.

CHAPTER XIV.

ST. VICELIN, BISHOP OF OLDENBURG.

BESIDES the efforts in Pomerania which have formed
the subject of the last chapter, attempts were made to
win over to the Christian fold other tribes belonging
to the great Sclavonic family.

In the countries bordering on the Elbe, the Oder,
and the Saale dwelt the Wends. Hemmed in on the
one side by the rapidly-increasing German empire,
on the other by the Scandinavian Vikings, they long
resented all efforts to curb their independent spirit
and to plant the seeds of Christian civilization.

The clergy, moreover, who came amongst them,
having but the scantiest acquaintance with the Sclavonic language, were too often regarded as mere
political agents of the German emperors, and their
work was too often identified with a settled design of
perpetuating their national bondage. Under these
circumstances it is not surprising that such scanty
seeds of knowledge as were sown amongst them fell
on the stoniest ground, and having no depth of
earth in which to strike root speedily withered away.
Once and again, perhaps, a few monks or an in-

dividual bishop might acquire a knowledge of the Sclavonic tongue; but their efforts, though comparatively successful, were inappreciable amidst the general ignorance.

With the year A.D. 936, however, there dawned a somewhat brighter epoch. The emperor Otho I., anxious for the conversion of his Wendish subjects, founded bishoprics at Havelburg, Aldenburg, Brandenburg, and other places, and made them subordinate to the metropolitan see of Magdeburg.

For these posts the emperor used his utmost endeavours to select men who had been tried in other fields of missionary labour, and Boso, bishop of Merseburg, one of his chaplains, applied himself diligently to acquire the Sclavonic language, and was eventually able to preach in it with some success. He also translated some of the liturgical forms into the Sclavonian dialect, but failed to make even the Kyrie Eleison intelligible to the people, who, caught by a somewhat similar jingle of sounds, changed it into Ukrivolsa, or "the adder stands in the hedge."[1]

The partial success, however, of such prelates, was rendered abortive by the cruel oppressions to which the Wends were subjected, and the persistency of the German clergy in levying from them ecclesiastical dues.

Every fresh conquest, therefore, of the German empire, was succeeded by a fresh rebellion, and ceaseless efforts were made to throw off the yoke of the

[1] Thietmar, "Chron.;" Pertz, "Mon. Germ." vol. v. p. 755.

stranger. Thus, in A.D. 983, a Sclavonic chief named
Mistawoi embraced Christianity, and was attached
to the emperor's court. But so exasperated did he
become at the personal injuries inflicted upon him,
that he summoned his countrymen to Rethre, the
centre of the Sclavonic idolatry, and, unfurling the
banner of open rebellion, wasted Northern Germany
with fire and sword, razing to the ground every
church and monastery that came in his way.

Again his grandson Gottschalk, though he had
received a Christian training at Luneburg, stung to
the quick at the cold-blooded murder of his father,
the Wendish prince Udo, flew to arms, gathered
round him the Wendish youth, and spread havoc over
Hamburg and Holstein. One day, however, as he
surveyed a district, formerly covered with churches,
now lying waste and desolate, he is said to have
been filled with remorse, and to have vowed to
make atonement for the evil he had done, by propagating the faith he had been taught in his earlier
years.

Under his auspices arose, in A.D. 1047, a great
Wendish kingdom, into which he invited a large staff
of ecclesiastics from Bremen, and even expounded
the Scriptures himself to his subjects, or interpreted
to them in their own tongue the words of the foreign
clergy. At this period, the palace of Albrecht,
archbishop of Bremen, would appear to have been
a harbour of refuge for ecclesiastics of all grades,
whom the distractions of the times had driven from
their dioceses. Here they were sure of a welcome,

and, in return for the kindness and hospitality of the archbishop, were ready to go forth at his bidding into such parts of the mission-field as promised the slightest hope of success. The goodwill of Gottschalk naturally encouraged many to diffuse a knowledge of Christianity amongst his subjects; but though several churches and mission-stations were erected, the results of their exertions were only too speedily obliterated.

The heathen party, who would never forgive their king for favouring a hostile faith and allying himself with the German princes, at last rose in fury, stoned many of the clergy, murdered Ebbo, the priest of Lutzen, at the altar, and their king Gottschalk himself.

In this persecution perished one of the last representatives of the earlier Irish missionaries, in the person of John, bishop of Mecklenburg. Leaving Ireland, he had travelled into Saxony, and had been hospitably received by the archbishop of Bremen. This prelate induced him to take a share in the mission to the Wends, and recommended him to Gottschalk, by whom he was stationed at Mecklenburg.

His labours are said to have been unusually successful, but in the end he fell a martyr to his zeal. The Wends seized him, and after beating him cruelly with clubs, carried him about as a show through the chief towns, and at Rethre, when he refused to deny the faith, cut off his hands and feet, and then beheaded him. Not satisfied with this, they flung his body into the street, and fixing his head on a pole, carried it in triumph to the temple of Radegast, and there offered it as an atonement to the offended deity. This cruel murder was the signal for a general revolt, during which nearly every vestige of the mission was swept away; and during the subsequent rule of Cruko, a chief determinately hostile to Christianity, the old idolatries regained their former ascendancy.

After an interval, however, of somewhat more than fifty years, the Wendish Christian kingdom was re-established. But the period of its true independence was very limited. Year after year, in consequence of internal dissensions, it became an easier prey to the princes of Germany. At length Henry the Lion and Albert the Bear invaded the country, and while the latter founded the Margravate of Brandenburg, the former vanquished the Obotrites, and colonized the devastated districts with German settlers, who, assisted by foreign clergy, reorganized the Wendish sees.

Amidst, however, the ceaseless din of arms, we come across one true missionary, who strove to soften the hearts of the vanquished Wends, and to win them over by other arms than those of the military oppressors. This was St. Vicelin, afterwards bishop of Oldenburg.

Born at Quernheim, on the banks of the Weser, he was first educated at the flourishing school of Padeborn. Thence he was removed to take charge of an educational establishment at Bremen, and after succeeding there, studied for three years at the University of Paris. Having received holy orders, and heard of

the need of missionary efforts in the Wendish kingdom, he betook himself, in the year A.D. 1125, to the
archbishop of Bremen, who gave him a commission
to preach amongst the Wends.

His first efforts at Lubeck were cut short by
political disturbances and a heathen reaction. The
old idolatries still retained a great hold over the
people, and sacrifices not only of sheep and oxen, but
even of human beings, in honour of the native gods
Prone and Radegast, were renewed, while the Christians
were in many instances crucified and exposed to
revolting tortures. From Lubeck, therefore, Vicelin
removed to Faldera, or, as it was afterwards called,
Neumünster, as being a convenient outpost for evangelizing the districts north of the Elbe. The neighbouring country lay waste and desolate under the
repeated ravages of war, and the impoverished
inhabitants, despairing of aid and protection, had
relapsed in many instances into their old idolatries.

Vicelin, however, settled down amongst them, and
so won the hearts of many by his zeal, that a number
of laymen and ecclesiastics rallied round him, and
formed themselves into a fraternity, who vowed to
devote their lives to prayer, charity, and good works,
to visit the sick, relieve the poor, and especially labour
for the conversion of the Wends. For nine years this
pious band toiled on amidst every kind of obstacle;
and when the province of Holstein was visited, in
A.D. 1134, by the emperor Lothaire II., they could
point to many proofs that their exertions had been
largely blessed, and Lothaire was so gratified by the

success that had attended Vicelin's efforts, that he committed to him the superintendence of the churches of Lubeck and Segeberg, and encouraged him with much earnestness to persevere in his work.

But it was only by slow and painful stages that the Wendish mission could gain a secure footing. On the death of Lothaire, in A.D. 1137, the Wends again rose in rebellion against their German rulers, fell upon the churches and monasteries, and expelled every missionary from the country. Vicelin was constrained to fall back upon Faldera, and there *persecuted, but not forsaken, cast down, but not destroyed*,[1] he continued for several years to animate the faith of his flock. A brighter day dawned when Adolph, count of Holstein, succeeded in restoring the German supremacy. His church at Segeberg was now restored to him, but, in prospect of too probable interruptions, he removed the monastery he had established to Högelsdorf. There, aided by Dittmar, a canon of Bremen, he presided over the little society, and on the occurrence of a grievous famine was enabled, by his welcome charity, to supply the wants of many who crowded round the gates of the monastery.[2]

Meanwhile the wave of German conquest again swept over the districts whence it had been obliged to recede during the late rebellion, and the archbishop of Bremen found himself able to re-establish the ruined sees. Vicelin, therefore, was nominated, in A.D. 1148, to the see of Oldenburg, and continued for

---

[1] 2 Cor. iv. 9.
[2] "Chron. Sclav." cap. xxii.

some years to set an eminent example of devotion to the true object of missionary labour till his death, A.D. 1154. After this a still larger number of German colonists were introduced into the country, who displaced the original inhabitants, consolidated the influence of the German emperors, and established more and more at least a nominal form of Christianity.

About this time the important island of Rügen, which has been already mentioned as one of the chief fortresses and asylums of Sclavonic superstition, was brought within the widening circle of Christian civilization. Ever since the conversion of the Pomeranians by Bishop Otho, sanguinary feuds had arisen between the new converts and the pagan islanders. Resenting the apostasy of Stettin and Julin, the natives of this Mona of the northern seas had menaced them again and again with the direst vengeance, and in the terror of Otho's companions, when he proposed to visit the island, we saw a striking proof of the reputation in which they were held.

At length the Danes resolved to subjugate the island, and Waldemar I. king of Denmark, assisted by the chiefs of Pomerania and of the Obotrites, set out in the year A.D. 1168, and after frequent engagements succeeded in reducing the people to subjection. One spot, however, long resisted all their efforts to effect its reduction. This was Arcona, the capital, situated on the most northern point of Rügen, at a height of one hundred and seventy-three feet above the level of the sea, and commanding from its rugged chalk cliffs an extensive view many miles round.

Here was the stronghold of the Wends, consisting of a circular intrenchment from thirty to forty feet in height, within which was the temple of the gigantic four-headed idol Swantevit.[1]

Round this sole remaining stronghold of the national faith the islanders rallied in great numbers, and resisted with the utmost ferocity all the efforts of the Danes to capture it. At length, after a long siege, King Waldemar took the place, and the inhabitants, finding it impossible to withstand the Danish arms, agreed to surrender, and permit the introduction of Christianity according to the usage of the Danish Church.

The introduction of Christianity was entrusted to Bishop Absalom of Roeskilde, in Zealand. His first care was the destruction of the idol Swantevit, for until this had been effected it was certain that no progress could be made.

A vast crowd surrounded the inclosure within which the temple stood, expecting that a sudden and awful death would be the inevitable penalty of violating the sanctity of the ancient shrine. But Absalom and his retinue entered the temple and removed the purple curtains, mouldering with age,[2] which were suspended before the idol. Then they plied their axes against the feet of the enormous image. These appear to have been fastened firmly to the platform on which it stood, but after a few blows it fell with a crash to the ground; and at

---

[1] See above, pp. 25—27.
[2] "Saxo-Grammaticus," lib. xiv.

the same moment, according to the common mediæval belief, the demon which haunted the temple was suddenly seen to dart from the shrine in the form of a black animal and disappear.

But though the idol lay prostrate on the ground, the awe with which it had for ages been regarded was not entirely removed. No native of the island dared to touch it. Thereupon Bishop Absalom prevailed on certain captives and foreigners to make the dangerous experiment. Ropes were fastened to the image, and amidst some lamentations, but not a little mockery and laughter, it was dragged into the Danish camp, hewn in pieces, and converted into fuel for cooking the soldiers' provisions.

Other temples were then attacked, and other images destroyed. Amongst these was an enormous one of oak with seven heads, and of such size that the bishop, though he stood on its feet, could scarcely reach the chin of the image with his axe. It fell, however, like that of Swantevit, and with it the nests, which generations of swallows had built round its head and neck, so as wellnigh to hide the outline of the features of the deity. Besides this, another idol was destroyed with five heads, and a third with four, all which stood in shrines contiguous to that of Swantevit.

These objects of idolatrous superstition having been removed, Bishop Absalom employed himself zealously in laying the foundations of several churches, which were served by ecclesiastics whom he procured from Denmark, and supported at his own cost. The distribution of these clergy in various parts of the island, added to the exemption of the natives from ecclesiastical dues, considerably facilitated the reception of this ancient stronghold of Sclavonic heathenism within the advancing circle of Christendom, and the sound of prayer and praise rose from amidst the beech forests which once, in all probability, witnessed the worship of the ancient Hertha, goddess of the earth.[1]

[1] See Tacitus, "Germania," chap. xl.

CHAPTER XV.

BEYOND the Wends, and along the eastern coast of the Baltic, extending to the Gulf of Finland, dwelt the Livonians, or Lieflanders, another branch of the Sclavonic family, though considerably intermixed with the Ugrian race of Finns.

Like other tribes already mentioned, the Livonians were addicted to the worship of groves and trees, the practice of magic and sorcery, and the immolation, on occasions of great necessity, of human victims.

Till the year A.D. 1158, when Henry II. was king of England and Thomas à Becket was rapidly rising into notice, Livonia was wellnigh utterly unknown to the rest of Europe. Some traders of Bremen then visited it, and formed several settlements along the coast.

These commercial relations with their western neighbours first opened up the country to missionary enterprise, and in the year A.D. 1186 one of the merchant-ships of Bremen brought to the mouth of the Düna a venerable canon named Meinhard. He had been trained in one of Vicelin's monasteries at Sege-berg, and having obtained permission from the Russian prince Vladimir of Plozk founded the first Livonian church at Yxhull on the Düna, where the Bremen merchants had already erected a fort for the protection of their trade.[1]

Though the people were sunk in the grossest ignorance, Meinhard did not find it impossible, by care and patience, to instil amongst them the seeds of civilization. A fortunate incident served to secure their goodwill. On one occasion the Livonians at Yxhull were attacked by a hostile army, and the fort erected by the Bremen merchants proved unequal to protect them. Thereupon Meinhard instructed them how to construct a larger fort for their permanent defence and security. Grateful for these benefits, not a few professed themselves willing to listen to the doctrines which he preached, and even to receive baptism.

Having thus made a satisfactory commencement, Meinhard repaired to Bremen, and announced to Hartwig, the archbishop, the result of his endeavours, and was appointed to the see of Yxhull.

But on his return to his diocese he found nothing but disappointment. No sooner had their immediate wants been relieved, than the fickle multitude relapsed into their heathen errors, and the utmost efforts of Meinhard were vainly spent in attempting to induce them to forsake their old superstitions.

Soon afterwards a Cistercian monk, named Theodoric, came to his aid, and began to cultivate some land in the neighbourhood of the mission station. His crops were remarkably productive, far more pro-

[1] "Origines Livoniæ," ed. Gruber, pp. 1—5.

ductive, indeed, than any in the fields of the Livonians, while the corn they had cultivated was unfortunately destroyed by a flood of water which inundated the land. Filled with jealousy, they rose up against the more fortunate Cistercian, and determined to offer him in sacrifice to their gods. It was thought expedient, however, to ascertain the will of the native deities before proceeding to this extremity. Accordingly, the sacred horse was thrice led by the attendant priest over the rows of spears, and on each occasion the omens favoured the sparing of his life, and he escaped.

But shortly afterwards he incurred similar or even greater perils. An eclipse of the sun took place, and the superstitious people could account for it in no other way than by ascribing it to sinister influences which he had exercised over the source of light. This, added to the success of his agricultural labours, rendered his stay in the country more and more hazardous, and he was constrained to fly; while Meinhard, after much fruitless labour, died at Yxhull, in the year A.D. 1196.

Meinhard was succeeded by Berthold, abbot of a Cistercian monastery in Lower Saxony. The new-comer thought to conciliate his flock by a distribution of provisions and numerous presents. So long as his stock lasted, their goodwill was readily secured, but no sooner had they come to an end than a revulsion of feeling ensued. Like Bishop Bernard, at Wolgast in Pomerania,[1] he was despised as a beggarly stranger,

---

[1] See above, p. 213.

and various schemes were proposed as to the mode of dealing with him. Some suggested that he should be burnt, together with his church; others wished to fling him into the Düna; others to slay him with the sword.[1]

Accordingly he was fain to leave the country, but returned after the lapse of a year, A.D. 1198, at the head of an army of crusaders, whom Pope Innocent III. had summoned to his aid from the neighbouring countries, directing those who had taken upon them a vow of making a pilgrimage to Rome to substitute for it a crusade against the Lieflanders.

On his arrival at the head of his martial array, Berthold bade the people surrender without delay, and not provoke a useless contest. Undeterred by the sight of the warriors in his retinue, they replied by bidding him dismiss his forces and enter peacefully on his duties, and advised him to try and compel those who had espoused Christianity to remain faithful to their new creed, and induce others to adopt it by good words instead of violent blows.

Thereupon a battle ensued, in which Berthold fell. But the rude pagans, unable to cope with a disciplined force, were soon defeated, promised obedience to the demands of their conquerors, and consented, in some instances, to receive baptism. The change, however, was not destined to continue. The crusaders had no sooner departed than, as might naturally be expected, a reaction immediately followed. The heathen party rose and wreaked their vengeance with terrible effect

[1] "Orig. Livoniæ," ii. 2.

on the new converts and such clergy as had been left
amongst them, and many of those who had consented
to be baptized now flung themselves into the Düna,
and strove to efface the effects of their baptism by
washing in its waters.

The successor of Berthold was Albert von Apeldern
of Bremen. With a fleet of twenty-three ships and a
numerous army of crusaders he sailed up the Düna
and strove to accomplish what his predecessor had
failed to achieve. He laid the foundations of the
town of Riga, and transferred thither, as being a more
secure locality, the bishopric of Yxhull.

His efforts, however, to secure any permanent
results, were not more successful than those of his
two predecessors, and, harassed by the incursions of
neighbouring pagan tribes, he determined to establish
a permanent military force, at once to defend his own
diocese and overawe the Lieflanders into a reception
of Christianity. Accordingly he instituted, in the year
A.D. 1201, with the concurrence of the emperor Otho
IV. and the approbation of the Pope, the knightly
" Order of the Sword," and placed it under the special
protection of the Virgin Mary. The members of this
Order bound themselves by solemn vows to hear mass
frequently, to abstain from marriage, to lead a sober
and chaste life, and to fight against the heathen. In
return for these services they were to have and to
enjoy whatever lands they might wrest with their
swords from their pagan adversaries.

Remorseless war was now waged against the
Lieflanders for upwards of twenty years. In vain

they courted alliances with other tribes, and strove
to resist their oppressors.   Castle after castle was
erected in their territory, and German colonists in
ever-increasing numbers flocked into the country,
and, taking up their residence, extended German
influences far and wide.

Albert von Apeldern made Riga the starting-point
of his operations.   Thence, aided by Waldemar II. king
of Denmark, he directed the arms of his crusaders
against Esthonia, and the neighbouring countries
of Semgallen and Courland.   On these war-wasted
districts he succeeded in imposing a nominal form
of Christianity, and the bishoprics of Revel, Dorpat,
and Pernau were so many ecclesiastical fortresses
strengthening the power of the " Order of the Sword,"
and securing the fruits of their victories.

As might naturally be expected from the character
of the efforts thus made, there was no such thing
as any vernacular literature, in which the Livonians
could learn the elements of the Christian faith.   Curious means were consequently adopted for diffusing
amongst them a glimmering knowledge of their new
creed ; and of these miracle-plays formed a conspicuous part.

Thus at Riga, in the year A.D. 1204, a miracle-play
was performed, representing scenes from the Old
and New Testaments, and an attempt was made to
enlist the sympathy of the eye with events which the
uninstructed ear of the rude people was unable to comprehend.   Accordingly, while the exploits of Gideon,
David, and Herod were visibly enacted before their

wondering gaze, interpreters from time to time explained the meaning of the dramatical representations.
But they do not appear to have been uniformly
successful in their endeavours to do this. On one
occasion, the spectators interpreting the scenes more
literally than their instructors intended, fled in terror
at the sight of the Midianites attacked by Gideon's
army, and imagined that the next assault would be
directed against themselves.

During the following winter, Archbishop Andreas
of Lund, who had come into the country with the
allied army of the Danes, set an example which many
of his clergy would have done well to follow.   He lectured to the people, in their own tongue, on the Book
of Psalms ; and proofs were not wanting that, whenever an attempt was made in a meet and becoming
spirit, the Leiflanders were not unwilling to listen to
the words of those, who addressed them in a language
suitable to the faith they sought to propagate.

CHAPTER XVI.

THE MARTYR ADALBERT OF PRUSSIA.

CLOSELY bordering on Livonia was Prussia, which was at this time inhabited chiefly by Sclaves, with a Lithuanian and German admixture, and divided into eleven petty independent states.

Nowhere, perhaps, was the ancient Sclavonic superstition more deeply rooted. Nowhere had the Sclavonic priesthood more undisputed sway.

The people worshipped not only the heavenly bodies and the elements of nature, but also a number of divinities, of whom the three held in chiefest estimation have been already mentioned,[1]—Percunos the god of thunder, Potrimpos the god of corn and fruits, Picullos the god of the infernal regions.

Every town and village possessed a larger or a smaller temple, but the sanctuary of the nation was at Romove, not far from the present Königsburg. Here also resided the chief pontiff, who was held in such veneration that not only he himself, and many of his connexions, but even a herald bearing his staff, or other insignia, was accounted sacred.[2] The priests

[1] See above, p. 25.
[2] Hartknoch's "Dissertations," vii.

were required to live in celibacy, and possessed unbounded influence over the people, and they did
not scruple, at particular seasons, to exact of them
human sacrifices, especially in honour of Picullos
and Potrimpos.

Every native of the country was allowed to have
three wives, who were regarded as slaves, and on
the death of their husbands they were expected to
ascend the funeral pile or otherwise put an end to
their lives.[1] Infanticide, especially of female children,
was common, and it was the custom to destroy or sell
all the daughters of a family save one. Children
also that were deformed, aged persons, and all whose
recovery was doubtful, were put out of the way, and
male and female slaves were burnt with the corpse of
their master, as also his horses, hounds, hawks, and
armour.

One of the earliest preachers who endeavoured to
proclaim amongst the Prussians the word of life was
Wogteich, or Adalbert, bishop of Prague. Born of
a respectable family about the year A.D. 956, he was
educated at Magdeburg, and was chosen bishop of his
native town in the year A.D. 983.

The rough heathen manners of too many in his
diocese, added to their addiction to their old superstitions, caused him the greatest anxiety. Full of
zeal and ardour, but lacking moderation and patience,
he frequently declared his intention of leaving a flock
which would not lay aside their lawless customs and

[1] In the "Origines Livoniæ," p. 31, we have an instance of fifty
women hanging themselves on the death of their husbands.

follow his guidance and directions. At length, anxious
to embrace the monastic life, he undertook a journey
to Italy and sought out the venerable monk Nilus,[1]
who was frequently visited by men of every rank and
station seeking his counsel and direction. But after
a while he left his adviser, and returning to his
diocese resumed his labours amongst his people.

After a few years, however, attracted by a favourable opportunity of missionary work, he repaired to
Bohemia, and, with the aid of Boleslav the Pious,
sought to extinguish the remains of paganism in that
country. But the natural hastiness of his character,
added to the harshness of the measures he adopted,
marred all hopes of real success. His stringent disciplinary measures provoked opposition, and he resigned
his post and retired to a convent.

In the year A.D. 994 the Roman synod ordered
him to resume his labours, and, obeying the injunction
with reluctance, he returned to Bohemia, only to be
a second time expelled by the Sclavonic population,
who disliked his German nationality as much as the
harshness of his measures. He now passed into
Hungary, and was welcomed by the duke Geisa, who
was persuaded by the influence of his wife to be
baptized. But here, also, his success was limited to
the effect which his life and conversation appear to
have exercised over their son Stephen, the first king
of Hungary, who afterwards so widely established
Christianity amongst his subjects.

[1] See a notice of him in Neander's "Memorials of Christian Life,"
p. 492.

And now his restless spirit prompted him to penetrate into Prussia, where as yet no missionary had
set his foot. Boleslav I., duke of Poland, granted
him an escort of soldiers, and in the year A.D. 997 he
proceeded to Dantzic, then a border-town between
Poland and Prussia. His landing was not opposed,
and he succeeded in inducing not a few to listen to his
message. Leaving this district, accompanied only by
a priest named Benedict, and one of his own pupils,
Gaudentius, he landed at the Frische Haff, and thence
in a little boat proceeded to a small island at the
mouth of the river Pregel. There his landing was
opposed, and the natives fell upon him and his
companions with clubs. Struck with an oar while
engaged in chanting the Psalter, Adalbert fell stunned
to the bottom of the boat.

After a while they succeeded, though with much
difficulty, in making their way to the other side of the
Pregel, and into the district of Samland. Here they
were met by a chief of one of the villages, who brought
them to his house, and, summoning the inhabitants,
bade the strangers explain the object of their visit.

Thereupon Adalbert declared who he was and
whence he had come, and proceeded to say: "It is
for the sake of your salvation that I have made my
way amongst you. The gods ye worship neither
hear, nor speak, nor see. I come to bid you turn from
these deities to the worship of the one true God,
your Creator, beside whom there is no other God, in
order that ye may put your faith in his name, and
may receive hereafter eternal life, and partake, in the

mansions he has prepared for them that love and fear him, of everlasting joy."

These words roused the furious wrath of his hearers, and they gnashed upon him with their teeth. "Away," they exclaimed, "with such fellows from our land! These are they that cause our crops to fail, our trees to decay, our herds to sicken. Let the strangers deem themselves fortunate that they have come thus far unhurt. Let them now depart before night comes on, or expect instant death as the penalty of any further delay."[1]

Thereupon Adalbert and his companions departed and made their way to the coast. He himself was inclined to linger in the country, and thought that, if they suffered their hair to grow, laid aside their clerical garb, and took to working with their own hands, they might hope to disarm the prejudices of the people, and be enabled in time to obtain greater success. But such ideas were not destined to be realized.

When they awoke on the next day, Gaudentius told the bishop a dream which he had had in the night. "I beheld," said he, "an altar, and in the middle a golden cup half filled with wine. When I looked, I saw no one near on the watch. I therefore wished to drink of the wine, but one drew near and said, "It cannot be. Of that cup it is not meet that thou or any man shouldst drink. This wine is reserved for the spiritual refreshment of thy bishop at some future day." Adalbert, who deemed this an intimation of approaching martyrdom, replied, "My son, may God

[1] Brunonis "Vita S. Adalberti;" Pertz, "Mon. Germ." vol. ii. p. 608.

bless to us this vision! But let us not repose too
much confidence in what may deceive." At daybreak
they plunged into a thick forest and pursued their
journey, chanting psalms and invoking the protection
of the Lord.

About noon they halted, and Gaudentius celebrated
mass, and the bishop partook of the Lord's Supper.
Then they took some refreshment, after which Adalbert essayed to proceed still further. But, feeling
wearied, he repeated a verse of Scripture, chanted a
psalm, and fell asleep. His companions followed his
example. But they had not slept long before they
were roused by the loud shouts of a troop of the
natives of the district, who bound them prisoners and
clamoured for their instant execution.

Still preserving his coolness, Adalbert bade his two
friends not to be discouraged. "Be ye not troubled,"
said he ; "we know for whom we are thus called
to suffer, even for our Lord. His might surpasses
all might, his beauty exceeds all beauty, his grace
transcends all expression. What can be a nobler
death than to die for him ?" He had scarcely spoken,
when a priest appeared from amongst the infuriated
crowd and pierced him with a lance in the breast;
others followed his example and plunged their spears
into his body. Thus, raising his eyes to heaven, and
offering up prayers for his murderers, Adalbert perished
on the 23d of April, A.D. 997.

Another attempt to carry the word of life into this
dangerous region was made by Bruno, chaplain to the
emperor Otho III. Instigated, it is said, to under-

take the mission by the sight at Rome of a picture of
Archbishop Boniface, the great Apostle of Germany,
he procured a commission from Pope Sylvester II.
empowering him to preach to the heathen Prussians,
and was consecrated regionary bishop at Magdeburg.
With eighteen companions he entered Prussia in the
year A.D. 1008, but within twelve months he and all
his retinue had shared the fate of Bishop Adalbert.

After the death of Bruno a period of nearly two
centuries elapsed, during which the national repug-
nance of the Prussians to Christianity was still further
intensified by long and persistent wars with Poland.
At length, in the year A.D. 1207, a Polish abbot named
Gotefried penetrated into the country with one of his
monks, and had succeeded in achieving a scanty success, when his companion fell a victim to the hostility
of the people, and he himself was obliged to give up
in despair.

Three years afterwards, A.D. 1210, a monk named
Christian, from a Pomeranian convent near Dantzic,
accompanied by several brethren, and accredited with
the express authority of Pope Innocent III., determined to make another attempt.   For a space of four
years he prosecuted his task in peace, and then set
out for Rome, accompanied by two converted chiefs,
the firstfruits of his mission.

The Pope received them cordially, and appointed
Christian bishop of the new community.   He also
wrote to various Cistercian abbots in the country,
desiring them to aid instead of impeding the efforts
of the new bishop, and to the Polish and Pomeranian

dukes, inveighing strongly against the oppressive burdens they had laid upon the Prussian converts, which only tended to irritate the people and prejudice them against the Gospel.

Thus accredited, Christian once more returned to his diocese. But the suspicions of the heathen party had been aroused, and the new converts themselves groaned under the taxes and imposts exacted from them by the authorities of Poland and Pomerania. The consequence was a general reaction. The Prussians rose in fury, destroyed nearly three hundred churches and chapels, and put many Christians to the sword.[1]

Other agencies were now invoked by Bishop Christian, and the "Order of Knights Brethren of Dobrin," formed on the model of that which we have already encountered in Livonia, was bidden to coerce the people into the reception of Christianity. But they failed to achieve the task assigned them, and then it was that the famous "Order of Teutonic Knights," united with the "Brethren of the Sword" in Livonia, concentrated their energies on this European crusade.

Originally instituted for the purpose of succouring German pilgrims in the Holy Land, the "Order of Teutonic Knights," now that the old crusades had become unpopular, enrolled numbers of eager adventurers determined to expel the last remains of heathenism from the face of Europe. After the union of the two Orders had been duly solemnized at

[1] "Chronicon Prussiæ," p. 29 ; Hartknoch, "Dissert." xiv.

Rome, in the presence of the Pope, in the year A.D. 1238, they entered the Prussian territory, and for a space of nearly fifty years continued a series of remorseless wars against the wretched inhabitants. Slowly but surely they made their way into the very heart of the country, and secured their conquests by erecting castles, under the shadow of which rose the towns of Culm, Thorn, Marienwerder, and Elbing, which they peopled with German colonists.

The authority of the Order knew scarcely any bounds. Themselves the faithful vassals of the Pope, they exacted the same implicit obedience, alike from the German immigrant, or colonist, and the converted Prussians. Baptism was made the one condition of admission to the enjoyment of any rights, individual or social.[1] The baptized proselyte might regard himself as a freeman, might boast that, in some sense, he was a man. The Prussian who still persisted, in spite of being conquered, to adhere to his old superstitions, forfeited all claim to personal freedom, and was as much the property of his master as his horse or his hound.

In A.D. 1243 the conquered lands were divided by the Pope into three bishoprics, Culm, Pomerania, and Ermeland, each of which was again divided into three parts, one being subject to the bishop, and the other two to the brethren of the Order. With this subdivision there gradually sprang up a number of churches and monasteries, and the Prussians began to discontinue many of their heathen customs, such as

[1] See Milman's " Latin Christianity," v. 404.

sacrifice to idols, infanticide, the practice of poly-
gamy, and the burning of their dead. In return for
these concessions, a greater degree of personal liberty
was guaranteed to them, the Polish laws were introduced, and the Popes, who to the utmost of their
power befriended the new converts, enjoined an
equable distribution of the country into parishes,
impressed upon the clergy the duty of instructing the
people, and on the knights a due regard to the
gentler precepts of the Gospel. In A.D. 1251 schools
also began to be erected, though numbers of the
Prussian children were sent for instruction into Germany, and especially to Magdeburg, and numerous
Dominican monks laboured for the more effectual
conversion of the people.

Paganism, however, was not yet extinct. In the
year A.D. 1260 the Teutonic knights found themselves confronted by a formidable invasion of Lithuanians. The polytheism of these tribes assumed even
a more degraded form than that of the heathen
Prussians. Not only the heavenly bodies and the
god of thunder, but even serpents were regarded with
superstitious veneration, and were actually worshipped
with human sacrifices.[1]

The Lithuanians utterly defeated the knights, and
eight of the Order who were taken prisoners were
burnt alive in honour of the gods. This was the signal
for another rebellion. Aided by the Lithuanians, the
Prussians rose and wasted the country far and wide,

[1] Adam Brem. "de Situ Daniæ;" Æneas Sylvius "de Statu
Europæ," cap. xxii. p. 418.

murdered the clergy, and pillaged the monasteries and churches. Thereupon the knights retaliated. The favourable terms granted to the Prussians ten years before were cancelled, and a sanguinary war was carried on for upwards of twenty-two years.

Aided by armies of crusaders sent to them by the Popes, the knights at length gained the mastery. Many of the Prussian chiefs were deprived of their freedom, and reduced to the condition of serfs, and the bulk of the population consented, in sheer despair, to recognise the sovereignty of the Order, and to receive at least a nominal form of Christianity.

CHAPTER XVII.

AMONG the letters of St. Boniface to numerous friends in England is one addressed to the abbess Eadburga, in which he dissuades her from undertaking a pilgrimage to Rome in consequence of the perpetual incursions of the Saracens.

Meagre, doubtless, were the tidings which the Apostle of Germany received respecting the limitation of the Church in the distant East, but events had occurred far nearer Europe itself calculated to excite in his mind deep musings as to the designs of Providence.

Bursting from its home in the Arabian deserts, the wave of Mahometanism had swept on unchecked over Persia, Syria, Egypt, and Northern Africa, nor, stopping there, had inundated the length and breadth of Spain, save only a little Gothic kingdom in the inaccessible fortresses of Asturia. Restless even here, the Moslem warriors had crossed the Pyrenees, and the sword of Charles Martel alone saved the Frankish churches from the fate which had already befallen those of Augustine and of Cyprian.

Strange indeed and sad must have been the reflection of the early pioneers of Christian civilization
among the Teutonic nations, when they heard that
churches which a Paul or an Apollos had planted and
watered had been swept away before the austere
monotheism of Arabia.   Little could they understand
at the time that this sudden revolution was no less a
judgment on the decrepit Eastern churches for their
disunion and moral corruption, than a means destined
to minister, and that not ineffectually, to the ultimate
civilization of modern Europe.

On the history, however, of mediæval missions the
conquests of the Saracens exercised a sinister influence.   For a time they seemed to change the very
spirit of Christianity, and taught the soldiers of the
Cross to imagine that the weapons of their warfare
were not spiritual but carnal.   When, moreover, as
years rolled on, and stories began to be circulated
throughout the length and breadth of Europe of
the cruelties practised on Christian pilgrims by the
Moslem warriors, and thousands roused by the frenzied
hermit, Peter, poured forth from every land to rescue
the Holy City from the infidel, the crusading spirit
penetrated into the very heart of society, animating
the solitary monk no less than the follower of God-
frey, the peaceful burgher no less than the steel-clad
soldier.   Before the fiery propagandism of the Crusades the gentler spirit of true missionary enterprise
fled away, and the record of its triumphs seems to
have come to an end.

Still from time to time we come across traces of

some, who even now, while the din of arms was perpetually sounding around them, did not forget that there was a voice more potent in appealing to the hearts of men than the fire, the earthquake, and the storm.

Let us first take an instance in the life of St. Francis of Assisi.

In the year A.D. 1219 the champions of the Cross, numbering two hundred thousand Franks, lay encamped under the walls of Damietta.[1]

It was the tenth year of the Franciscan era, and the founder of the Franciscan Order was in the camp. He had just returned from his second general chapter, and had seen upwards of five thousand mendicants marching in long procession from the Porzioncula, two miles from Assisi, to Perugia. The cardinal Ugolino had quailed before the stern and menacing words, in which the " Spouse of Poverty" had rebuked his attempt to weaken, by tempting offers of mitres and even of the purple, the allegiance of his followers.

To turn their thoughts into other channels Francis proposed, as an object worthy of their ambition, the spiritual conquest of the world, and had reserved for himself the seat of war between the champions of the Cross and of the Crescent. The Christian camp itself was in a state of unutterable confusion, and an effort to quell its anarchy would have been worthy of all his energies.

But St. Francis burnt with an ardour which nothing could quench, to go alone and unattended into the

---

[1] Gibbon, vii. p. 268.

Moslem camp, and attempt the conversion of the
Soldan himself. After spending many hours in rapt
devotion, he went forth in the squalid robe of a mendicant and crossed the boundary lines between the
rival armies, chanting the words of the Psalmist :
*Though I walk through the valley of the shadow of
death, I will fear no evil, for thou art with me.*[1]
Apprehended by the Saracen outposts, he was conveyed to the tent of their leader and asked the reason
of his coming. " I am sent," he replied, " not of man,
but of God, to show thee the way of salvation." The
Soldan, we are assured by an eye-witness, received the
brave monk with respect, and not only permitted him
for several days to preach before himself and his
officers, but listened to his words with attention, and
sent him back to the Christian camp, saying, " Pray for
me, that God may enlighten me to hold fast that faith
which is most acceptable in his sight."

Other authorities inform us that, when asked by the
commander of the faithful to remain in his tent, the
intrepid monk replied, " Yes, I will remain, if thou
and thy people will become converts for the love of
the Saviour my Master. If thou art unwilling, kindle
a furnace, and I and thy priests will enter it together,
and let God determine whether the true faith is on
thy side or on mine." The most venerable of the
imauns trembled, and the commander declared his
fears that none of his priests would be willing to face
such an ordeal. " Only promise then," replied St.
Francis, " to become a Christian, and I will enter the

[1] Ps. xxiii. 4.

fire alone. If I come forth unharmed, acknowledge Christ ; but even should I be burnt, conclude not that my faith is false, but that on account of my sins I am unworthy to receive this honour."

The commander of the faithful courteously declined the proposal, and dismissed the enthusiastic monk with ample presents, and the Bishop of Acco, then present with the army, assures us that the Saracens were far from unwilling to listen to the preaching of the followers of St. Francis. They only complained when, in a spirit utterly alien from that which the greatest of Christian missionaries displayed towards the Athenians on Mars Hill, they resorted to coarse abuse and fanatical declamation.

The spirit of the Apostle of the Gentiles, rare at all times, was especially rare at this period. It is pleasant, therefore, to meet with another eminent man, who in a still more striking manner displayed all the attributes of the true Apostle, and whose life and labours mark an era in the missionary history of the Middle Ages.

This was the once famous, now almost forgotten, Raymund Lull.

This celebrated man was born of noble parents at Palma, the capital of Majorca, about the year A.D. 1236.[1] His father had served with great distinction in the army of James I., king of Arragon, and the boy was introduced at an early age into the royal court, and there rose to the post of seneschal.

The traditions of his youth represent him as gifted with extraordinary mental accomplishments, and an

[1] "Vita D. Raymundi Lulli Mart. ;" "Acta Sanct." June 30.

ardent cultivator of poetry, but addicted to gross sensual pleasures. He married, but this did not restrain him from gratifying lawless passions, and the theme of his poetical effusions was seldom any other than the joys of guilty love. " I see, O Lord," he writes in his work on *The Contemplation of God*, " that trees bring forth every year flowers and fruit, each after their kind, and from them mankind derives pleasure and profit. But thus it was not with me, sinful that I am. For thirty years I brought forth no fruit in this world. I cumbered the ground, nay, was noxious and hurtful to my friends and neighbours."

But on reaching his thirtieth year, the seneschal was one day sitting on his couch composing an erotic song, when suddenly, as he tells us, there appeared to him the image of Christ hanging on the cross. So deep was the impression made upon his mind that he was absolutely unable to write any more. Some days passed away, and he was again similarly engaged, when once more the same divine image presented itself, and he was fain for the second time to lay aside his pen. On this occasion the effect was not so transitory; and when it returned a third time, he was unable to resist the conviction that a special message was intended by it for himself; that the Saviour of men, who died upon the cross, was thus inviting him to conquer his lower passions, to come to him, and devote himself to his service.

But then, he tells us, arose the difficulty. " How can I, defiled with impurity, rise and enter on a holier life?" Night after night he lay awake, a prey to doubt and despondency. At length the thought occurred to him, "Christ is meek, and full of compassion and tender mercy. He invites all to come to him, and whosoever cometh to him, he will in no wise cast out. Sinful as thou art, peradventure he will accept thee, if thou wilt turn to him."

With that thought came peace and consolation. He concluded that he was indeed invited to forsake the world, to renounce its transitory pleasures, and follow his Saviour. At length he resolved to give up everything for his sake, and as this resolution gained a hold upon him, he began to feel that he was walking in the right path. Old things began to pass away. Powers long dormant, or dwarfed and stunted by devotion to lower aims, put forth greater activity. The flower at the bottom of the long sunless cavern had caught at last the quickening ray of the Sun of Righteousness, and was beginning to expand and put forth its bloom.

After long reflection, he came to the conclusion that he could not devote his energies to a higher work than that of proclaiming the message of the cross to the Saracens.

His thoughts would naturally take such a direction. The Balearic Isles had long been in the possession of the Saracens. His father had served in the wars and shared the triumphs of the King of Arragon, and had been rewarded for his bravery by the grant of a portion of Majorca. It occurred to his son that possibly the sword of the Spirit might conquer foes, whom the arms of mailed knights had failed to win over to the Christian fold.

" I see," he writes in one place, "many knights who cross the sea on their way to the Holy Land. They think that they shall conquer it by force of their arms, but one after another they are constrained to leave it without accomplishing their purpose. It seems to me, therefore, that the Holy Land can be won in no other way than that whereby thou, O Lord Jesus Christ, and thy holy Apostles won it, even by love, and prayer, and shedding of tears and blood. The Holy Sepulchre and the Holy Land can be won back far more effectually by proclaiming the word of truth than by force of arms. Let then spiritual knights go forth thither; let them be filled with the grace of the Holy Spirit. Let them announce to man the sufferings which their dear Lord underwent, and out of love to him shed forth their blood, even as he shed his for them."

But now there arose another difficulty. How could he, a layman and uninstructed, enter upon such a work? Thereupon the idea struck him that at least a beginning might be made by composing a volume, which should demonstrate the truth of Christianity, and convince the warriors of the Crescent of their errors.

But even if such a volume were composed, of what avail, he reflected, would it be in the hands of the Saracens, who understood no other language but Arabic. As he pondered over this, he was filled with the idea of calling upon the Pope and the monarchs of Christendom, instead of spending blood and treasure in bootless martial enterprises against the Saracens, to join in founding monasteries and schools, where men might learn the language of the Saracens, and so be enabled to go forth to preach the word to some purpose. Full of such thoughts, he repaired on the following day to a neighbouring church, and poured forth his whole soul to God, beseeching him, if he did indeed inspire these thoughts, to enable him to carry them out, and to give him strength and courage for the work.

This was in the month of July, A.D. 1266. But though old things were passing away, all things had not yet become new. Former passions rose and struggled afresh for the mastery, and so far succeeded in thwarting and baffling higher aspirations, that for three months his great design was laid aside.

The fourth of October came round. It was the festival of St. Francis of Assisi. Lull went to the Franciscan church at Palma, and heard from the lips of the preacher the tale of the "Spouse of Poverty"; how the son of Pietro Bernadone di Mericoni, once foremost in all deeds of arms, and gayest at the gay festival, was taken prisoner at Perugia, and brought by disease to the very gates of death; how, in sight of the awful portals of the tomb, he learnt to weigh the things of time and sense in the balances of eternity, and, recovering, arose to live no more to himself but to his Lord; how he exchanged his gay apparel for the garb of the mendicant; how he visited the sick, tended the lepers, and, renouncing the world, achieved the victory that overcometh it.

The words of the preacher rekindled the resolutions of the listening seneschal. He now made up his mind once and for ever, sold all his property, save a scanty sustenance for his wife and children, assumed the coarse garb of the mendicant, made pilgrimages to various churches in the island, and prayed earnestly for grace and assistance in the work he had resolved to undertake.[1]

At one time he thought of repairing to Paris, and there, by close and diligent study, training himself for controversy with the Saracens. But he was induced to remain at Majorca by his kinsman the Dominican Raymund de Pennaforte, who a few years before had urged the famous St. Thomas Aquinas to compose his work in four volumes, " On the Catholic Faith, or A Summary against the Gentiles." He next proceeded to purchase a Saracen slave, and entered on the study of Arabic, with which he occupied himself for upwards of nine years, till a tragical incident interrupted his studies. On one occasion the Saracen uttered words of blasphemy against Christ. Lull, unable to control his indignation, struck him violently on the face. The Moslem, roused to fury, attempted his life. For this he was flung into prison, and there committed suicide.

Still Lull persevered in his resolution, and retired for a period of eight days to a mountain to engage in prayer and meditation. While thus employed, the idea occurred to him of composing a work which should contain a strict and formal demonstration of all the Christian doctrines, of such cogency that the Moslem doctors could not fail to acknowledge their

[1] " Lib. Contemp." xci. 27.

truth and to embrace the faith. With such force did
this thought take possession of his mind, that he
could regard it in no other light than a divine revelation, and having traced the outline of such a work,
which he called the "Ars Major sive Generalis," he
returned to the spot where the idea had first burst
upon him, and remained there for four months,
developing the argument, and praying for the divine
blessing upon his work. This treatise, while primarily
intended for the special work of convincing the Moslems, was to include "an universal art of acquisition,
demonstration, and confutation, to cover the whole
field of knowledge, and to supersede the inadequate
methods of previous schoolmen."

In the year A.D. 1262 the Balearic Isles had been
erected into a kingdom under the name of Majorca.
With the monarch of the islands Lull, as soon as his
treatise was completed, held an interview, then published the first book, and lectured upon it in public.
At length he persuaded the king to found and endow
a monastery in Majorca, where thirteen Franciscan
monks might be instructed in the Arabic language, and
trained to become able disputants among the Moslems.

The success of his request to the king encouraged
him to hope that the Pope might evince a similar
interest in his plans. He therefore undertook a
journey to Rome, expecting to obtain from Honorius IV. the approbation of his treatise, and efficient
assistance in founding missionary schools and colleges
in various parts of Europe. But on his arrival at
Rome he found that Honorius was dead, and that men

were busied with one thing only, the election of his successor.

He resolved therefore to wait for calmer times; but impediments were always thrown in his way, and his plans received little encouragement. The heads of the Christian world cared for none of these things. Accordingly, he repaired to Paris, lectured on his treatise at the University, and composed another work on the "Discovery of Truth."

At length, tired of seeking aid for plans in which no one took any interest, he determined to set forth himself, and attempt alone and single-handed the propagation of the faith among the Moslems in Northern Africa. For this purpose he betook himself to Genoa, and finding a ship bound for the African coast, engaged his passage thither.

At Genoa the story of his life was not unknown. Men had heard with wonder of the change that had come over the once gay and dissolute seneschal. It was now whispered that he had devised an entirely new method for the conversion of the infidel, and was about to set forth alone for the shores of Africa. The expectations of the Genoese were raised to the highest pitch, and the utmost interest was taken in his project. The ship was lying in the harbour. The missionary's books had been conveyed on board, and everything was ready for the voyage.

But at this juncture a change came over him. He was overwhelmed with terror at the thought of what might befall him in the country whither he was going. The idea of enduring torture or lifelong imprisonment presented itself with such force to his mind, that he could not control his emotions. His books were ordered to be removed from the vessel, and she sailed without him. But no sooner had he received tidings that this was the case, than he was seized with the keenest remorse. The thought that he had proved a traitor to his Master, slighted a divine call to a special work, and given a handle to all scoffers at religion, threw him into a violent fever.

While, however, he was yet suffering the greatest bodily and mental prostration, he heard that another ship was lying in the harbour ready to sail for Tunis. Weak as he was, he implored his friends that his books might again be put on board, and he himself suffered to essay the voyage. He was conveyed to the ship, but his friends, convinced that he could not live, insisted on his being again landed. He returned to his bed, and his troubled mind found no peace, and his bodily sufferings no alleviation.

Before long another ship was announced as on the point of sailing, and he determined at all risks to be put on board. His wishes were complied with, and the vessel had hardly lost sight of land before he felt himself a different man. His conscience no more rebuked him for cowardice, his peace of mind returned, and to the surprise of all he seemed to have regained perfect health.

He reached Tunis at the close of the year A.D. 1291, or the beginning of A.D. 1292. His first step was to invite the Mahometan literati to a conference. When they came, he announced that he had diligently studied

the arguments which were commonly urged in support
not only of the Christian but also of the Mahometan
religion. He was anxious for the fullest and freest
discussion, and was willing, if they succeeded in convincing him by fair argument, to espouse their faith.
The Imauns eagerly responded to the challenge, and
flocking to the place of conference in great numbers
exhausted their whole store of arguments in the hope
of winning him over to the religion of the Prophet.

After a lengthened discussion the missionary advanced the following propositions :

" Every wise man," he said, " must acknowledge
that to be the true religion which ascribed the greatest
perfection to the Supreme Being, and not only conveyed the worthiest conceptions of all His attributes, such as his goodness, wisdom, power, and
glory, but also demonstrated the harmony existing
between them. Now their religion was defective in
acknowledging only two active principles in the Deity,
his will and his wisdom, whilst it left his goodness
and greatness inoperative, as though they were in-
dolent qualities, and had not been called forth into
active exercise. But the Christian faith could not be
charged with this defect. In its doctrine of the Trinity
it conveyed the highest conception of the Deity, as the
Father, the Son, and the Holy Spirit, in one essence
and nature. In that of the Incarnation of the Son it
evinced the harmony that exists between God's goodness and his greatness, and in the person of Jesus
Christ displayed the true union of the Creator and
the creature. In his Passion, which he underwent

out of his great love for man, it set forth the divine harmony of infinite goodness and infinite love ; even the love of him who, for us men and for our salvation, underwent these sufferings and died upon the cross." [1]

This argument, whatever else was thought of it, was deemed worthy of drawing down persecution on the head of its author. A learned Moslem pointed out to the king the danger likely to beset the law of Mahomet, if such a zealous propagandist was allowed to go on disseminating his opinions, and therefore suggested that he should be put to death. Accordingly Lull was thrown into prison, and only escaped the capital penalty by the intercession of a less prejudiced counsellor, who reminded his sovereign that a professor of their own faith would be held in high honour if he imitated the self-devotion of the prisoner in propagating *their* doctrines among the Christians. Let him, then, be fairly dealt with, and let them do as they would be done by.

This timely intervention saved him, and the sentence of death was commuted to banishment from the country. He was placed on board the vessel which had conveyed him to Tunis, and warned that if he ever made his way into the country again, he would assuredly be stoned to death. But Lull, unwilling to relinquish the hopes of a lifetime, managed to return to Tunis unawares, and for three months concealed himself in the neighbourhood of the harbour.

[1] " Vita Prima," p. 665 : comp. also "Lib. de Contempl. in Deum," liv. 25—28.

Finding, however, no opportunity for disseminating
the doctrines of the faith, he sailed to Naples, and
there remained several years teaching and lecturing
on his new method, till, hearing of the elevation of
Cœlestine V. to the papal chair, he betook himself to
Rome, hoping to obtain that assistance in establishing
his favourite plan of missionary colleges, which he
had vainly besought before. But Cœlestine's reign
was brief, and his successor, Boniface VIII., failed to
show him any encouragement.

Seeing that his journey to Rome was likely to lead
to no practical results, he resolved to travel from place
to place, and preach wherever he might have an opportunity. After endeavouring, therefore, to convince
the Mahometans and Jews in Majorca of their errors,
he sailed for Cyprus, and thence, attended only by a
single companion, penetrated into Armenia, and strove
to reclaim the various Oriental sects to the orthodox
faith. Ten years having been thus spent, he returned
and lectured in several of the universities of Italy
and France ; and then in A.D. 1307 made his way once
more to Northern Africa, and standing up at Bugia,
then the capital of a Mahometan kingdom, proclaimed
publicly in the Arabic language that Christianity was
the only true faith, that the religion of the Prophet
was false, and he was ready to prove this to the satisfaction of all.

A commotion ensued, and not a few hands were
lifted to stone him to death. The Moslem literati
however, rescued him, and expostulated with him on
his madness in thus exposing himself to imminent

peril. "Death has no terrors," he replied, "for a sincere servant of Christ, who is labouring to bring souls to a knowledge of the truth." Thereupon certain Moslems, who were well versed in the Arabian philosophy, challenged him to produce his proofs of the supcriority of his religion to that of the Prophet.

Lull fell back upon his favourite position, and dilated on the beauty and harmony of the Christian doctrine of the Trinity. But, as before, his arguments only entailed upon him bitter persecution. He was flung into a dungeon, and for half a year remained a close prisoner, befriended only by some merchants of Genoa and Spain. Meanwhile riches, wives, high places, and power were offered him, if he would consent to abjure the faith. To all such temptations he replied, "And I will promise you wealth, and honour, and everlasting life, if you will forsake your false creed, and believe in the Lord Jesus Christ." He also proposed that both parties should compose a written defence of their respective tenets, and he was engaged in fulfilling his part of the engagement, when a sudden command of the king directed that he should be sent out of the country.

During the voyage a storm arose, and the vessel was driven on a point of the coast not far from Pisa. Here he was received with all the respect that became so eminent a champion of the faith. Though upwards of seventy, his old ardour was not abated. The same high aspirations still animated him. "Once," he writes, "I was rich; once I had a wife and children; once I tasted freely of the pleasures of this life. But

all these things I gladly resigned that I might spread
abroad a knowledge of the truth.   I studied Arabic,
and several times went forth to preach the Gospel to
the Saracens.   I have been in prisons.   I have been
scourged.   For years I have striven to persuade the
princes of Christendom to promote the common good
of all men.   Now, though old and poor, I do not
despair.   I am ready, if it be God's will, to persevere
even unto death."

Full of his former ardour, and in keeping with the
spirit of the age, he conceived the idea of founding a
new order of spiritual knights, who should be ready
to embark at a moment's notice, to war against the
Saracens, and attempt the recovery of the Holy
Sepulchre.   Pious noblemen and ladies at Genoa
offered to contribute towards this object the sum of
thirty thousand guilders.   Thus encouraged, he set
out for Avignon, to lay his scheme before Clement V.
But the same fate befell this appeal that had attended
all the rest.   He repaired, therefore, to Paris, and
there heard that a general council was to be summoned at Vienne.   A general council might support
what Popes had scarcely deigned to notice.   Accordingly he betook himself to Vienne, and proposed that
missionary colleges should be established in various
parts of Europe ; that the different order of spiritual
knights should be consolidated, with a view to another
effort to recover the Holy Land ; and, lastly, that men
duly qualified should be invited to combat the opinions
of Averroes.   The first of these propositions was favourably received, and the council passed a decree that

professorships of the Oriental languages should be endowed in the universities of Paris, Salamanca, and Oxford, and in all cities where the Papal Court resided.

Thus, at last, he lived to see some portion of the labours of his life brought to fruition. When the deliberations of the council were over, it might have been thought he would have been willing to enjoy the rest he had so well deserved. But such was not his wish. "As the needle," he says, "naturally turns to the north when it is touched by the magnet, so is it fitting, O Lord, that thy servant should turn to love and praise and serve thee, seeing that out of love to him thou wast willing to endure such grievous pangs and sufferings." Or, as he says again, "Men are wont to die, O Lord, from old age, from the failure of natural warmth, and excess of cold. But thus, if it be thy will, thy servant would not wish to die. He would prefer to expire in the glow of love, even as thou wast willing to die for him."

Animated by these sentiments, he crossed over once more to Bugia on the 13th of August, A.D. 1314, and for nearly a year laboured secretly among a little circle, on whom, during previous visits, he had prevailed to listen to his teaching. To them he continued to expatiate on the theme, of which he never seemed to tire, of the inherent superiority of the Christian religion to that of the Jews or of the Mahometans. "If the latter," he still argued, "according to their law, affirm that God loves man because he created him, endowed him with noble faculties, and pours his blessings upon

him, then the Christians, according to their law, affirm
the same. But inasmuch as the Christians believe
more than this, and affirm that God so loved man that
he was willing to become man, to endure poverty,
ignominy, torture, and death for his sake, which the
Jews and Saracens do not teach concerning him ;
therefore is the religion of the Christians, which thus
reveals a love beyond all other love, superior to
that of those, which reveals it only in an inferior
degree."

On the length and breadth and depth and height
of this love, a love which passeth knowledge, he never
ceases to expatiate in his work on the contemplation
of God, and now it was the one theme of his earnest
converse with his little flock. At length, longing for
the crown of martyrdom, he came forth from his
seclusion, and presenting himself openly to the people,
proclaimed that he was the same man they had once
expelled from the town, and boldly denounced their
errors. The consequences can be easily anticipated.
Filled with fury the populace seized him, dragged him
outside the town, and then, by command of the king,
stoned him to death on the 30th of June, A.D. 1315.
There under a pile of stones the body remained, till a
few faithful merchants of Majorca succeeded in obtaining permission to remove it, and conveyed it for
interment to their native land.

CHAPTER XVIII.

WITH this notice of the famous Raymund Lull we must close our account of some of the more eminent Apostles of Mediæval Europe.

At this point, therefore, it may not be amiss to look back and gather up some of the chief lessons which their lives enforce, and that with special reference to the missionary history of the Middle Ages.

I. And first let us make a remark respecting the Mediæval period itself.

It is always useful to bear in mind that this period was one of transition, that it was not ultimate but intermediate and preliminary. Trite and commonplace as the observation may seem, it is one which deserves recollection, if we would form a just estimate of the efforts then made to spread a knowledge of Christianity.

We started at that point when the Christian Church had absorbed into herself whatever was good and valuable in the culture of the Greek and Roman world. We have paused just before the dawn of the bright

morning of the last three hundred years, which
have given birth to what has been not inaptly called
Teutonic, as contrasted with *Latin*, Christianity.

The missionary history, therefore, of the Middle
Ages partook of the characteristics of the Mediæval
period itself.   To a great extent it was disciplinary
and preparatory.   During the earlier portion of the
period, the Church was called upon to undertake one
of the most difficult tasks that could have been presented to her energies and her zeal.   In her contact
with the world she herself had lost somewhat of her
original simplicity, and the form of Christianity which
she presented to the new races for their reception was
not that of purer and Apostolic times.   The stage of
culture which the nations had reached whom she
was called to civilize was low; they were little
capable of discerning the outward from the inward,
the letter from the spirit; and before learning the
simplest lesson of the Christian faith, they had to
unlearn a ferocity and a lawlessness which made
them at first a terror even to their teachers.

However defective, therefore, may have been the
development obtained during this period, it may be
pleaded that on the one hand it was almost inevitable
from the nature of the case, and on the other that it
was adapted as a transitory stage for the childhood
of the new races.   They needed parental discipline
before they could learn or value independence.   They
needed to be governed before they could govern
themselves.

At the first promulgation of Christianity, the old

Roman empire had, in the providence of God, supplied the framework that held together the various masses of social life, which the Gospel was intended to pervade. During the Mediæval period, a great Latin Christian empire was, if not needed, at least overruled, to address the nations in language legal and formal, and, so to speak, to naturalize Christianity in the West.

The Primitive Church has been compared to the Patriarchal period of Jewish history, and the Mediæval Church to the Mosaic Dispensation.[1] If the latter comparison is allowed, we may conclude that like that Dispensation the Mediæval Church was destined, after performing its office of legal discipline, *to vanish away;* but that, while needed, it was " of great consequence and undeniable aptitude." " The task," observes Professor Ranke, " of bending the refractory spirit of the Northern tribes to the pure laws of Christian truth was no light one. Wedded, as these nations were, to their long-cherished superstitions, the religious element required a large predominance before it could gain possession of the German character; but by this predominance that close union of Latin and German elements was effected, on which is based the character of Europe in later times. There is a spirit of community in the modern world which has always been regarded as the basis of its progressive improvement, whether in religion, politics, manners, social life, or literature. To bring about this community it was necessary that the Western

---

[1] Dean Stanley's " Sermons on the Apostolic Age," p. 105.

nations should at one period constitute what may be called a single politico-ecclesiastical state."[1]

II. If from this notice of the Mediæval period itself we turn to its most eminent Apostles, we cannot but be struck with the immense influence of individual energy and the subduing force of personal character.

Around individuals penetrated with Christian zeal and self-denial centred not merely the life, but the very existence of the Churches of Europe. In the most troubled epochs of these troublous times they always appeared to do the work of their day and their generation.

I am with you always, even to the end of the world, said the ascending Saviour to his first Apostles.[2]

Again and again we have seen that promise fulfilled.

While the Roman world was sinking in an abyss of decrepitude, and the continent of Europe was a scene of the wildest disorder and confusion, still there were men, like Ulphilas and Severinus, to sow amongst the new races the seeds of civilization, before they took up their positions on the ruins of the Empire.[3]

When the light of the Frankish Church grew dim, and its missionary zeal waxed cold, a beacon was kindled in the secluded Celtic Churches of Ireland and Scotland, whence, in the words of Alcuin, "the light of truth might give shine to many parts of the world," and the disciples of St. Columba might go

---

[1] Ranke's "History of the Popes," i. p. 22.
[2] St. Matt. xxviii. 20.
[3] See above, pp. 29, 30.

forth in troops to the forests of Switzerland and of Southern Germany.[1]

When the British Church, in our own island, failed to evangelize her Teutonic invaders, a Gregory was ready to send an Augustine to her shores, whose disciples laboured here side by side with the Celtic missionaries from Iona, till the conversion of the Anglo-Saxon kingdoms was complete.[2]

Then when the Teuton of the Continent was crying from his native forests, like the Macedonian of old to the great Apostle of the Gentiles, *Come over and help us*,[3] the members of the churches which Roman and Celtic missionaries had founded throughout the length and breadth of England were prepared to go forth and emulate the zeal which had already founded the monasteries of Luxeuil and St. Gall, and, Teutons themselves, to evangelize the Teutons of Friesland and Northern Germany.[4]

When again an opportunity was offered of carrying the word into the forests of Central Germany, a Winfrid[5] was raised up to go forth and labour with unwearied zeal in Thuringia and Hessia, to persuade numbers of devoted women to leave their homes in England and join him in the work, and to bequeath his martyr spirit to numerous scholars and disciples, like Gregory of Utrecht and Sturmi of Fulda.[6]

When, lastly, on the death of Charlemagne, the barks of the terrible Northmen were prowling round every coast, and carrying havoc and desolation into

---

[1] See above, pp. 57, 58.　　[2] Ib. p. 98.　　[3] Acts xvi. 9.
[4] See above, pp. 99—110.　　[5] Ib. p. 110.　　[6] Ib. pp. 129—138.

the fairest fields of France and England, even then an Anskar was found willing to go forth with dauntless bravery and lay the foundations of the Churches of Denmark and Sweden, carrying the Gospel into the very home of the Scandinavian Vikings.[1]

It was the same with the Sclavonic nations. A Cyril and a Methodius were prepared to preach the word in Bohemia and Moravia,[2] a Vicelin to toil amidst perpetual discouragements among the savage Wends,[3] a Meinhard to labour in Livonia,[4] an Adalbert to suffer martyrdom in Prussia,[5] an Otho to penetrate into the furthest recesses of fanatical Pomerania.[6]

Nay, when the crusading spirit had sunk deeply into the heart of European society, and the patience of an Anskar was exchanged for the fiery zeal of the Champion of the Cross, we have seen how even then there was a Raymund Lull to protest against propagandism by the sword, to develop *a more excellent way*[7] towards winning over the Moslem warriors than the argument of force, and to seal his constancy with his blood outside the gates of Bugia.[8]

Thus, even in the darkest times, there were ever some streaks of light, and the leaven destined to quicken the whole lump of society was never altogether inert or ineffectual. Take away these men, blot out their influence, and how materially would events have varied, how much the entire history of

[1] See above, pp. 151—171.   [2] Ib. pp. 202—206.   [3] Ib. pp. 244—246.
[4] Ib. pp. 250—254.   [5] Ib. pp. 258—263.   [6] Ib. pp. 220—239.
[7] 1 Cor. xii. 31.   [8] See above, p. 288.

the Middle Ages would have been altered! They
had their defects, the defects of their day and generation. But it becomes us always to speak with gratitude and kindness of men who counted not their lives
dear unto them if they might win over to the truth the
Teuton and the Sclave, and to whom modern Europe
owes much of its present civilization.

III. If we turn from the agents themselves to the
work they accomplished, we cannot but notice a
striking contrast between the Mediæval and Apostolic
missions.

During the Apostolic period, we are chiefly struck
by the presence of direct miraculous agency and
spiritual gifts, and by the corresponding absence of
temporal aid.

In the Sub-apostolic age, again, Christianity found a
point of contact with the Greek and Roman mind, as
well as a distinct national culture which it could purify
and transfigure. It found also a language long prepared for its service, in which it could everywhere
address itself to the intellect and the reason as well as
to the conscience of its hearers.

It was the season, too, of its *first love*.[1] Hence the
attitude of complete antagonism of its first believers
towards paganism, their repudiation of all compro-
mise, their studious renunciation of all heathen principles and practices. It was the season also of the
Church's struggle, always for toleration, sometimes for
existence. Hence her conversions were individual
rather than national; the new faith made its way from

[1] Rev. ii. 4.

below rather than from above; *not many wise, not many mighty, not many noble were called.*[1]

But even before the beginning of the period, whose chief Apostles we have chronicled, all this had passed away.

The consolation of the slave or of the fugitive in the catacombs had become the creed of the Emperor. Instead of pleading for toleration, the Church herself had learnt to be aggressive. The Greek Fathers had moulded her Creeds, Rome had regulated her laws, and bequeathed to her its own love of organization and government. No longer in dread of the caprice or malice of the occupant of the imperial throne, she awaited, with fixed institutions, magistrates, and laws, the incoming of the new races.

For a while, indeed, her own safety seemed in peril ; but when the agitated elements of society had been calmed, she emerged to present to the world the single stable institution that had survived the shock.

In her dealings, therefore, with the new races, there was a great change from the missions of the first age. Whereas the latter had, from the necessity of the case, worked upwards from below, till at length the number of converts became too great and too influential to be ignored by the ruler, and the voice from the catacombs found an echo in the palace, during the Mediæval period all this was reversed.

With an almost monotonous uniformity, in Ireland and England, in Southern and in Northern Germany, among the Sclavonic no less than the Scandinavian

[1] 1 Cor. i. 26.

nations, the conversion of the people followed that of the king or chief.

The fourth century, indeed, presents the somewhat anomalous spectacle of the emperor Constantine, as yet unbaptized, taking an active part in Christian preaching.[1] But turn where we will in this age, we cannot but be struck by the religious aspect of the temporal rule. The Apostle of Ireland addresses himself to Irish, the founder of Iona to Pictish princes. Columbanus rebukes Thierri and Brunehaut; Boniface discusses plans for his Thuringian missions in the courts of Austrasian kings; his disciples follow in the track of Charlemagne's victorious armies. It is with a prince of Denmark that Anskar embarks on his first missionary voyage. It is to Bogoris, the Bulgarian chief, that Methodius displays the awful picture of the Judgment Day. A Polish duke supplies all the necessities of the Apostle of Pomerania, while another welcomes him on entering the land he had come to evangelize, and offers to protect him with a regiment of soldiers. Moreover, if anything were wanting to complete the picture, it is supplied by the record of the visit of the missionaries of the Eastern Church to the Russian court, where the religious aspect of the temporal ruler finds its highest expression, and Vladimir bears the same title as the emperor Constantine, Isapostolos, *Vladimir, equal to an apostle.*

Various explanations have been offered to account for this feature of the Mediæval missions.

Some have ascribed it to the deliberate policy of

[1] Dean Stanley's "Eastern Church," p. 198.

the missionaries themselves. Others have dwelt on the aristocratic character of society amongst the Germanic tribes, and have drawn attention to the docile and imitative tendencies of the Sclavonic races.

But we need not linger over these speculations. The success of the Mediæval missionary did not more depend on the will of princes than that of the Reformation movement in every country that became Protestant in the sixteenth century. St. Boniface only expresses the experience of many eminent missionaries of more recent times when he writes, "Without the patronage of the Frankish chiefs, I can neither govern the people, exercise discipline over the clergy and monks, nor prohibit heathen writers."

And if these national conversions depended so much on the smile or favour of the prince, we cannot fail to observe how often the conversion of the prince himself was due to his alliance in marriage with a Christian queen. The story of Clovis and Clotilda, of Ethelbert and Bertha, of Vladimir and Anne, repeats itself again and again.

It has been noticed that the interpretation so generally adopted by early Christian writers of the words of St. Paul, *What knowest thou, O wife, whether thou shalt save thy husband? or how knowest thou, O husband, whether thou shalt save thy wife?*[1] exercised no small influence in early times in promoting the conversion of unbelieving husbands by believing wives. At any rate, the saying of St. Chrysostom, that "no teacher has so much effect in conversion as a wife,"

[1] I Cor. vii. 16.

has been verified not only in the instance of the two great kingdoms of France and England, but accounts, in some measure, for these rapid conversions of whole tribes, which form so characteristic a feature in the missionary annals of this period. The intermarriage of the Goths with their Christian captives in the days of Ulphilas, of the Saxons with the conquered Britons in England, of the Northmen with the Franks in Normandy, hints at a solution of what is otherwise perplexing. In the latter case, moreover, it suggests a reason why the followers of Rollo ceased to be Teutons as well as Pagans, why they became Frenchmen as well as Christians.[1]

[1] Milman's "Latin Christianity," ii. 434.

CHAPTER XIX.

WE have noticed the chief characteristics of the Mediæval period itself, the Providence which decreed a succession of Apostles for Mediæval Europe, and the national character of the conversions they effected.

I. Another feature now demands attention, namely, the prominence in the execution of the work of the Monastic Orders.

Monasticism founded the Celtic Churches in Ireland and Scotland; already existed in England when the Saxon invader appeared on her shores; fled with the British Church to the fastnesses of Wales and Cumberland; returned with Augustine to the coast of Kent; with Aidan spread to the Farne Islands; with Columbanus penetrated the forests of Switzerland; with Winfrid civilized Thuringia and Frisia; with Sturmi opened up the forests of Buclomia; with Anskar found an entrance into Denmark and Sweden; with Methodius and Cyril visited Bulgaria, Moravia, and Bohemia; with members of the Cistercian Order penetrated Lithuania and Prussia; with ardent disciples of St. Francis and St. Dominic confronted the Moslem soldiery.

We have already[1] glanced at the physical necessities, so to speak, which dictated the employment of
these heroic pioneers. We have seen how many of
the fairest provinces of the Roman empire, groaning
under the weight of merciless taxation, had wellnigh
ceased to till the soil; how many tracts had been utterly
depopulated by the ceaseless levies for the imperial
armies; how before the inroad of barbarous invaders
village life had ceased, and towns, forsaken by their
inhabitants, had gradually disappeared; how dense
woods had arisen, and completely concealing the ruins
of temples and baths, villas and streets, spread onwards
till at length ·they joined the immense and impenetrable forests which covered the whole extent of France,
Switzerland, Belgium, and both banks of the Rhine.

The question, we have said, was, Who would plunge
into the gloom of these forests, proclaim the word
of life to the wild tribes that dwelt around them,
and teach them the first principles of civilization?

It was a momentous question, but the lives of the
Apostles of Mediæval Europe tell us how it was
answered. Armed with none of the inventions of
modern industry, strong only in invisible protection,
the monastery sent forth hundreds of devoted men to
undertake the work. "It is an ugly thing for an
unarmed man," writes Professor Kinsgley, "to traverse
without compass the bush of Australia or New
Zealand, where there are no wild beasts. But it was
uglier still to start out under the dark roof of those
primæval Germanic forests. Knights, when they rode

[1] See above, pp. 5—8.

thither, went armed *cap-à-pie*, like Sintram through
the dark valley, trusting in God and their good swords.
Chapmen and merchants stole through it by a few
tracks in great companies, armed with bill and bow.
Peasants ventured into it a few miles, to cut timber,
and find forage for their swine, and whispered wild
legends of the ugly things therein—and sometimes,
too, never came home. Away it stretched, from the
fair Rhineland, wave after wave of oak and alder,
beech and pine, God alone knew how far, into the
land of night and wonder, and the infinite unknown,
full of elk and bison, bear and wolf, lynx and glutton,
and perhaps of worse beasts still." [1]

But the disciples of St. Columba and St. Boniface
did not hesitate to penetrate the darkness of these
primæval forests, there to live and pray and study,
and till the waste.

Strange indeed, passing strange, must these pioneers
of civilization have appeared to heathen Suevians and
Allmannen. They themselves knew of no power save
physical force. These wanderers seemed to hold
physical force in utter contempt. They themselves
acknowledged no influence but that of the sword and
the battle-axe, the club and the spear. These soldiers
of an Invisible King seemed to acknowledge no such
weapons in their warfare. And yet out of weakness
they were made strong. Where others trembled, they
showed no fear ; where others ventured nothing, they
ventured everything. It was clear that they made
little of Frankish count or Suevian king. In their

[1] "The Monks and the Heathen," *Good Words*, Jan. 1863.

palaces they were no reeds shaken by the wind. A Thierri quailed before them. A Brunehaut could not endure their pure and upright life. A Radbod was forced to acknowledge the fearlessness with which they rebuked cruelty and barbarity. Such men the simple people could not but revere, and believe to be possessed of mysterious power. They might at times be austere; they might with more zeal than love protest against their idolatries; but to the widow and the orphan, to the lame and the blind, to the sick and the afflicted, they were ever fast and patient friends, and for them they ever had words of true comfort and mysterious consolation.

The wisdom of Providence assigned the order in which these Apostles of Civilization were to enter upon the work.

The Celtic disciple of St. Columba went first. The Anglo-Saxon disciple of St. Boniface followed. Eager, ardent, impetuous, the Celtic anchorites seemed to take the Continent by storm. With a dauntless zeal that nothing could check, an enthusiasm that nothing could stay, they flung themselves into the gloomiest solitudes of Switzerland and Belgium, and before long their wooden huts made way for the statelier buildings of Luxeuil and St. Gall.

These Celtic pioneers laid the foundations. The disciples of St. Boniface raised the superstructure. With practised eye they sought out the proper site for their monastic home, saw that it occupied a central position with reference to the tribes amongst whom they proposed to labour, that it possessed

a fertile soil, that it was near some friendly water-
course.

These points secured, the word was given, the trees
were felled, the forest was cleared, the monastery
arose. Soon the voice of prayer and praise was heard
in those gloomy solitudes. The thrilling chant and
plaintive litany awoke unwonted echoes amidst the
forest glades. The brethren were never idle. While
some educated children, whom they had redeemed
from death or torture,[1] others copied manuscripts, or
toiled over the illuminated missal, or transcribed a
Gospel; others cultivated the soil, guided the plough,
planted the apple-tree and the vine, arranged the
bee-hives, erected the water-mill, opened the mine,
and thus presented to the eyes of men the kingdom
of Christ as the kingdom of One, who had redeemed
the bodies no less than the souls of His creatures.

Such were the modes in which these Apostles of
Mediæval Europe accomplished the work of their day
and their generation.

Their numbers, their union, their singular habits,
could not fail to make a deep impression on the
heathen tribes whom they addressed. The contrast
between the teachers and the taught was sharp and
startling. On the one side was a horror of all dependence, and an indomitable spirit of restlessness;
on the other was a life of continued self-sacrifice and
obedience.

Grant that the institutions which they founded,
though "clear in the spring," proved "miry in the

[1] See above, pp. 104, 105.

stream ;" grant that, in the days of their prosperity and ease, when the original necessities which had called them forth had ceased to operate, they forgot their original simplicity, and became too often a by-word and a proverb; yet we must never forget what European civilization owes to the self-devotion of a Columbanus and a Gallus, a Boniface and a Sturmi. "The monks," writes Livingstone, "did not disdain to hold the plough. They introduced fruit-trees, flowers, vegetables, in addition to teaching and emancipating the serfs. Their monasteries were mission-stations which resembled ours in being dispensaries for the sick, almshouses for the poor, and nurseries of learning. Can we learn nothing from them in their prosperity as the schools of Europe, and see naught in their history but the pollution and laziness of their decay ?"

II. Next to the prominence of the monastic orders in the missionary work of the Middle Ages, the most noteworthy feature is the important aid afforded (1) by Episcopal Supervision, and (2) by Ecclesiastical Councils, in directing and consolidating the efforts of the various missionary bodies.

1. During the Mediæval period, from first to last, the introduction of Christianity amongst any tribe was followed up as speedily as possible by the establishment of episcopal government. The first seeds of the Gospel may have been sown by inferior ministers, by the influence of a Christian queen, by Christian captives in the land of their captivity, by Christian merchants during trading voyages. But uniformly

the management of the infant churches when formed
was entrusted to a local episcopate. Sometimes a
bishop headed from the first a body of voluntary
adventurers. More often, as soon as any considerable
success had been achieved, one of the energetic
pioneers was advanced to the episcopal rank, and
in this capacity superintended the staff of monks or
clergy around him, and ordained, as soon as possible,
a native ministry from amongst the converted tribes,
and established a cathedral or corresponding ecclesiastical foundation.

Such a course it is not necessary to attribute to an
empty craving after hierarchical display. It had other
recommendations of the most practical character.

Already, before the inroad of the new races, the
bishops had become not only a kind of privy council
to the emperor, but were regarded in almost every
town as the natural chiefs. They alone stood bravely
by their flocks when the barbarous host appeared
before a defenceless city. When the civil magistrate
and the military leader often sought safety in flight,
they alone were found able and willing to mediate
between the people and the heathen chief.

It is no wonder, then, that, on the reception of
Christianity by any tribe, the native prince was glad
to have near him one who could assume the functions
of the pagan high-priest, and advise him in any
matter of civil or religious moment.

To say that, when placed in this position, and in his
priestly character regarded as superior to the prince
himself, the bishop was prone to abuse his influence,

and to foster many corruptions he ought to have checked, is only to say that he was not superior to the ordinary temptations of human nature. At any rate we know what his own generation expected of him. We know how it was required of the bishop that "he should ever be busied with reconciliation and peace, as he best might; that he should zealously appease strife, and effect peace with those temporal judges who love right; that in accusations he should direct the *lád*, so that no man might wrong another, either in oath or ordeal; that he should not consent to any injustice or wrong measure or false weight; that every legal right should go with his counsel and with his witness; that together with the temporal judges he should so direct judgments that, as far as in him lay, he should never permit any injustice to spring up there; that he should ever exalt righteousness and suppress unrighteousness; that he should flinch neither before the lowly nor the powerful, because he doeth naught if he fear or be ashamed to speak righteousness."[1]

This was certainly no mean standard of duty, and however far the bishops may at times have come short of it, it was a matter of the utmost importance to have in the court and by the side of the newly-converted chieftain one, who by the duties of his office was bound to be a counterpoise to the rude and capricious government of a military aristocracy, a mediator between the noble and the serf, a defender of the weak and the down-trodden. The interposition

[1] Kemble's "Saxons in England," ii. p. 393.

of Boniface in the matter of Gewillieb's succession to the bishopric of Mayence is one instance out of many, which must often have occurred in those times of constant warfare, when a bishop's exalted position enabled him to speak out boldly against a positive wrong, and to speak with effect.

2. And in carrying on their work they were materially aided by the provincial and diocesan synods which they assembled.

For these synods not only decided doctrinal questions, but dealt also with some of the most important social problems of the age. Not merely did they regulate the life and manners of the clergy, but they defined the degrees of affinity within which marriage could be contracted, determined the mutual relation of master and servant, laid down rules concerning false coin, theft, and homicide, and sometimes enacted sumptuary laws and sanitary regulations.

Our Indian Government boasts that during the last forty years the enormities of Thuggee and Dacoitee have been suppressed, that piracy has been put down, that female infanticide has been checked, that Suttee has been made criminal, that slavery as a legal status and compulsory labour have been abolished.

But the Mediæval synods can point to no less satisfactory results. They forbade the Teutonic and Scandinavian custom of exposing weak and deformed children ; they interdicted sacrifice of men and animals in honour of the gods, and witchcraft and sorcery of all kinds. They inculcated a due regard for the sanctity of human life, and taught the necessity for

punitive justice and regular forms of law, in contra-
distinction to the low and unworthy notions which
would condone all crimes, even murder, by pecuniary
fines. They elevated the peasant class, and bent all
their efforts to abolish slavery.

The means employed towards the attainment of
the latter object were necessarily and wisely gradual,
instead of sudden and violent. The example of the
Jewish legislator, who, while obliged to recognise
slavery as an institution, yet endeavoured by all the
means in his power to mitigate its evils, was followed
by the Apostles of Mediæval Europe. As even in the
Decalogue the slave in respect to his spiritual relation was pronounced equal before God, and was admitted to the enjoyment of all religious privileges,
and was never regarded as a mere thing or chattel,
so the Church never faltered in her proclamation that
the image of God was to be discerned in every human
creature, and that the blessings of redemption were
designed for all alike, whether bond or free.

The change brought about was gradual, but sure.

At first monks, especially Eastern monks, refused
to be waited upon at all by slaves. Then, as we have
so often seen in the preceding pages, missionaries
never lost an opportunity of redeeming slaves, and,
after giving them suitable instruction, of admitting
them, if qualified, to offices in the Church. Practical
teaching like this, in the course of time, could not fail
to leave its mark. The heathen proprietor was forced
to regard his slave with other and higher feelings
than those of the Roman master, with whom it was

an axiom incapable of disproof, that all men were by nature free or bondmen.

Thus more and more the tone of public feeling was pervaded with the spirit that dictated the noble words of Gregory the Great, in a deed manumitting two slaves :

"As our Saviour," he writes, "the Author of all created beings, was willing for this reason to take upon him the nature of man, that he might by his grace set us free from the chains of bondage by which we were enthralled, and restore us to our original freedom, so a good and salutary thing is done when men, whom Nature from the beginning had created free, and whom the law of nations has subjected to the yoke of servitude, are presented again with the freedom in which they were born."[1]

Penetrated with these sentiments, the Mediæval synods restored many of the earlier edicts of Constantine, declaring the slave to be a *man*, and not a *thing* or *chattel*. They laid it down that his life was his own, and could not be taken from him without public trial. They imposed on a master guilty of the involuntary murder of his slaves penance and exclusion from the rites of the Church; they opened asylums to those who fled from their masters' cruelty; they declared the enfranchisement of the serf a work acceptable to God; they demanded it from time to time of princes on their death-beds, as a necessary preparation for their release; they hallowed manumission at all times with the sanctity of a religious rite.

[1] Greg. Ep. vi. 12.

The abolition of domestic slavery was one of the most important duties incumbent on the Mediæval missionaries. It is to their exertions we owe the fact that political Helotry no more interposes to perpetuate the severance of race from race in an attitude of bitter, enduring hostility. Theirs is the credit that "prædial serfdom, the true gulf before the Roman senate-house, which the devotion of no Curtius might close, no longer swallows up people after people, draining into its abyss the springs of free industry which are the sap and sustenance of maturer civilization."[1]

[1] "Secularia, or Surveys on the Main Stream of History," G. Lucas. P. 25.

CHAPTER XX.

IT is impossible to close a review, however brief, of the work of the Apostles of Mediæval Europe, without noticing one or two additional points.

I. And the first which calls for remark is the national and seemingly indiscriminate baptisms which the influence of various princes secured, and the Church did not hesitate to administer.

It is obvious that in the Middle Ages necessity would often dictate a departure from ordinary rules. But it is hardly possible to read of the multitudes admitted to baptism after a very limited preparation without suspecting that there was at times a far greater anxiety to multiply the number than to enlighten the minds of the proselytes.

It is true, indeed, that we ought to bear in mind the fewness of the teachers, the great masses of the people, and the general ignorance; still the habitual practice of thus administering the sacred rite must have been the reverse of an adequate preservative against the danger of relapse. The baptism of the ten thousand subjects of Ethelbert in the waters of the Swale, of the many thousand Teutons by the Apostle of

Germany, of the Russians in the waters of the Dnieper, of the Pomeranians by Bishop Otho, the absence of adequate preparation, and the influence of the prince or king, will cause such administrations to be regarded by some as a subject for a compassionate smile rather than for regard or forgiveness.

But in forming a fair opinion on the subject, it ought to be borne in mind that the Mediæval missionaries had to contend with unusual difficulties. To say nothing of the relaxed condition of society, of the constant wars which were ever setting tribe against tribe and people against people, of the fact that the administrators of the baptismal rite were in many cases themselves but recently converted, there were other and more formidable difficulties in regard to the recipients of the rite themselves.

For they had known nothing of that long education under a preliminary Dispensation, which had exerted its influences over those three thousand converts whom the Apostle Peter admitted into the Church in one day. The revelation of an external law and the warnings of the prophets had not made Monotheism natural to them, or taught, "here a little, and there a little, line upon line, and precept upon precept," those elementary religious truths which appear to us so easy to apprehend, because we have lived from childhood in an atmosphere permeated with their influence.

They were not proselytes of the gate, to whom, like the Ethiopian eunuch, a Philip could explain the true meaning of sacred prophecy, and receive into the Christian Church on the simplest profession of belief.

Neither were they in a condition analogous to that of the Græco-Roman world at the first promulgation of the faith, convinced of its inability to regenerate itself, and wearied of its long tossing on the ocean of Uncertainty. The utter failure of Art, and Science, and Philosophy to solve the deepest problems of life, had not brought them as proselytes in riper years to "the True Philosophy."

Infants alike in knowledge and civilization, they were admitted to infant baptism by teachers themselves in many cases but imperfectly educated, whose whole theology was often contained in the Creed and the Lord's Prayer. It was "the day of small things," and the men who did not despise that day, but acted up to the extent of their knowledge, hoping for a future day of greater things, accomplished no mean work, and reaped no inconsiderable harvest.

II. We have abundant evidence, however, of the use of a course of instruction by the Mediæval missionaries as preparatory to baptism, which was far from being unworthy of its object. Their biographers, it is true, have not given us such full and complete information on the subject as might have been desired ; still such information as we possess is full of interest.

Much, indeed, has been said of a peculiar natural and national predisposition on the part of the Teutonic nations towards Christianity.

We admit freely that under the poetic legends of Teutonic mythology there lay a residuum of truth, to which the new faith could attach itself, and which it could transfigure. We admit that in its ideas respecting the origin of the world, in its distorted legends of the Creation, in its conception, however much afterwards overlaid, of a great Allfadir, in its belief in the final triumph of good over evil, in its traditions of a conflict between Balder, the lord of light and life, and the goddess of death, and in its hope of an ultimate restoration of all things, there may have been scattered seeds which Christianity might quicken and make fruitful. Yet it must be conceded that there were few amongst the missionaries of this period who could, even if they had been willing, have seen the matter in this light.

That largeness of heart, that more than human wisdom, which suggested to the great Apostle of the Gentiles, when he stood on Mar's Hill, the propriety of "taking his smooth stone," as Chrysostom expresses it, " out of the Athenians' own brook," and of finding a common ground between himself and those whom he addressed, are qualities rare at all times, and which it would be folly to expect in the period with which we are concerned.

The teaching, however, of the Apostles of Mediæval Europe, so far as it has come down to us, had one great merit. From first to last it was eminently *objective*. It dealt mainly with the great *facts* of Christianity. It proclaimed the incarnation of the Saviour, his life, his death, his resurrection, his ascension, his future coming to judge the quick and dead, and then it proceeded to treat of the good works which ought to flow from the vital reception of these Christian truths.

To the Celtic worshippers of the powers of nature, and especially of the sun, we saw how the Apostle of Ireland proclaimed the existence of one God, the Creator of all things, and then proceeded to dwell upon the life, death, resurrection, and ascension of his only-begotten Son, Jesus Christ, whom he declared to be the *true Sun*, of whom, and by whom, and to whom, are all things.[1]

Similarly we saw how Augustine directed the attention of the royal worshipper of Odin and Thor in Kent to the picture of the Saviour on the cross, and then told him of such events in his wondrous life as were likely to make an impression on his mind; how at his birth a star appeared in the East; how he walked upon the sea; how at his death the sun withdrew his shining; how at his resurrection the earth trembled and the rocks were rent; how, having been looked for as the Great Deliverer of mankind from the beginning of the world, and having sealed his mission as divine, he ascended up on high, and was now worshipped everywhere as the only-begotten Son of God.[2]

From the sermons of Eligius we have already offered some quotations, which sufficiently illustrate the same objective mode of preaching, as also the earnest way in which he sought to warn his flock against heathen errors.[3]

[1] See above, p. 37.

[2] See above, p. 92, and compare "Vita S. Augustin." Migne, "Patrologia," Sæc. vii. p. 61.

[3] See above, pp. 81—85.

The sermon of Gallus on the occasion of the consecration of his disciple to the see of Constance is
interesting from the testimony it bears to his intimate
acquaintance with the Old Testament history, and the
order of the events in the Saviour's life, and the knowledge it displays is far in advance of that which is
popularly ascribed to the period in which he lived.[1]

The correspondence of Daniel, bishop of Winchester, with his friend and fellow-countryman, St.
Boniface, is peculiarly deserving of notice, as illustrating
the way in which he would have him deal with the
errors and superstitions of their Teutonic kinsmen,
and win them over to the right faith.[2] If from this
prudent advice we turn to the fifteen sermons of the
great Apostle of Germany which have been preserved
to us,[3] we have ample proof that he desired something
far more real than a mere superficial form of Christian
belief.

The first of these treats of the right faith, of the
doctrine of the Trinity, the relation of baptism to
the remission of sins, the resurrection of the dead,
the future judgment, and the necessity of repentance.

The second, preached on Christmas Day, is concerned with the creation of man, the history of his
fall, the promise of a Saviour, and his first Advent
in great humility.

The third has for its subject the twofold operation
of justification.

The fourth treats of the Beatitudes.

---

[1] See above, p. 75.   [2] Ib. pp. 114, 115.
[3] Migne, "Patrologia Latina," Sæc. viii. p. 813.

The fifth of faith and the works of love.

The sixth, seventh, eighth, and ninth of deadly sins and the Ten Commandments.

The tenth and eleventh are mainly concerned with further explanations of man's original state, of his fall and redemption through Christ, of the hope of the world to come, and the necessity of preparation by leading a fresh and holy life for the Day of Judgment. The subject of the twelfth and thirteenth is an explanation of the necessity of observing the season of Lent; while the fourteenth is an Easter sermon.

The last appears to have been preached on the occasion of the celebration of the Sacrament of Baptism, and illustrates the simple missionary character of the rest.

"Listen, my brethren," it begins, "and consider attentively what it was ye renounced at your baptism. Ye renounced the devil and all his works. What are the works of the devil? They are pride, idolatry, envy, backbiting, lying, perjury, hatred, variance, fornication, adultery, theft, drunkenness, sorcery, witchcraft, recourse to amulets and charms. These and such like are the works of the devil, and all such ye renounced at your baptism, and, as the Apostle saith, 'They who do such things are worthy of death, and shall not enter into the kingdom of heaven.' But because we believe that through God's mercy ye renounce all these sins in heart and life, therefore, that ye may deserve to obtain pardon, I warn you, brethren beloved, to remember what ye promised unto God Almighty.

"For ye promised to believe in God Almighty, and in Jesus Christ his Son, and in the Holy Spirit, One God Almighty in a perfect Trinity.

"These are the commandments of God, which we ought to observe and keep: ye must love the Lord, in whom ye have professed your belief, with all your heart, and mind, and strength. Be ye patient, tender-hearted, kind, chaste, and pure. Teach your children to love God, and your household in like manner. Reconcile them that are at variance. Let him that judges give righteous judgment, let him not receive bribes, for bribes blind the eyes even of the wise.

"Observe the Lord's Day, assemble yourselves at church, and there pray, not making vain repetitions. Give alms according to your means, for as water extinguisheth the flame, so almsgiving blotteth out sin. Observe hospitality, visit the sick, minister to widows and orphans, give tithes to the Church, and what ye would not men should do unto you, that do ye not unto them. Fear God, and him only. Servants, be obedient unto your masters, and maintain the rights of your master among your fellow-servants. Learn diligently the Lord's Prayer and the Creed, and teach them to your children, and to those for whom ye stood sponsors at their baptism. Practise fasting, love righteousness, resist the devil, receive the Eucharist at the stated seasons. These, and such like, are the commands that God bade you do and keep.

"Believe that Christ will come, that there will be a resurrection of the body, and a general judgment of mankind. Then the wicked will be separated from the good, and the one will go into eternal fire, the other into eternal bliss, and they shall enjoy everlasting life with God without any more death, light without darkness, health without sickness, happiness without fear, joy without sorrow; there shall be peace for evermore, and the righteous shall shine forth as the sun, for *eye hath not seen, nor ear heard, neither hath it entered into the heart of man to conceive, what things God hath prepared for them that love him.*"[1]

Such was the missionary instruction which the Apostle of Germany imparted to his flock.

Further information on the same point is supplied by the correspondence of Alcuin with the emperor Charlemagne, who had entrusted Arno, archbishop of Salzburg, with a mission amongst the Avars. He congratulates the emperor on his success and the prospect of the speedy spread of the faith, but impresses upon him the necessity for due attention to public preaching and an orderly celebration of baptism.[2] A mere external washing of the body, he reminds him, will avail nothing, unless the mind has first duly received.

"The Apostolic order," he observes, "is first to teach all nations, then is to follow the administration of baptism and further instruction in Christian duties. Therefore in teaching those of riper years, that order should be strictly observed, which the blessed Augustine has laid down in his treatise on the very subject :[3]

[1] 1 Cor. ii. 9.   [2] See Migne, " Patrologia," Sæc. ix. p. 187.
[3] " De Catechizandis Rudibus."

" 1. First, a man ought to be instructed in the immortality of the soul, in the future life, and its retribution hereafter of good and evil.

" 2. Secondly, he ought to learn for what crimes and sins he will be condemned to future punishment, and for what good and beneficial actions he will enjoy eternal happiness with Christ.

" 3. Thirdly, he ought to be very carefully instructed in the doctrine of the Trinity, in the advent of the Saviour for the salvation of mankind, in his life, his passion, his resurrection, his ascension, and future coming to judge the world. Strengthened and thoroughly instructed in this faith, let him be baptized, and afterwards let the precepts of the Gospel be further unfolded by public preaching, till he attain to the measure of the stature of a perfect man, and become a worthy habitation for the Holy Ghost."

In another letter, after exhorting the emperor to provide competent instructors for his newly-conquered subjects, he remarks that they ought to follow the example of the Apostles in preaching the word of God. "For they," he says, "were wont at the beginning to feed their hearers with milk, that is, with gentle precepts, even as the Apostle Paul saith : *And I, brethren, could not speak unto you as unto spiritual, but as unto carnal, even as unto babes in Christ. I have fed you with milk, and not with meat : for hitherto ye were not able to bear it, neither yet now are ye able.*[1] And thereby that great Apostle of the whole world, Christ speaking in him, signified, that

[1] I Cor. iii. 1, 2.

newly-converted tribes ought to be nourished with simple precepts, like as children are with milk, lest if austerer precepts be taught at first, their weak mind should reject what it drinks. Whence also the Lord Jesus Christ himself in the Gospel replied to those asking him why his disciples fasted not : *Men put not new wine into old bottles : else the bottles break, and the wine runneth out, and the bottles perish : but they put new wine into new bottles, and both are preserved ;*[1] 'for,' as Jerome saith, 'the virgin purity of the soul which has never been contaminated with vice is very different from that which has long been in bondage to foul lusts and passions.' "

III. And here a few remarks on the policy of the missionaries as regards heathenism may not be out of place, especially as they have sometimes been accused of too great accommodation to the weaknesses and scruples of their pagan converts.

A review of the efforts made during this period does not tend to substantiate the charge at least against the missionaries themselves. Again and again we have seen them hewing down the images, profaning the temples, and protesting with vehemence against sorcery, witchcraft, and other heathen practices. The Apostle of Ireland did not, as we saw, spare the great object of Celtic worship ; his countrymen, Columbanus and Gallus, provoked the grievous wrath of the Suevians by their hostility to Thor and Odin ; Willibrord, at the peril of his life, polluted the sacred fountains of Fosites-land ; Boniface risked not

[1] Matt. ix. 17.

only personal safety, but all his influence over the
people of Hesse by hewing down the sacred oak
of Geismar; the address of Lebuin to the Saxon
assembly did not betray one easily "shaken by the
wind;" Bogoris flung away his idols at the first
request of Methodius; Vladimir flogged the huge
image of Peroun, and flung it into the waters of the
Dnieper before the face of his people; Olaf and
Thangbrand overthrew the monuments of Scandinavian idolatry with a zeal worthy of a Jehu; Bishop
Otho in Pomerania insisted, in spite of imminent
danger to himself, on destroying various Sclavonic
temples.

As far as such external protests against idolatry
could avail, their missionary zeal did not err on the
side of laxity. It cannot be said that there was any
accommodation here to the views of the heathens, or
anything like the policy of the unworthy followers of
Xavier, in India.

In several cases, however, the advice of Gregory the
Great to Augustine appears to have been mainly followed, at least by the Anglo-Saxon missionaries.
From the letter of that Pope to Mellitus[1] it seems
that the question of the destruction of the heathen
temples had caused him considerable anxiety, and
had long occupied his thoughts. The conclusion to
which he at last came was that, instead of being
destroyed, they should be ".cleansed from heathen
pollution by being sprinkled with holy water," and

[1] Epp. Greg. lib. xi. 76 ; Bede, i. 30, "*Diu* mecum de causa Anglo-
rum cogitans tractavi."

consecrated to Christian purposes by the erection of the Christian altar and the "deposition of relics of the saints."

Whatever may be the reason of the strange contrast between the policy advocated in this letter and in that addressed to Ethelbert, it is certain that Gregory was wisely anxious to facilitate the transition from heathenism to Christianity. In this spirit, therefore, he advised Augustine to deal cautiously with the heathen festivals which were celebrated in or near the temples; he would not have them abolished altogether, but suggested that on the anniversaries of the Martyrs, whose relics had been placed in the temples now converted into churches, booths should be erected, and the people permitted to celebrate their feasts in honour not of the old pagan deities, but of the True God, the Giver of all good.

Gregory, whose spirit is said to have yearned towards the old heathen sages who had died without hearing of the work of Christ, considered that he had found a precedent for the advice he now gave in the divine system of educating the Jewish people after their departure from Egypt. "They had been wont," he remarks, "to sacrifice to false gods; they were not forbidden now altogether to abstain from offering sacrifice. The object only of their worship was changed, and the same animals they had been wont to sacrifice to idols, they now sacrificed in honour of the Lord their God."

Grant that he may have regarded the Jewish sacrificial system from far too low a point of view, still, in the circumstances of the Anglo-Saxons just emerging from heathenism, there was much to remind him of the Jewish nation in its long contact with idolatry in Egypt. The latter, unfitted, as the very genius of their language attests, for abstract thought or metaphysical speculations, absolutely required material symbols, and with a Book of Symbols they were mercifully provided.

The same mode of proceeding, Gregory was of opinion, was requisite in the case of the Anglo-Saxon converts, and if existing ceremonies could only be exalted and purified, a gradual ascent might be supplied towards understanding higher truths. Where, as in England, and probably on the Continent, every town had its religious establishment, the Mediæval missionaries, themselves in many cases but lately converted, may be pardoned for the natural desire to make as much as possible of the *religio loci*, and to avail themselves, so far as it was practicable, of old associations.

Architectural reasons may very probably have prevented in many cases a compliance with Gregory's advice, but its spirit was obeyed, wherever the Teutonic missionary went forth to evangelize Teutons. And independently of the sound principle which was thus taught, "that the evil spirit can be cast out of institutions without destroying them," the early missionaries must have found that it is easy to destroy the image or fling it into the stream, but very hard to extirpate a faith, and eradicate time-honoured superstitions.

They to whom they preached were, as we have already seen, worshippers of all above them and around them ; in the skies, the woods, the waters, they found their oracles and sacred books; they revelled in spirits of the grove and of the fountain, of the lake and of the hill ; they believed devoutly in divinations, and presages, and lots. Imagine, then, one who from his earliest years had lived and moved in the atmosphere of a faith like this, which identified itself with all the associations of nature and the world around, which taught him to hear voices from another world in the forest roaring round his cottage in the wintry night, or on the lake where he flung his net ;— imagine such an one, out of deference to the will of his chief, or the stern command of the conqueror, in an age of " implicit, childlike, trusting, fearing, rejoicing faith," exchanging his early creed for that of the Christian ; and can we wonder that the old ideas long retained their sway, or that councils were obliged to denounce, and the missionary to inveigh against, lingering traces of well-worship and tree-worship, against divination and witchcraft ?

Can we wonder that in an age when the old divinities were still regarded as real powers, which were not entirely bereft of all influence over their apostate votaries, even after they had bowed before the uplifted cross, or been signed with the same symbol in the baptismal stream, the missionary was tempted, almost unconsciously, to meet heathenism halfway, and to Christianize superstitions he found himself powerless to dispel ?

Can we wonder that many, unable to resist the glamour of old beliefs, in the midst of which their forefathers "had lived and moved and had their being," were still prone at times to offer the ancient sacrifices, and, as we gather from the letters of Boniface, to resort to the old magic and soothsaying? When we remember that as late as the fifteenth century the Church was engaged in eradicating the remains of Sclavonic heathenism, and protesting against a rude fetishism and serpent worship, it is surely no matter of surprise that the boundary line between the old and the new faith was not very sharply defined, that a continual interchange long went on between Christian legends and heathen myths.

It was no settled policy on the part of the forefathers of European civilization, but the spirit of the age itself, which refused to disjoin the judicial assembly from its old accompanying heathen rites ; which kept heathen festivals on Christian holidays, and celebrated heathen festivals, purified of their grosser elements, under a Christian guise; which exchanged the remembrance cup once drunk at the banquet in honour of Thor and Woden for a similar salutation of the Apostles, and in place of the image of Frigga caused the staff of some saint to be carried round the cornfields to drive away the fieldmice or the caterpillars ; which preserved the heathen names of the days of the week, and inextricably united the name of a Saxon goddess with the most joyous of the Christian festivals : names which have survived all the intervening changes of thought and feeling, and remain to the present day the undying memorials of the period of twilight between heathendom and Christianity.

IV. Our retrospect has, from the nature of the case, been chiefly concerned with the more legitimate efforts made during the earlier period of the Middle Ages to propagate the Gospel. But during the later period we noticed how other agencies besides the holy lives and eloquent tongues of devoted men, besides the monastic colony and the missionary school, were employed to complete the circle of European Christendom. We saw how the genuine missionary spirit became tinged with fanaticism, and was succeeded by violent and coercive propagandism.

The wars of Charlemagne against the Saxons are the subjects of legitimate censure. That these wars were carried on with relentless severity, that the Saxon territory was invaded from year to year, that on one occasion four thousand five hundred prisoners were beheaded for sharing in an insurrection, that on another ten thousand Saxons were forcibly removed from their own country into the older Frankish territory, cannot be denied.

Still the peculiarities of Charlemagne's position must not be overlooked. Other causes than the simple lust of conquest promoted these wars. Antipathies of race and divergences of religious belief lent a peculiar bitterness to the conflict between the Frank and the Saxon. Charlemagne knew well that if these hardy pirates of the North gained the upper hand, all order and security in Europe would be at an end. At the root of the new civilization, whereof he was the champion, lay the Christian faith. In the Christian Church, he felt, were the only elements of order, and he had strengthened his own power by the most intimate relations with it. It is no wonder, therefore, that he believed himself bound, as a Christian king, to impose that faith, which alone promised any definite union or concord, on races that still clung to the blood-stained rites of Odinism.

"That the alternative, 'Believe or die,' was sometimes proposed by Charlemagne to the Saxons," writes Sir James Stephen, "I shall not dispute. But it is not less true that, before these terms were tendered to them, they had again and again rejected his less formidable proposal, 'Be quiet and live.' In form and term, indeed, their election lay between the Gospel and the sword. In substance and in reality, they had to make their choice between submission and destruction. A long and deplorable experience had already shown that the Frankish people had neither peace nor security to expect for a single year so long as their Saxon neighbours retained their heathen rites and the ferocious barbarism inseparable from them. Fearful as may be the dilemma, 'Submit or perish,' it is that to which every nation, even in our own times, endeavours to reduce a host of invading and desolating foes ; nor, if we ourselves were exposed to similar inroads, should we offer to our assailants conditions more gentle or less peremptory."[1]

[1] Lecture i. p. 92.

These considerations may tend to modify our view of Charlemagne's policy, but the wholesale and indiscriminate mode of administering the rite of baptism on the conclusion of his compaigns cannot possibly be defended, and drew forth, as we saw, the indignant expostulations of Alcuin, and men of kindred spirit.

The violent efforts of the Norwegian princes to enforce Christianity as the national faith have a grotesqueness of their own, which relieves them from the imputation of those darker motives which prompted the Albigensian Crusades and the establishment of the Inquisition. As for the violence of the Viking, it may be pleaded that, however low and unworthy the conceptions he had formed of the Christian faith, his mode of enforcing his new creed on his rough and hardy subjects was at least straightforward. He had believed once in the might of Thor's great hammer, "the crusher and smasher," and force was the only weapon he could conceive capable of effecting his purpose. To expect maxims of toleration from a Viking would indeed be absurd ; but the fact that, in spite of the violence with which Christianity was introduced into the Scandinavian and other kingdoms, the leaven was found able to work mightily, and to do great things for their advancement, is surely an encouragement as regards the future of modern missionary efforts. When we reflect how long a period even the partial evangelization of Europe occupied, how slow, how gradual was its progress, how at times it seemed to have come to a standstill altogether, we shall not be impatient for immediate results of missionary work in modern times.

Whenever the Church effected anything real or lasting, it was when she was content to persevere in a spirit of absolute dependence on him who has promised to be with her *always, even unto the end of the world;* when in the person of a Columba, a Boniface, a Sturmi, an Anskar, a Raymund Lull, she was contented to go forth and sow the seed, and then leave it to do its work, remembering that if " earthly seed is long in springing up, imperishable seed is longer still." Whenever she failed in her efforts, it was when she forgot in whose strength she went forth, and for whose glory alone she existed, when she was tempted to resort to other means and to try other expedients than those which her great Head had sanctioned when, instead of patiently leaving the good seed to grow of itself, she strove to hurry its development, and was impatient of small beginnings and weak instruments.

For if the retrospect of the missionary efforts of the Middle Ages teaches one lesson more than another, it is the value of those " slender wires " on which the greatest events are often hung, and the importance of not despising the day of small things. " Let any one," writes the author of the " Historical Memoirs of Canterbury," " sit on the hill of the little Church of St. Martin at Canterbury, and look on the view which is there spread before his eyes. Immediately below are the towers of the great Abbey of St. Augustine, where Christian learning and civilization first struck root in the Anglo-Saxon race ; and within which now, after a lapse of many centuries, a new institution has arisen, intended to carry far and wide, to countries of which Gregory and Augustine had never heard, the blessings which they gave to us. . . . . From Canterbury, the first English Christian city—from Kent, the first English Christian kingdom—has, by degrees, arisen the whole constitution of a Church and State in England, which now binds together the whole British Empire. And from the Christianity here established in England has flowed, by direct consequence, first, the Christianity of Germany, —then, after a long interval, of North America,—and lastly, we may trust, in time, of all India and Australasia. The view from St. Martin's Church is indeed one of the most inspiriting that can be found in the world ; there is none to which I would more willingly take any one who doubted whether a small beginning would lead to a great and lasting good,—none which carries us more vividly back to the past, or more hopefully forward to the future."[1]

[1] Stanley's "Memorials of Canterbury," p. 39.